RESEARCH IN CORPORATE SOCIAL PERFORMANCE AND POLICY

Volume 4 ● 1982

RESEARCH IN CORPORATE SOCIAL PERFORMANCE AND POLICY

A Research Annual

Editor: **LEE E. PRESTON**
College of Business and Management
University of Maryland

VOLUME 4 ● 1982

 **JAI PRESS INC.**

Greenwich, Connecticut   *London, England*

CONTENTS

LIST OF CONTRIBUTORS

Patti N. Andrews

School of Management,
Boston University

Robert J. De Fillippi

Department of Management and
Administrative Systems, College
of Business and Economics,
Washington State University

George Greanias

Graduate School of Business
Administration,
Rice University

Robert Hogner

School of Business and
Organizational Sciences,
Florida International University

John F. Mahon

School of Management,
Boston University

Barry M. Mitnick

Graduate School of Business,
University of Pittsburgh

Edwin A. Murray, Jr.

School of Management,
Boston University

James E. Post

School of Management,
Boston University

Jeffery A. Sonnenfeld

Graduate School of Business
Administration,
Harvard University

Duane Windsor

Graduate School of Business
Administration,
Rice University

Richard E. Wokutch   College of Business,
                                Virginia Polytechnic Institute and
                                State University

Elliot Zashin   College of Liberal Arts and
                                Sciences, University of Illinois,
                                Chicago Circle

EDITOR'S INTRODUCTION

The research papers published in this volume reflect a very substantial evolution in the substance and significance of corporation and society studies. They should be a source of pride to their authors, and a source of stimulation to scholars and students working in this field. Each of the papers rests on a substantial methodological base, and some treat methodology explicitly as their principal focus. Each of them also has significant empirical content—from systematically gathered collections of new data, individual field observations and interviews, syntheses of materials from the existing literature, or combinations of all of these. Many of the papers involve the use of multiple methodologies and data sources in search of insights and answers to significant analytical or substantive questions. Each of them is well-documented and grounded in the prior literature. The time when casual dabbling could pass for scholarship in this area has clearly passed.

The first four papers in this volume are primarily conceptual and methodological. The introduction to Volume 3 of this series noted that a substantial amount of the new research in this field consists of case studies, and that it appeared likely that case research would continue to play an important role in the field's development. In response to this stimulus, Post and Andrews have developed a major paper that sets forth in considerable detail a methodology of case research, and demonstrates the strengths and limitations of both individual projects and an entire field of knowledge based on a case-study approach. This paper should become a handbook for a generation of doctoral candidates and new investigators, as well as a source of ideas, techniques and warnings for more experienced scholars.

The papers by DeFillippi and Mahon are useful companions to the Post-Andrews piece. DeFillippi has reviewed a large conceptual literature, and attempts to develop a comprehensive "map" relating basic concepts to implementing research designs and data requirements. His analysis extends very substantially the organizational effort attempted in my own paper in Volume 1 of this series. Again, students and newcomers should find this presentation extremely valuable as they attempt to gain a basic orientation to the field of study. By contrast, Mahon returns to the work of one of the earliest and most influential conceptual contributors, James Thompson, and shows how some of his initial ideas were extended and implemented in work by one of his students (Thomas Page) that has not heretofore been available in the literature. Mahon links this early work with several more recent studies to show its continuing relevance. All of these papers deal with the systematic pursuit of a research strategy, from the initial identification of subjects and concepts through the selection and development of implementing methods, and finally to results.

Windsor and Greanias combine an extensive conceptual presentation with a substantial empirical survey to explore the role of environmental scanning in the corporate strategic planning process. This subject has received little systematic research attention, yet it is of central importance. General social awareness within an organization, and even systematic scanning studies, will influence neither strategic nor routine behavior unless the results of external analyses are integrated directly into planning and management. Windsor and Greanias construct a framework for analyzing this process, and assess the extent to which it is actually taking place within a number of actual firms. Their paper should provide a basis for the design of planning systems to accomplish this integration and for the conduct of systematic field studies of their effectiveness.

The remaining papers in this volume are primarily empirical, yet each of them develops conceptual themes as well. Sonnenfeld's extensive field study of public affairs in the forest products industry emphasizes the importance of internal structure and process in determining both the receipt of external stimuli and the initiation of responses to the external environment. It is thus in some ways an additional and more detailed example of the type of situation more briefly discussed by Windsor and Greanias.

Murray and Wokutch each report systematic empirical surveys involving extensive statistical documentation. These studies differ entirely in subject matter—organization of the corporate public affairs function in major firms, and the use of "ethical investment" guidelines among Roman Catholic orders—but they share similar purposes and methodology. Both are intended to supply comprehensive factual information about subjects that have been previously discussed primarily on an anecdotal or prescriptive basis. Both also use multiple data sources—secondary literature, interviews, and direct observation—to interpret and validate their basic questionnaire results.

The papers by Zashin and Mitnick share a common subject—government regulation of business—and also a common perspective: That the corporation possesses great discretion, and therefore great opportunity for strategic behavior, in the regulatory environment. These authors emphasize that the firm's response to regulation is as much an aspect of managerial policy as more familiar actions involving marketing, finance and production. Zashin reports on a single well-known case experience—the recall of the Firestone "500" tire—and contrasts the actual record of company and regulator behavior in this case with a proposed "ethnic of fair-dealing" in the regulatory process. Mitnick further emphasizes the freedom of action prevailing for both regulators and regulatees, and the extent to which both can frustrate or advance the fundamental goals of regulatory policy; his analysis is based on a detailed study of regulatory implementation in the strip mining of coal.

The final paper by Hogner is an historical note, documenting an early concept and record of social involvement on the part of U.S. Steel. The somewhat parternalistic forms of corporate social policy evidenced here may have been commonplace among other firms during the earlier decades of this century, and are certainly prevalent in Europe and elsewhere at the present time. Important possibilities for historical and comparative research are suggested by Hogner's chance discovery of this interesting material.

Once again, it is appropriate to thank the authors and others who have contributed to the development of this volume. I also take this opportunity to invite readers and potential future contributors to communicate directly concerning their reactions to the volumes in this series, their ideas for future subjects or improvements, and their own research studies that might be included in future volumes.

Lee E. Preston
Series Editor

CASE RESEARCH IN CORPORATION AND SOCIETY STUDIES

James E. Post and Patti N. Andrews

INTRODUCTION

Today, some fifteen years since its beginning as a recognizable area of management scholarship, the business and society field can cite much progress, even while acknowledging that a number of problems continue to pose a challenge. The academic successes include curriculum development, teaching materials, and an expanding cadre of teachers and scholars identifying with the field. The number and variety of courses and approaches to curricula continue to expand. Faculty have increasing number of texts, case collections, and visual tools on which to draw in designing their courses. Additionally, the membership of the Social Issues in Management Division of the Academy of Management has grown from a handful of members in 1970 to nearly 500 today.

The most serious continuing challenge involves the research base of the field. Few things have proven as consistently frustrating to interested

Research in Corporate Social Performance and Policy, Vol. 4, pages 1–33
ISBN: 0-89232-259-4

scholars, students, and observers as the substance and methodology of business and society research. The diversity of research questions, the variety of theoretical perspectives from which those questions have been approached, the number of different research tools employed, and the unevenness with which they are applied have all provoked serious and substantial criticism.

While some of this criticism seems unjustified for a field still in search of a central focus (Preston, 1975), a considerable amount is warranted. To the extent that anecdote, opinion, and ideology have characterized much of the published material, subjectivity and bias are real problems. "Informed speculations" dominate the methodology landscape. An occasional survey, statistical analysis of time series data, or other quantitative analysis can be found in the early literature of the field. Today, while more of the latter can be found, case research remains a vital form of inquiry. By "case research," we mean a whole range of research methodologies in which the case study is central, whether singly, in sequence, comparative, or as part of a larger research effort.

The criticisms of case research—poor generalizability, subjectivity bias, no degrees of freedom—are familiar but have not significantly diminished the volume of research that employs this approach. Of thirty reports published from original research in Volumes 1-3 of *Research in Corporate Social Performance and Policy,* for example, eighteen employed case research as a major methodological part of the study. Case research remains a popular approach to inquiry in the field because it is well-suited to the study of many important questions about the corporation and society where sheer complexity of issues renders other methodologies inappropriate.

Case analysis as a research effort can yield much more than mere description of facts. What this field can learn from neighboring disciplines is to use a case for its full theoretical potential. Its potential for theoretical payoff comes in part from the variety of techniques which fall under the umbrella of the general term "case research": the single case study, a sequence of case studies, comparative case analysis, or phased research in which cases play a major role.

- The *single case study* has a familiar but tainted image in the corporation and society field. In the broader world of research single cases—such as the contribution to anthropology of the "Lucy" discovery (the "missing link")—have lead to powerful theories. So have *sequential cases*—such as successive single case studies of dying patients—contributed to theories of death in sociology. Corporation-society research that proceeds in phases may use single or sequential cases as well (see Taylor, 1979 and 1981).

- *Comparative cases* are familiar in the corporation-society field. A number of comparative case analyses may be examined in the first three volumes of this series as well as in Randall (1972), Murray (1974), Jesaitis (1969), and Unterman (1968).
- *Phased research,* in which cases play a limited role—e.g., pilot study—use cases in conjunction with other research techniques. A recent example of the potential contribution of cases to a larger study may be found in Mahon (1982) where cases were used early in the research effort to generate research questions. This was followed by an extensive quantitative analysis of the public affairs data[1] and used to build some theory about public affairs structures and activities. The theory was then examined in the context of another case study.

A PERSPECTIVE ON CORPORATION-SOCIETY RESERACH

The literature of the corporation-society field can be organized along two principal dimensions. The first relates to whether the researcher's focus is primarily on the corporation, either individually or as an institution, or society, as manifested in its institutions, for example, government— or in specific social problems or issues—e.g., environment protection. Only a few studies have emphasized the interaction process between business and its environment, thereby bridging the boundary between the two (Epstein, 1969; Post and Mahon, 1980).

A second dimension of the literature of the field ranges from theoretical to applied. It is possible to distinguish between those studies which are relatively more theoretical in their approach to the corporation-society relationship (Galbraith, 1967; Lindblom, 1977; Friedman, 1962; Rawls, 1971) and those which are relatively more applied or practical in nature (Ackerman, 1975; Ackerman and Bauer, 1976; Murray, 1974; Stone, 1975; Sethi, 1977). These studies have in common a concern with either corporate management of a changing social and political environment or societal management—e.g., regulation, direct action, or public policy— of important problems of corporate social and economic performance.

The central themes of the corporation-society field as reflected in the literature can be illustrated in terms of the dimensions mentioned above. The typology is illustrated by topics in Figure 1A and by reference to specific studies in Figure 1B.

The Applied Perspective

The topics and studies in Quadrant I of each of the figures are those which tend to have a managerial focus and which are primarily concerned

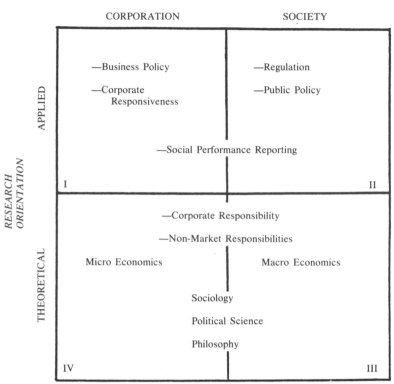

Figure 1A. Literature of the Corporation-Society Field

with questions of how companies manage their responses to a changing social and political environment. Many "corporate responsiveness" studies fall squarely into this area, as do studies from business policy which deal with the strategic impact of regulation, social trends, and public issues. The literature of this entire area emphasizes a concern with the running of private sector organizations, and the way in which those organizations do or should respond to environmental change. The writings of Ackerman (1973, 1975), Ackerman and Bauer (1976), Hanson (1979), Murray (1976), and Post (1978) all manifest a concern with organizational repsonsiveness to external change.

Quadrant II also reflects an applied perspective, but from a societal or public sector orientation rather than the private one that characterizes Quadrant I. Unlike Quadrant I studies, in which the research generally adopts a perspective from within the firm, the researcher's perspective in Quadrant II studies is "in society"; and the dominant concern is a

Figure 1B. Literature of the Corporation-Society Field

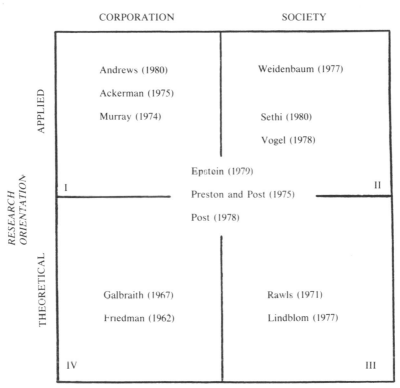

RESEARCH FOCUS

CORPORATION   SOCIETY

Andrews (1980)   Weidenbaum (1977)

Ackerman (1975)

Murray (1974)   Sethi (1980)

Vogel (1978)

Epstein (1979)

I   Preston and Post (1975)   II

Post (1978)

Galbraith (1967)   Rawls (1971)

Friedman (1962)   Lindblom (1977)

IV   III

APPLIED

THEORETICAL

RESEARCH ORIENTATION

social problem or the external effects of corporate performance. The literature of antitrust, industrial organization, and regulatory policy generally speaks to the way in which society, through public policy, can alter, influence, and shape corporate performance.

Spanning the boundary between Quadrants I and II are various studies of corporate social performance measurement. Ranging from Bauer and Fenn's (1972) discussion of the corporate social audit to more sophisticated attempts to match internal and public performance on a common set of measurement dimensions (Preston, 1978; Kelly, 1978; Rey, 1980; Dierkes, 1980), the literature of corporate performance measurement represents applied studies that span the private sector/public sector boundary. In addition, a number of studies have examined the responses of both private and public sector organizations to the same phenomenon. For example, the Investor Responsibility Research Center (IRRC) annually publishes analyses of issues that are the subject of stockholder resolutions. It includes descriptions of the positions of the businesses involved, those of regulatory agencies, public action groups, and other institutional actors. Moreover, there are a number of especially interesting studies from an applied perspective that deliberately examine what actions both corporations and society can (should) take with regard to specific events or issues. Epstein's (1979) analysis of political action committees (PACs), for example, stresses both the considerations that should govern a corporate management's commitment to a PAC and the considerations society, through the Federal Election Commission and the Congress, must give to the PAC phenomenon.

The Theoretical Perspective

Although the applied literature of the field is extensive, a far greater number of analyses take theoretical perspectives (Quadrants III and IV). Quadrant III includes an emphasis on the societal consequences and aspects of business and modern economics, while Quadrant IV identified studies that tend to focus more sharply on business as an institutional force in society. Scholars from such disciplines as economics (Marris, 1974; Friedman, 1962; Galbraith, 1967), sociology (Zeitlin, 1978), political science (Orren, 1974), and philosophy (Rawls, 1971; Nozick, 1975) have analyzed the relationship between the corporation and society or the issues spawned by that relationship. The abundance of this literature and the continuing efforts of political scientists, sociologists, economists, and historians to undertake research that deals with questions of corporation and society underscores both the importance of the subject and the opportunities for discipline-based research.

Summary

The research dimensions and perspectives discussed in this section have two important implications for research design. First, they can help a researcher clearly specify whether it is the corporation, society, or the interactive processes that are the principal focus of analysis. Whatever the reason for undertaking a case research project, the researcher is well advised to be explicit about what is to be accomplished and why he or she has selected to use a case approach rather than some other alternative. The more explicit the researcher can be in answering these questions, the better the job she/he will have done in framing the research question itself.

Second, the researcher will be forced to clarify the relationship between theory and data. The design of a research study will differ greatly according to its primary concern—whether to simply explore the "what is" of a particular social problem or to examine that problem in light of *a priori* theoretical statements. It is against this background of substantive focus (corporation, society, or both) and research perspectives (theoretical, applied) that the discussion of case research must proceed.

TYPES OF CASE RESEARCH

Case research can be used in many areas in need of systematic inquiry for a range of theoretical purposes. One aim of this paper is to entice the researcher who has made a choice about focus to make a similarly explicit choice about whether the primary effort should be to describe, explore, explain, or predict. With so much description and exploration already in the literature, many areas of research may be ready for the latter two aims.

There are four broad categories of case analysis, each of which describes a distinct genre of research. While in reality these categories overlap, sharp distinctions are drawn here to emphasize differences in primary purpose. *Descriptive* case research attempts to present a coherent picture of the facts that constitute a particular problem, organization, or object of study. Descriptive case research is characterized by an accurate representation of events, and while they may include some interpretation of data or drawing of inference, there is little evidence of conscious analytical purpose to the case report.

Exploratory case research is a deliberate form of "mucking around," done for the purpose of identifying issues, problems, or unique facets of a complex situation or organization. Exploratory case research has a more deliberate analytical purpose than the descriptive focus in that the researcher is undertaking the accumulation of facts for the purpose of identifying or clarifying research questions, or developing hypotheses for further study. Certain implicit ideas inevitably guide the researcher's exploration.

The descriptive and exploratory types of case research are characterized by a primarily inductive approach that requires assembling all available facts that together render a description without major gaps. The principal methodological problem with descriptive and exploratory case research involves the need for a guarantee [embodied in Churchman's (1971) "guarantor"] that the factual landscape has been swept sufficiently clean. If there are important facts that have escaped the researcher's net and these leave holes in the picture, the representations made about the case will be inherently flawed, and the conclusions drawn suspect. Nothing undermines the credibility of descriptive or exploratory case research as seriously as disclosure that important factual evidence was excluded or never sought. Hence, the critical need in such descriptive or exploratory case research is comprehensiveness of data collection and truthfulness in representation to the reader.

Explanatory case research is somewhat less grounded in factual presentation than the descriptive and exploratory types. The distinctive feature of the explanatory case research is its starting point: an explanatory work begins with a proposition, hypothesis, or conflicting statements of theory that the case study is used to test or prove. In this context explanatory case research is a device for advancing theory by empirical testing of theoretical propositions.

An extension of the explanatory studies, *predictive* analysis is the ultimate form of case research. Such a research study will have gathered together all relevant factual data, identified and analyzed key issues, and concluded with one or more hypotheses or predictions about future developments. Usually, such predictions take the form of scenarios. These scenarios may focus on external events or they may focus on clusters of internal characteristics—such as, Bruce Scott's (1971) analysis of the stages of growth through which companies evolve and of the characteristics which distinguish each stage of development.

Not surprisingly, case research is most frequently found in inquiry of an applied nature. The concern with "practical"questions of organizational and social functioning has led scholars to study questions that have a substantial impact on the operations or organizations or the smooth functioning of society. Thus, in terms of Figure 1, case research is most prominently found in applied/corporation and applied/society quadrants. The business policy, corporate responsiveness, and applied public policy literature frequently highlight descriptive and explanatory case analyses that focus on important research topics and/or key events—for example, Chrysler bailout, Love Canal, or Bay of Pigs invasion.

It is important to note that case research has also been used to build or to test theory in the study of the corporation and society. Max Weber's (1947) study of bureaucracy, and formulation of ideal types, can well be viewed as a theoretical construct built upon extensive case research. The Miles and Snow (1978) study of organization/environment relationships repeatedly draws on case studies to develop key conceptual propositions. Unlike Thompson (1967), whose discussion of organization/environment relations was almost wholly theoretical in its original presentation, and subsequently tested through the empirical case research of others (Page, 1972), the distinctive feature of the Miles and Snow work is their systematic building of theory through a series of explanatory and predictive case analyses.

The usefulness of case research to both the building and verification of theory underscores Henry Mintzberg's (1977) assertion that research is really a continuous process of inductive and deductive analysis. Case research may be undertaken either for the purpose of building an empirical base upon which hypotheses and research propositions can be predicted or used as a device to test and examine previously articulated hypotheses or propositions. It is important for the researcher to know what is to be accomplished with the research and to refrain from misusing the findings developed from one type of case research as "proof" at other levels. A well-done descriptive case research effort ought not to be used for predictive purposes, and an explanatory case research effort, which has not attempted to sweep in all relevant available facts to adequately describe, ought not to be cited as factual example for propositions other than those tested. Much of the methodological criticism of case research stems from the careless citation of case research for purposes other than that for which the case was researched and written.[2] Table 1 presents the four categories of case research to help the individual(s) planning research to be clear on the primary purpose of the effort.

DEFINING THE SUBJECT OF CASE RESEARCH

What is the appropriate subject (object) of case research? The question is important, for the researcher must provide some boundaries that define the subject being researched. This becomes difficult in practice, however,

Table 1. Types of Case Research

Types of Case Research	Focus	Characteristic Uses
Descriptive	*What* occurred?	Develop an empirical baseline for studying the subject. Occasionally used to illustrate a theoretical point.
Exploratory	*How* did the event develop, or the organization act?	Pilot study; provide insight for structuring a larger analysis. Used to clarify variables, so as to permit more focused analysis in subsequent stages of research.
Explanatory	*Why* did the event or organizational action occur?	Build a theory. Test two conflicting theoretical propositions. Add new variables to the analysis of previously studied questions.
Predictive	*What* will happen when such conditions arise again?	Test and verify theoretical propositions. Articulate a new theory?

for researchers often find themselves with the proverbial ball of twine that continues to unravel in ways that reveal new connections and directions. So, while it is true that bounding is an essential step in case research, there is a reality that everything is related to everything else and that the effort to delimit the scope of case research is somewhat arbitrary.

Case research can be focused in a number of ways. It is always best to search for a "natural" or recurrent context in which a case can be defined. The bounding will always be factual in nature but will inevitably require some conceptual abstraction to make the definition precise. "Natural" configurations are easiest to work with because they require the least amount of conceptual abstraction and definition. Thus, cases that are limited to an entity, such as a particular organization, are easier to define than those dealing with an issue, trend, or social phenomenon. Preston (1978) has argued that good research in the study of corporate social policy and performance requires that the researcher have a firm grasp of the organization, the environment, and the processes by which they interact. It is possible to select any of these components as the basis for bounding the case, though the degree of abstraction necessary to clarify the boundaries may differ considerably depending on the choice.

Listed below are some of the common boundaries given cases in the corporation and society field. The first four concentrate on the corporation as the focal unit of analysis, the next four concentrate on society, and the last two focus on processes of interaction among institutions. The ten types of case research subjects are summarized in Table 2.

Table 2.   The Subjects of Case Research

Focus on the Corporation

1. *A Single Organization.*   Case studies of business firms, regulatory agencies, or public groups. Little abstraction necessary to define boundaries—i.e., a highly natural configuration. Evaluation criteria are comprehensiveness of factual material.

2. *An Organizational Subunit.*   Focus is on a particular department or structural subunit of the organization. Bounding is more difficult than in #1, because organizations do not include the same scope of activities in departments of the same name. Evaluation criteria are comprehensiveness for descriptive studies, subtlety for explanatory and predictive studies.

3. *An Organizational Practice.*   Case studies of programs, activities, or policies. Bounding is made difficult by definitional difference among organizations. Evaluation criteria rest on factual completeness and comparison with other organizations.

Table 2. (Continued)

4. *An Industry.* Some definitional difficulty, but generally includes competitors, potential competitors, and producers of substitute goods/services. Bounding is generally based on product line definitions. Criteria for evaluation rest on factual completeness and comparison with other industry analyses.

Focus on Society

5. *Segment of Society.* Focus on specific stakeholders in society. Bounding problems are definitional in nature—i.e., need to specify who is within the definition and who is outside. Criteria for evaluation rest on precision of definition as measured against alternative definitions (e.g., does "community" mean only groups and institutions, or general citizenry?).

6. *A Social Phenomenon.* Focus on a significant event or happening in society (e.g., the drive to put a man on the moon, "corporate Watergate" disclosures, or new conservatism). Bounding problem is one of definition—i.e., distinguishing the phenomenon from the general history of the period. Evaluation criteria include precision of definition, and comparative insight into phenomenon.

7. *A Social Issue.* The most popular subject for case studies in business and society field. Definitional problem is significant—i.e., what is a social issue? Bounding will be an increasingly relevant criteria in evaluating such studies.

8. *Society as a Whole.* Occasionally the subject of case studies, an entire country or culture (e.g., Japan) is most difficult to bound properly. Evaluation criteria must include comprehensiveness or factual presentation, and comparative insights into multidimensional cultural aspects.

Focus on Processes of Interaction

9. *Public Policy Process.* How actors of different, often conflicting interests find bases to accommodate one another and resolve problems. Difficult to separate the process from the organizations or institutions that are directly involved. Evaluation should focus on the author's skill in distinguishing the process aspects from the substantive aspects of the subject.

10. *Direct Action.* Campaigns, boycotts, and so forth to influence other institutions. Bounding is often done by focusing on events (e.g., Campaign GM, Nestlé Boycott). Evaluation criteria include comprehensiveness of factual presentation, and comparison with alternative explanations.

1. A Single Organization

Case studies of business firms, regulatory agencies, or other organizational units in their entirety are among the most common forms of case research. The organizational case study requires very little abstraction to define the boundaries of the case, the organization being a very natural unit for analysis. More difficult to meet is the criterion of comprehensiveness of factual information because of the sensitivity and confidentiality of internal documents, interviews, and so forth. An alternative is to organize a case around only objectively verifiable data—such as publicly available. This approach allows the researcher to comment on "operative policies" of the organization, even while unable to comment on its "stated policies" and intentions (Post, 1978). Such an approach may be satisfactory for explanatory or predictive case research although insufficiently comprehensive for descriptive case research. For examples of explanatory case research see Chatov, 1978; Post, 1978; and Sethi, 1977.

2. An Organizational Subunit

This type of case research concentrates on a particular department or structural subunit—such as division—of an organization. The researcher's concern may be with the manner in which a particular staff unit relates to operating divisions on social issues matters—e.g., equal employment opportunity—the way in which a subunit functions within the framework of the whole organization—e.g., Competition Bureau within the Federal Trade Commission—or the degree to which the internal functioning of a subunit within the organization depends upon its relations to external entities—for example, community relations office. Research at the subunit level can create more pitfalls than organizational units in their entirety. A subunit's boundaries are more fluid and less easily fixed for research than those of an entire organization; in addition, subunits across different organizations may have more differences than similarities. Under such circumstances, the researcher must take care to be as explicit as possible in defining the subunit within the context it operates.

3. An Organizational Practice

Specific organizational practices are frequent targets for social issues researchers. Single case and comparative case analyses of such practices as affirmative action programs (Taylor, 1979), corporate philanthropy (Callaghan, 1975), and political activities (Brenner, 1980; Epstein, 1980) are representative of the approach. Problems often occur because of the difficulty of precisely defining the practice, or class of practices, to be researched. For example, philanthropy is often a part of a business firm's community relations or public affairs activities, providing a rationale for the actual disbursement of charitable gifts. Case research on philanthropic practices would have to relate philanthropic practices to the community affairs or public affairs efforts of the organization. The limitations of the research must be clearly specified. The field research itself may be the first indication that the practice as originally defined encompasses several seemingly discrete areas. The practice may be only understood in the context of some other area of corporate behavior, and the researcher must be prepared to revise the original conception of the topic—e.g., philanthropic practices—in favor of a more precise definition of the subject—for example, philanthropy in the service of community relations goals.

4. An Industry

While product line definitions may be quite appropriate in some case research, there are situations in which the definition of the topic may call for a broader definition of the industry. Case research on the political impact of the oil industry, for example, requires inclusion of not only the integrated major producers but also the independent producers, marketers, and refiners, the wildcat operators, oil service companies, and so forth. What drives the determination of the industry definition is the theoretical requirement that the definition meet the needs of the research question and the theory being pursued.

Definitions that meet such needs are important to search for in case research, for they frequently have a bearing on the behavior of firms in response to social issues. For example, the infant formula industry consists of firms which do not exclusively manufacture and sell infant formula products. Rather, some are food companies which sell formula as part of a line of milk-based products, while others are pharmaceutical manufacturers which sell formula as a health care product through a medical sales system (Post and Baer, 1979). As suggested, the behavior of these firms varies in ways related to their differing orientations to conducting business.

In addition to case research which concentrates on the firm or industry, it may concentrate primarily on society or some portion thereof as the focal unit for analysis. Listed below are several categories of "society-oriented" types of case research.

5. Segment of Society

The study of specific social groups, "stakeholders," or "relevant publics" can also be made using case research. Institutional investors (Purcell, 1979), church organizations (Vogel, 1978), and public interest networks (Gerlach, 1978) have all been the focus of case research efforts. Familiar definitional problems exist. For example, are churches institutional investors or proponents of shareholder resolutions? In terms of the topical definition, such choice will make a difference. If the focus is on institutional investors, churches may be a subset of such investors in the research. If, however, the researcher's real interest is the behavior of churches, their investment behavior regarding resolutions must be viewed as one of a number of social activities in which they engage. This specification of the context in which the focal segment is to be analyzed is a crucial research step that too often is seen as secondary in importance to gathering information. In truth, it is quite important that the researcher may be reasonably specific in placing the facets of the project into a logically appropriate arrangement. Thus, one more precise way of defining the example study mentioned above so that behavior is the focal question would be as a study of "the institutional investor behavior of denominational churches in the United States." The initiation of shareholder resolutions may be left to be considered as one type of behavior.

6. A Social Phenomenon

Case research often focusses on major events or social phenomena. The creation of NASA and the drive to put man on the moon, the aborted campaign to build the SuperSonic Transport (SST) (Horwitch, 1982), grass roots politics as reflected in the TVA (Selznick, 1965), the economic regulation of the New Deal (Chatov, 1978), or the present development of a synthetic fuels industry are but a few examples of social phenomena that have been examined in ways that emphasize the business/government/society relationship. A critical problem in such research is to define the phenomenon at the outset in sufficient detail so as to distinguish the case analysis from a general history. A conceptual proposition or hypothesis can facilitate case research. Sethi's study of advocacy advertising (1973), identifies a phenomenon, describes it in detail, and then uses organizational studies to further elucidate the significance of the advocacy advertising phenomenon. See also Sethi's study of executive liability trends (1981) and Horwitch's (1980) research on large scale social projects such as synfuels. In each, the key is a clear description of the phenomenon followed by research that illuminates the complexity of that phenomenon and enriches understanding of factors and forces affecting it.

7. A Social Issue

The most prevalent of all types of case research in the business and society field is the study of specific social issues, which have long dominated the published literature of the field. Methodological problems exist with respect to these studies. The thoroughness and subtlety of analysis has often been in question. Too often, these studies have been little more than scrapbook collections of material gleaned from secondary sources with little or no primary investigation. At the same time, with appropriate controls and theoretical guidance, quality research with useful theoretical payoff may and should be designed using materials already published in an astute manner. Social issue case studies and research can make a greater contribution if they rise beyond the purely descriptive level.

Today, research on social issues should focus on the identification of explanatory variables and prediction of future developments, beginning with a conceptual definition of what constitutes an issue. For example, the senior author has argued that a social issue exists whenever a gap exists between the public's expectations of an organization or industry's proper performance and the actual performance of that organization or industry (Post, 1978). Thus, redlining practices, doing business in South Africa, worker exposure to toxic substances, marketing infant formula in developing nations, and dumping taconite in lakes and streams all have in common a definitional similarity. Whereas the analysis of one more incident of industrial effluent discharge is not very helpful research for the business and society field, and analysis of a pollution control problem in terms of a given definition or concept—e.g., public issue life cycle may serve to illuminate a new facet of business/government/society relations or suggest a variation on the basic way public issues evolve which adds new knowledge to the field.

In the 1980s the scholarly significance of social issue analysis must come from the researcher's needs to be skilled at either doing an analysis of the larger problem in a context—for example, the substantive analysis of bank lending practices—or from systematic analysis in terms of an *a priori* definition or concept of the issue.

8. Society as a Whole

Occasionally, an entire society will form the basis of case research of corporation-society interaction; at the society level each society is one case. Most notable in this type of research are the efforts of Sethi (1978) and Lodge (1975) to compare the business/government/society relationship in Japan with that of the United States. As critical reviews of both efforts indicate, such analysis is fraught with conceptual, methodological, and factual problems. The most telling criticism may well be that institutional interrelationships are so culturally specific, and so entwined with the entire fabric of the society, that nothing less than expert treatment of each nation can produce a truly insightful analysis.

More promising than the inevitably broad national comparisons, however, is more narrowly focused study of an institution which arises out of a societal setting. Dickie's (1981) recent study of the interaction between government, multinational firms, and social interests in the development of the Indonesian securities market and Monsen and Walters' (1980) analysis of public enterprises in Western European nations suggest a direction such cross-cultural research might take.

Finally, there are case studies that focus primarily on processes of interaction among social institutions or between institutions and individuals. In particular, there are opportunities for case research on the public policy process and direct corporation/society interaction.

9. Public Policy Process

The political processes through which public and private interests are reconciled provide rich opportunities for case research. The bounding of the research can be accomplished by focusing on a particular piece of legislation (Redman, 1973), an administrative agency decision—e.g., FTC, NLRB—or a court opinion—(for example, First National Bank of Boston vs. Bellotti). Much legal research has concentrated on the judicial process as a way of defining and resolving social conflicts, and useful predictive analyses might be developed in this context. In evaluating such research, the researcher must distinguish the type of case research being undertaken—descriptive, exploratory, explanatory, predictive—and whether the author is attempting to analyze the process or the substantive issue on which the political process is acting.

10. Direct Action

Public action campaigns, boycotts, and so forth, represent distinct forms of direct social action taken against an organization or idea. Bounding may require that a stream of events be defined as a direct action campaign—e.g., Nestlé boycott, even if a formal campaign has not been announced (e.g., Moral Majority's review of television advertising). The researcher's explanation when compared with alternative explanations offered by participants or other observers needs to be balanced and to offer greater insight than any single viewpoint.

METHODOLOGICAL ISSUES

The process of case research must address a number of important methodological issues—for example, to what extent must the information be collected "systematically"? Must there be a uniform presentation? How does one identify and distinguish fact from interpretation or inference? These questions of methodology, in turn, are related to the purposes for which a case study is used. Issues of methodology are addressed in the process of inquiry.

Systematic inquiry can and has been done in many different, legitimate ways. C. West Churchman in the *Design of Inquiring Systems* (1971) argues that the key for the inquirer is to recognize that certain fundamental questions—what guarantees the value and validity of the work ("who is the guarantor"), and what is the relation between observed fact and *a priori* assumptions—must be answered in advance to insure the integrity of the inquiry. The models of inquiry in the field are relatively few in number, and researchers inevitably gravitate toward original research rather than the replication of other studies. Substantively, in the sense of covering the territory in numerous contexts, this is healthy for the field; but methodologically, there are perils for researchers.

There are a number of useful papers on methodology in a previous volume in this series and more in the present volume. In particular, Aldag and Bartol's (1978) article on empirical studies, Frederick's (1978) paper on social auditing methodology, and Bauer's (1978) paper on analyzing the corporate response process each present important insights into the problems encountered in designing research studies. Papers by Epstein (1980), Post and Baer (1980), Dierkes (1980), and Rey (1980) in Volume 2 also highlight methodological issues.

Three propositions about methodology can be set forth. First, most research in this field is "qualitative," rather than "quantitative," because the questions are more amenable to qualitative research. Second, many of the research questions require the use of multiple techniques rather than any single technique because the probability of a single technique providing a comprehensive answer is very low. Research is more appropriately viewed as a *process of inquiry* requiring many tools, rather than the application of a single technique in a series of replications. Third, case research has proven to be an especially useful approach because it is well suited to analysis of the complexity of business/government/society relations. The weaknesses of case research are not unique; they are the fundamental problems of all inquiry. With appropriate attention to those weaknesses, the case study is a legitimate form of research in this field.

"Quantitative research" in the sense of large sample-based research has been infrequently done in the business and society field, although it does achieve prominence in industrial organization and applied public policy areas, and in the study of such topics as corporate ownership and control and executive attitudes on social policy matters. The prerequisite for quantitative analysis is, of course, an adequate data base. Where time series data exist, as in the Economic Censuses or IRS collections, statistical analysis can be fruitfully pursued. But there have been relatively few such data bases in the business and society field. Recent collections of data on corporate boards of directors (Sethi, 1979), public affairs offices (Boston University, 1981), and political action committees (Epstein, 1979) improve the prospects for more quantitative research in the future.

"Qualitative research," particularly in the form of case studies, participant observation, and interviews, has been the foundation of most empirical work in the field. This is not unusual, since it has been necessary to create factual and descriptive documentation of what is actually occurring as a starting point. Today, a baseline of information has been created in many areas of the field, and the need for explanatory research is increasing. While qualitative research can continue to make significant contributiuons, it must become increasingly concerned with the testing of hypotheses.

An especially important example of the continuing importance of qualitative research can be found in Philip Burch's (1972) study of corporate ownership and control. For several decades following the Berle and Means (1932) study of corporate ownership patterns, more sophisticated quantitative studies of time series data concluded that there was a nearly total separation of stock ownership by family interests and effective control of management policy in those large corporations. Burch's study painstakingly drew on insider insights to reassess the influence of familiar ownership interests and produced a fundamental reexamination of the ownership/control relationship. More recently, Edward Herman (1981) has reexamined a portion of the data base and addressed anew the relationship of ownership and control and the social implications thereof.

The point, simply stated, is that the research technique to be used must fit the question being asked. Qualitative analysis does not sacrifice scholarly rigor by its mere use. Indeed, good qualitative studies are the key to the creation of useful and valuable bases for quantitative analysis.

THE PROCESS OF CASE RESEARCH

Case research is often a euphemism for qualitative research. While some authors view the case study as but one type of qualitative research (Duncan, 1979) on a par with interviewing and participant observation, such a conception is too narrow for this discussion of case research. Properly conceived and executed case research must incorporate the data acquired through interviews and observation but will also draw on available quantitative data. Although it is not a quantitative technique itself, case research that sweeps in all relevant data makes the inclusion— and analysis—of quantitative material inevitable. Thus, a research case study is more than just qualitative research, and something other than a simple qualitative technique. It is, rather, a basic way of thinking about complex issues.

The process of inquiry that distinguishes case research is different from but not entirely dissimilar to the process that guides experimental or more narrowly focussed research studies. Experimental and quasi-experimental research is characterized by a straight-line process which requires beginning with theory in the form of testable hypotheses. Such a process tends to place primary emphasis on the verification of existing theory. Generation of new theory from such a process is possible but is not the primary goal. This process is like that of Kuhn's (1962, 1970) "normal science." Figure 2 illustrates the major steps in the straight-line process and is derived from Isaac and Michael (1971) and Campbell and Stanley (1963).

Case research is one of a family of processes called by Glaser and Strauss (1967) the "constant comparative method." These processes differ most widely from the straight-line process in their *iterative* character. With the theory choice decisions made (see Figure 3) and the preconceptions and assumptions made explicit, the process begins with selection of data. Iteratively, each data "slice" is collected, coded, and analyzed. This process-within-a-process insures that the most theoretical value is extracted for the effort. The data is collected because the theory needs it. It is coded relative to the explicit theoretical goals and pre-conceptions, and previous data slices. It is analyzed for its potential contribution to concepts (categories and their properties).

Conceptually, there are several process-within-process cycles. Each cycle widens and moves the research in steps from 1) the collecting-coding-analyzing of the data; to 2) examining new data slices for their similarities to other data and categories; to 3) examining new data slices for their differences from other data and categories; and so on with repeated comparisons of new data and concepts to what has already been developed through the latter stages of hypothesis development and theory integration. Figure 4 illustrates the movement conceptually from the theory choice to the theory level and accompanying data.

Theory Choices

First choice. A central methodological question for the researcher is whether the case research is being undertaken to develop or to test theory. This decision on the primary purpose of the research will have dramatic impact on both what is to be done, and the sequence in which those activities are to be conducted. The choice is between "theory generation" and "theory verification." Either purpose can employ case research, but this choice of purpose will influence type (descriptive, exploratory, explanatory, or predictive) and the manner in which the subject (see Table 2, supra) is definitionally bound.

Figure 2.   Straight-Line Research Process[a]

Survey Literature

↓

Define Specific Problem Clearly

↓

Formulate Testable Hypotheses
and Competing Hypotheses;
Define Basic Concepts and Variables

↓

State Underlying Assumptions
which will Govern
Interpretation of Results

↓

Construct Research
Design to Maximize
Internal and External
Validity and to
Specify and Control
Data Procedures

↓

Data Collection

↓

Data Analysis

↓

Write Results
and
Conclusions

Note: [a]This schematic is a simplified picture of the process Isaac and Michael (1971) propose as necessary for carrying out valid, reliable, scientific research.

Figure 3. Two Primary Theory Choices

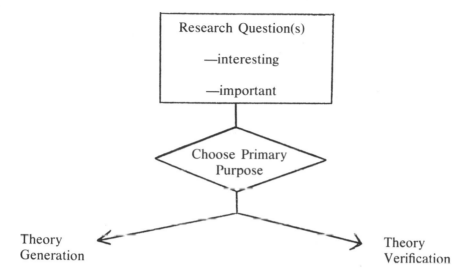

If theory verification is desired, the researcher may use either the familiar straight-line process (Figure 2) of literature review and hypothesis testing or explanatory or predictive case research as appropriate ways to test theory (Post, 1978; Merenda, 1981). If theory generation is the primary purpose, a different and less familiar process must be used which keeps the building of theory prominently first. Descriptive, exploratory, and explanatory case research may be employed to generate theory; but the research process begins with the question of what kind of theory the researcher is pursuing.

Second choice. Theory may range from substantive to formal in nature. That is, it may apply only to a specifically defined context(s), called substantive, or it may conceptually embrace a number of substantive areas, more formal. For example, a researcher might study the patterns of pricing behavior in one industry, and then proceed to develop a theory of pricing that was derived from known information about pricing behavior in many industries. This general theory of pricing would be a formal theory, embracing many substantive areas. The theory could then be verified by testing it in other industries, preferably not those used in its development.

Substantive and formal theory can be either developed through an inductive process or deduced from other theory areas. The researcher must recognize the importance of determining whether the questions are at a substantive or formal level; for example, is the purpose to develop

Figure 4.   Theory Level Choices and Beginning of Constant
Comparative Method for Theory Generation

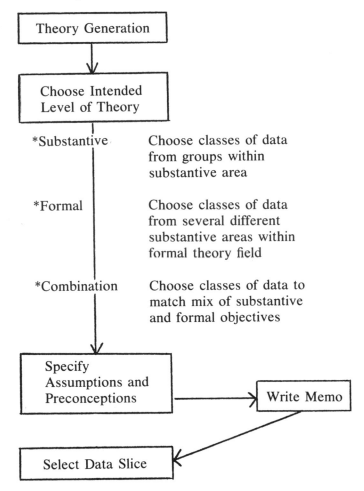

theory dealing with a narrower substantive area (e.g., social policy implementation), or more general theory (e.g., implementation of *all* corporate policies)? Similarly, one sometimes asks a question at a conceptual
level ("What is the model of corporate policy implementation?") and
then considers a specific context or substantive setting (e.g., affirmative
action programs) in which questions about policy implementation may
be examined.

In the study of the corporation and society, theory development has
usually been grounded in factual examples; and case studies of companies

and social issues have been the foundation of most conceptual propositions. Quite often, however, authors have proposed to leap from data analysis in one or two substantive areas to a general theoretical formulation. Sethi's (1975) comparison of social responsiveness in the United States and Japan, for example, suffers from an overly ambitious attempt to generalize to a model of social responsiveness from data on only two countries. Such "great leaps" would be more likely to succeed through a more systematic blending of formal and substantive theory development.

Between the extremes of purely substantive theory and purely formal theory lies a third possibility that is most appropriate in the social policy and performance area. This possibility is one of multiple layers of substantive theory between the descriptive data of an area and the formal theory. The analysis of patterns of corporate response (Post, 1976) provides an illustration. A detailed analysis of how one firm responded to many issues in the same time period provided a first collection of data and some initial concepts (reactive, manipulative, and interactive patterns). Using these definitions, a larger sample of cases organized by type of firm (manufacturing, service, trade) and by type of external change (economic, political, values, technological) was studied (Post, 1978). The analysis of this data helped sharpen the conceptual definitions and allowed the data analysis to be framed into a formal theory of how corporations behave in the face of external change. Mahon (1982), Sonnenfeld (1981), and Logsdon (1981) have since tested various facets of this theory in their own research.

The appropriateness of each of the theory-choice possibilities outlined above depends on the researcher's own goals and purposes. Glaser and Strauss (1967) reported that formal theory was infrequently developed directly from data, although there were a number of noteworthy instances in which such had occurred. The more familiar pattern was for theory to be developed first at a substantive level; then, the theory of several substantive areas was joined into a formal theory. The researcher needs to articulate this theoretical objective at the outset of a study, for it guides both the way the problem will be defined and the process of data collection. For these reasons it is desirable that the purpose be explicitly written out before data collection begins.

Case Research and the Comparative Method

As discussed previously, the single case study has its greatest value when used as a means to describe a complex phenomenon or as an exploratory device to discern possible dimensions of the issues that may lend themselves to more precise analysis. The single case study probably cannot serve as a basis for a broad generalization nor as the ground for disproving an established generalization (Lijphart, 1971:619). Comparative case analysis, however, has greater explanatory and predictive value. Indeed, comparative case analysis can be employed to either build theory from data or to verify an extant theory against additional facets of reality. Used in either way, legitimate comparative case analysis has a number of stringent methodological requirements similar to those already discussed.

First, the researcher's purpose—such as, to build theory or to verify theory—must be decided and made explicit. Second, the kind of theory being pursued—substantive, formal, or some combination—must also be made clear. A crucial aspect of these steps is the articulation of *a priori* assumptions and preconceptions that will inevitably guide the collection of data (see Figure 4). For example, a researcher who is studying the issue of plant closings must articulate both the analytical perspective (theoretical or applied) and the substantive perspective (corporation or society) being brought to the study. It is a matter of setting forth "where you're coming from" in the design of the research.

The third step is the identification of types and classes of data to be compared according to "theoretical relevance." Theoretical relevance is the criterion which continually guides data selection throughout the research process. The question being asked is "What do the concepts thus far developed tell us about (a) the next appropriate slice of data, and (b) where to look for it?" Usually, the researcher will have to decide which of several slices of data to examine next, a decision which should be made on the basis of greatest incremental contribution to the emerging theory.

The underlying method (see Figure 5) is an iterative process that moves the researcher through four stages, beginning with: Ⓐ *data;* whose Ⓑ *categories* and their properties are developed; until Ⓒ suggested *hypotheses* are formed, based on a reduction of the original categories and properties; and finally, all these Ⓓ for a dense, well-integrated *theory* with no more major modifications needed. Depending on the scope of the particular research project, this process can take months or years.

First in the process is a procedure of sampling in which the researcher collects, codes, and analyzes each data "slice" and decides what data slice to collect next and where to look (Figure 5, Ⓐ).

In a way that Churchman (1971) describes as Leibnitzian, the first step in the data search is to look for similarities in the data that suggest a category (Figure 5, Ⓑ), although differences which appear must also be noted. The next slice of data is then selected which has a similarity to the last in terms of the category or property under examination. This effort serves to verify the usefulness of the category, establishes its basic properties, and delimits where and when and to what extent the category

Figure 5. Interactive Constant Comparison Research Process[a]

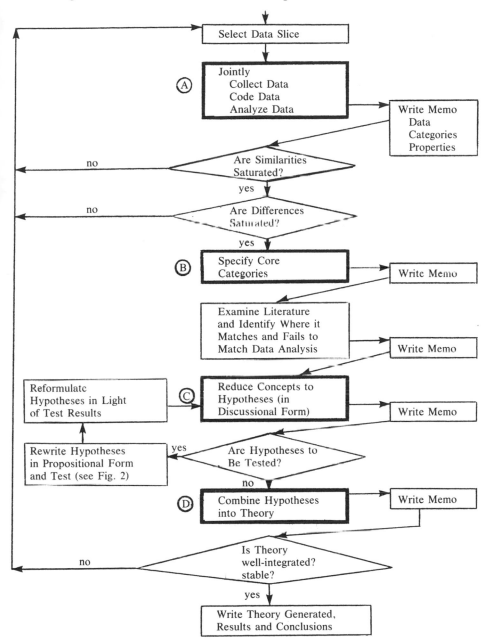

Note: [a]This schematic is a substantially simplified picture of the process Glaser and Strauss (1967) take their readers through. Glaser and Strauss do not present their process in flow chart form.

exists (thus, enabling prediction). Because differences are also being noted along the way, the conditions under which the category (or later in the process, hypotheses or theory) varies will also be articulated.

A second part to category development is also required where the data search is focussed on maximizing, rather than minimizing, differences. Diversity is sought to stretch a concept to its limits and push it to its depths. Simultaneously, similarities not previously noted are also taken into account. This effort forces a category conceptually tight and dense with well-defined properties, called "well-integrated."

These ideas of category development can be illustrated through a review of research undertaken by the senior author at Aetna Life & Casualty some years ago (Post, 1976). The study was concerned with patterns of response to social and political change. The company's responses to fifteen separate political issues were detailed and documented through archival research and participant interviews. Of the fifteen, the responses to twelve of the issues involved a corporate coping with problems over which the firm had no control, or in several instances, an effort to manipulate the process through which the issue evolved. The apparent or "contingent truth" was that the firms either reacted to, or attempted to shape the environment. This suggested two possible categories (reactive and manipulative); the careful examination of the organization-environment interchange during the evolution of each issue made it possible to both maximize and minimize the differences between responses. In so doing, two patterns of response were "defined". For those several issues which did not fit either category, close scrutiny of the organization-environment interaction suggested a possible third pattern. Since there was insufficient data to prove such a pattern, as with the others, a new issue was selected to clarify and distinguish the "interactive" pattern from the previously discussed reactive and manipulative patterns.

In Figure 5, ©, the third major part of concept development requires parsimonious creation of hypotheses from the categories and properties. It is here that testing may be appropriate as well as testing of the integrated theory (Figure 5, Ⓓ). A well-integrated theory with well-defined concepts will have a delimited scope, making it neither too narrow to be useful nor too general to be helpful. Delimiting bounds the contexts in which the theory applies.

According to Glaser and Strauss (1967), it is *after* core categories have been constructed from the data that similarities, convergences with, and divergences from the existing literature may be established. The reason this is done after core categories are constructed, is to minimize the amount of tunnel vision along one theoretical track brought to the analysis of the case. In their view the best theory is "grounded" theory, and the purer the grounding—that is, the less adulterated it is by pre-existing theoretical concepts—the greater its ultimate value.

The Guarantor

Case research most dramatically departs from large sample studies supported by sophisticated statistical analyses on the question of what guarantees the validity of the research. In addition to adherence to the straight-line process, statistical analysis gains its power from sufficient degrees of freedom, tests of significance, and confidence levels. Case research does not have any comparable features, and its validity is heavily dependent on the researcher's skill and depth of understanding of the subject studied. Indeed, it is the research process itself that is a key guarantor of the validity of case research. Here we must distinguish, once again, among the various types of case research.

Descriptive case research only intends to describe reality. It is valid, therefore, if all relevant facts are woven into the description, and other persons who are familiar with the subject acknowledge the comprehensiveness of each case. This is precisely where many case books used for teaching in the business and society field fall woefully short of acceptable research standards. (For example, having been a participant in the controversy over infant formula marketing in developing nations, the senior author has yet to see one published case study on the controversy that is adequate in terms of factual presentation. Thus, on a substantive level these are not good descriptive case *research* works because they do not meet the standard of comprehensiveness. This may, of course, be satisfactory for teaching and discussion purposes.)

The validity of *exploratory* case research rests more on the concepts than on specific facts. In a recent article Campbell (1975) describes how degrees of freedom in a single case study come from each piece of data which saturates (in our terms) a concept. When the research purpose is the illumnination of critical issues, the test of validity must be whether other scholars find the results illuminating. Occasionally, a researcher will undertake a single case study from a particular perspective in order to determine whether or not an issue exists *from that point of view*. Although this is a legitimate activity, it limits the validity test to one of whether others, with that same point of view, believe that critical issues have been raised. At some point the researcher can so narrow the peer group as to leave no outside guarantor available!

When the purpose of the research is to *explain* and/or *predict* behavior, it is essential that the researcher have in mind an appropriate process in advance and adhere to that plan throughout the project. Adherence insures valid control for which the process is designed. The constant comparative method is an especially powerful method to use in explanatory or predictive case research. The guarantor of validity is the density (to the saturation point) and delimited scope (for applicability and generalizability) of the resultant theory.

As the process of collecting, coding and analyzing successive "slices" of data and as category–, hypothesis–, and theory-building continue, a certain blurring of decisions or thoughts can occur. If during each iteration of each step in the process, however, the researcher takes care to write in memo form the categories and properties suggested by the data, a more consistent and logical analysis is likely to emerge. A similar practice of recording events and ideas as the process proceeds is used by the lab scientist who keeps carbon-copied notes in a spiral-bound book. The process of memo writing forces conceptualization early on and throughout the process. It is most valuable in dealing with conflicting evidence, so that the questions, puzzles, and apparent dilemmas suggested by the evidence are not lost. If preserved, these thoughts can become the clues to future conceptualization.

As Glaser and Strauss (1967) suggest and as others have subsequently demonstrated, case research, properly constructed and executed, can be both rigorous and credible in its quality and theoretical contribution. Moreover, the use of comparative case analysis—such as, several cases matched on theoretically relevant criteria—offers substantially more potential for generalizability than the single case study. None of this can be done very well from an "armchair," however. A process such as the one detailed in this paper is as demanding as many other forms of research. Most important, it provides a means of "building up" the base of substantive theory in the field.

LARGE PROJECTS, LITTLE STEPS

Perhaps the most intriguing aspect of case research is the way in which it can complement and enhance other research techniques. There are times when the holistic perspective of a case analysis is precisely what is needed to move the frontier of understanding forward. There are other times when surveys or other large scale methods are more appropriate. Most important, there are many important research questions that require, indeed demand, that a combination or sequence of techniques be employed to produce progress in knowledge about the subject. Examples of the different roles case research has played in recent research follow.

In 1976, the senior author began a study of the international infant formula industry and the conflict surrounding competitive marketing of formula products in less developed countries. Comparative descriptive cases of the competitive strategies and behavior of five companies provided an important factual and exploratory base. The research on these firms progressed to an explanatory level when the purpose was to understand how these industry leaders would respond to national legislation and the World Health Organization's code of marketing conduct (Post, 1980). Subsequent research steps were facilitated (and made possible by the filling of a "factual void") by this intensive work and have involved large surveys in a number of developing nations.

A second example involves the Boston University research project on "The Public Affairs Function in the American Corporation." As discussed by our colleague, E. A. Murray, Jr., elsewhere in this volume, exploratory case studies of how four individual companies managed their public affairs functions clarified important practices and internal relationships—for example, public affairs and corporate planning—and suggested a possible continuum of structures, shaping factors, and evolutionary development. The clarifications were important in the construction of a survey instrument, and the suggestions about the evaluation of public affairs units studied. In this manner case analysis has been used in concert with, and as a complement to, other types of inquiry. In so doing, it provides an excellent example of how the systematic pursuit of significant questions can yield a considerable improvement in our understanding of the corporation in society.

CONCLUSION

As the study of corporation and society relationships and interactions proceeds, it is to be expected that our research will become both more refined and more extensive. If our substantive theory continues to grow in systematic ways, the possibilities for formal theory development will improve as well. In both the generation of substantive theory, and the testing of formal theory, case analysis has much to offer. The systematic development, and extension, of research in the study of the corporation and society can become the hallmark of the second decade of this field. By focusing our research this way, we are likely to give to it the central focus and definition that it has needed. As we have argued in this paper, the key to systematic development lies not in the application of any single technique but in the creative and imaginative pursuit of an elusive truth.

NOTES

1.   The data from which this analysis was drawn is reported in *Public Affairs Offices and Their Functions: A Summary of Survey Results* (Boston University School of Management, Public Affairs Research Group, 1981).

2. Cases made available through the Intercollegiate Case Clearing House (ICCH) are almost universally prepared as "teaching cases." This purpose often results in a slanting or withholding of information for pedagogical reasons. Such gaps render these cases flawed for most research purposes.

REFERENCES

Ackerman, Robert W., "How Companies Respond to Social Demands." *Harvard Review* (July-August), 1973.

Ackerman, Robert W., *The Social Challenge to Business.* Cambridge, MA: Harvard University Press, 1975.

Ackerman, Robert, and Raymond Bauer, *Corporate Social Responsiveness–The Modern Dilemma.* Reston, VA: Reston Publishing Co., Inc., 1976.

Aldag, Ramon J., and Kathryn B. Bartol, "Empirical Studies of Corporate Social Performance and Policy: A Survey of Problems and Results." In Lee E. Preston (ed.), *Research in Corporate Social Performance and Policy,* vol. 1. Greenwich, CT: JAI Press Inc., 1978, pp. 165–200.

Bauer, Raymond A. "The Corporate Response Process." In Lee E. Preston (ed.), *Research in Corporate Social Performance and Policy,* vol. 1. Greenwich, CT: JAI Press, Inc., 1978, pp. 99–122.

Bauer, R. A., and D. H. Fenn, Jr., *The Corporate Social Audit.* New York: The Russell Sage Foundation, 1972.

Berle, A. A., and Gardner Means., *The Modern Corporation and Private Property.* NY: The Macmillan Co., 1933.

Boston University School of Management Public Affairs Research Group. *Public Affairs Offices and Their Functions: Summary of Survey Responses.* 1981.

Brenner, Steven N., "Influences on the Decision to Use Business-Government Relations: A Study of Computer Time-Sharing Firms." Unpublished doctoral dissertation. Harvard University, 1972.

Brenner, Steven N., "Corporate Political Activity: An Exploratory Study in a Developing Industry." In Lee E. Preston (ed.), *Research in Corporate Social Performance and Policy,* vol. 2. Greenwich, CT: JAI Press, Inc., 1980, pp. 197–236.

Burch, Philip H., *The Managerial Revolution Reassessed.* Lexington, MA: D. C. Heath, Inc., 1972.

Callaghan, D. W., "Management of the Corporate Gift-Giving Function: An Empirical Study of the Life Insurance Industry." Unpublished doctoral disseration. University of Massachusetts/Amherst, 1975.

Campbell, Donald T. III., "Degrees of Freedom and the Case Study." *Comparative Political Studies* 8 (July):178–193, 1975.

Campbell, Donald T., and Julian C. Stanley, *Experimental and QuasiExperimental Designs for Research.* Chicago: Rand McNally College Publishing Co., 1963.

Chatov, Robert, *Corporate Financial Reporting.* New York: The Free Press, 1975.

Churchman, C. West, *The Design of Inquiring Systems.* New York: Basic Books, Inc., 1971.

Dickie, Robert B., "MNC Responses to Equity-Sharing Policies: The Indonesian Experience." In Lee E. Preston (ed.), *Research in Corporate Social Performance and Policy,* vol. 3. Greenwich, CT: JAI Press, Inc., 1981, pp. 203–228.

Dierkes, Meinolf, "Corporate Social Reporting and Performance in Germany." In Lee E. Preston (ed.), *Research in Corporate Social Performance and Policy,* vol. 2. Greenwich, CT: JAI Press, Inc., 1979, pp. 251–290.

Duncan, Robert B., "Qualitative Research Methods in Strategic Management." In Dan E. Schendel and Charles W. Hofer (ed.), *Strategic Management: A New View of Business Policy and Planning*, Boston: Little Brown and Co., 1979.

Epstein, Edwin M., "Business Political Activity: Research Approaches and Analytical Issues." In Lee E. Preston (ed.), *Research in Corporate Social Performance and Policy*, vol. 2. Greenwich, CT: JAI Press, Inc., 1980, pp. 123–138.

Epstein, Edwin M., *The Corporation in American Politics*. Englewood Cliffs, NJ: Prentice-Hall, Inc., 1969.

Epstein, Edwin M., "The Emergence of Political Action Committees." *Political Finance: Sage Electoral Studies Yearbook*, Beverly Hills: Sage Publications, Inc., 5(1979):159–197.

First National Bank of Boston vs. Bellotti. 98 S Ct. 1407, 1978.

Frederick, William C., "Auditing Corporate Social Performance: The Anatomy of a Social Research Project." In Lee E. Preston (ed.), *Research in Corporate Social Performance and Policy*, vol. . Greenwich, CT: JAI Press, Inc., 1978, pp. 123–138.

Friedman, Milton with the assistance of Rose D. Friedman, *Capitalism and Freedom*. Chicago: The University of Chicago Press, 1962.

Galbraith, J. K., *The New Industrial State*. Boston: Houghton-Mifflin, paperback edition, Signet Books, 1967.

Gerlach, Luther P., "Milk, Movements and Multinationals: Complex Interactions and Social Responsibilities." In *Responsibilities of Multinational Corporations to Society*, vol. III. Proceedings of the Fifth Panel Discussion, Council of Better Business Bureaus, Washington, D.C.: (June 1–2) 1978.

Glaser, Barney G., and Anselm L. Strauss, *The Discovery of Grounded Theory: Strategies for Qualitative Research*. Observation Series (ed.), Howard S. Becker. New York: Aldine Publishing Co., 1967.

Hanson, Kirk, "Corporate Strategy and Public Policy." Paper presented at the Academy of Management Meetings, Atlanta, August, 1979.

Herman, Edward S., *Corporate Control, Corporate Power*. New York: Cambridge University Press, 1981.

Horwitch, Mel, "Uncontrolled and Unfocussed Growth: The U.S. Supersonic Transport, SST, and the Attempt to Synthesize Fuels from Coal." *Interdisciplinary Science Reviews* 5 (3):231–244, 1980.

———, *Clipped Wings: The American SST Conflict*. Cambridge, MA: MIT Press, 1982.

Isaac, S., and W. B. Michael, *Handbook in Research and Evaluation*. San Diego, CA: Edits Publishers, 1971.

Jesaitis, Patrick T., "Corporate Strategies and the Urban Crisis: A Study of Business Response to a Social Problem." Unpublished doctoral dissertation. Harvard University, 1969.

Kelly, Donald W., "Canadian Corporate Social Responsibility Survey." In Lee E. Preston (ed.), *Research in Corporate Social Performance and Policy*, vol. 1. Greenwich, CT: JAI Press, Inc., 1978, pp. 279–286.

Kuhn, Thomas S., *The Structure of Scientific Revolutions*. International Encyclopedia of Unified Science, Chicago: University of Chicago Press, 1962 (1970, 2nd ed.).

Lijphart, Arend, "Comparative Politics and the Comparative Method." *American Political Science Review* (65):682–693, 1971.

Lindblom, Charles E., *Politics and Markets: The World's Political-Economic Systems*. New York: Basic Books, Inc., 1977.

Lodge, George, *The New American Ideology*. New York: Alfred Knopp, 1975.

Logsdon, Jeanne M., "Organizational Responses to Environmental Regulation: Oil Refining Companies and Air Pollution." Unpublished paper, 1981.

Mahon, John F., "The Corporate Public Affairs Office: Structure, Process, and Impact." Unpublished doctoral dissertation. Boston University, 1982.

Marris, Robin, ed., *The Corporate Society*. London: Macmillan Press, 1974.

Merenda, Michael J., "The Process of Corporate Social Involvement: Five Case Studies." In Lee E. Preston (ed.), *Research in Corporate Social Performance and Policy*, vol. 3. Greenwich, CT: JAI Press Inc., 1981, p. 3.

Miles, R. E., and C. Snow, *Organizational Strategy, Structure and Process*. New York: McGraw Hill, 1978.

Mintzberg, Henry, "Process as a Field of Management Theory." *Academy of Management Review* (January):88–103, 1977.

Monsen, R. Joseph, and Kenneth D. Walters, "State Owned Firms: A Review of the Data and Issues." In Lee E. Preston (ed.), *Research in Corporate Social Performance and Policy*, vol. 2. Greenwich, CT: JAI Press, Inc., 1980, pp. 125–156.

Murray, Edwin A., Jr., "The Implementation of Social Policies in Commercial Banks." Unpublished doctoral dissertation. Harvard University, 1974.

Murray, Edwin A., Jr., "The Social Response Process in Commercial Banks: An Empirical Investigation." *Academy of Management Review* (July):1976.

Nozick, Robert, *Anarchy, State, and Utopia*. New York: Basic Books, 1974.

Orren, Karen, *Corporate Power and Social Change*. Baltimore: John Hopkins, 1974.

Page, Robert R., "Organizational Response to Social Challenge: Theory and Evidence for Two Industries." Unpublished doctoral dissertation. Indiana University, 1972.

Post, James E., *Corporate Behavior and Social Change*. Reston, VA: Reston Publishing Co., Inc., Prentice-Hall, 1978.

———, *Risk and Response: Management and Social Change in American Insurance Industry*. Lexington, MA: D. C. Heath, 1976.

Post, James E., and Edward Baer, "The International Code of Marketing for Breast-milk Substitutes: Consensus, Compromise, and Conflict in the Infant Formula Controversy." *International Commission of Jurists Review* 25(December):52–61, 1980.

———, "Demarketing Infant Formula: Consumer Products in the Developing World." *Journal of Contemporary Business* 7(1979):17–35.

Post, James E., and John Mahon, "Articulated Turbulence: The Impact of Regulatory Agencies on Corporate Responses to Social Change." *Academy of Management Review*, 1980.

Preston, Lee E., "Corporation and Society: The Search for a Paradigm." *Journal of Economic Literature* 13(June 1975): 434–453.

Preston, Lee E., "Corporate Social Responsibility Accounting: A Proposal for a Format and an Example of the State of the Art." *Journal of Contemporary Business* 7(Winter):1978.

Preston, Lee E. and James E. Post, *Private Management and Public Policy*, Engelwood Cliffs, N.J.: Prentice-Hall, Inc., 1975.

Purcell, T. V., "Management and the 'Ethical' Investors." *Harvard Business Review* 57 5(September-October):24–62 plus, 1979.

Randall, Frederic Dunn, "Corporate Strategies in the Drug Industry." Ph.D. dissertation, Harvard University Graduate School of Business Administration, 1972.

Rawls, John, *Theory of Justice*. Cambridge: Harvard University Press, 1971.

Redman, Eric, *The Dance of Legislation*. New York: Simon and Schuster, 1973.

Rey, Francoise, "Corporate Social Performance and Reporting in France." In Lee E. Preston (ed.), *Research in Corporate Social Performance and Policy*, vol. 2. Greenwich, CT: JAI Press, Inc., 1980, pp. 291–325.

Scott, Bruce R., "Stages of Corporate Development-Parts I and II." Boston Intercollegiate Case Clearing House, 9-371-294/BP998, 1971.

Selznick, Phillip, *TVA and the Grass Roots*. New York: Harper and Row, Inc., 1965.

Sethi, S. Prakash, *Advocacy Advertising and Large Corporations*. Lexington, MA: Lexington Books, 1977.

————, "An Analytical Framework for Making Cross-Cultural Comparisons of Business Responses to Social Pressures: The Case of the United States and Japan." In Lee E. Preston (ed.), *Research in Corporate Social Performance and Policy,* vol. 1. Greenwich, CT: JAI Press, Inc., 1978, pp. 201–221.

————, "Corporate Law Violations and Executive Liability." In Lee E. Preston (ed.), *Research in Corporate Social Performance and Policy,* vol. 3. Greenwich, CT: JAI Press, Inc., 1981, pp. 71–104.

————, "Dimensions of Corporate Social Performance: An Analytical Framework." *California Management Review* 17(1975):58–64.

Sonnenfeld, Jeffrey, *Corporate Views of the Public Interest: Perceptions of the Forest Products Industry.* Boston: Auburn House, 1981.

Stone, Christopher D., *Where the Law Ends: The Social Control of Corporate Behavior.* New York: Harper Colophon Books, Harper and Row, 1975.

Taylor, Marilyn L., "Implementing Affirmative Action: Impetus and Enabling Factors in Five Organizations." In Lee E. Preston (ed.), *Research in Corporate Social Performance and Policy,* vol. 3. Greenwich, CT: JAI Press, Inc., 1981, pp. 43–70.

————, "The Role of the Staff Specialist in the Public Implementation Process." Unpublished doctoral dissertation. Harvard University, 1979.

Thompson, James, *Organizations in Action.* New York: McGraw-Hill Book Company, 1967.

Unterman, Israel, "A Comparative Study of the Strategies of New Life Insurance Companies in New York State." Unpublished doctoral dissertation. Harvard University, 1968.

Vogel, David, *Lobbying the Corporation.* New York: Basic Books, 1978.

Weber, Max, *The Theory of Social and Economic Organization.* A.M. Henderson and T. Parsons (trans. and eds.), New York: Oxford University Press, Inc., 1947.

Zeitlin, Maurice, "Managerial Theory vs. Class Theory of Corporate Capitalism." In Lee E. Preston (ed.), vol. 1. Greenwich, CT: JAI Press, Inc., 1978, pp. 255–264.

CONCEPTUAL FRAMEWORKS AND STRATEGIES FOR CORPORATE SOCIAL INVOLVEMENT RESEARCH

Robert J. DeFillippi

A major challenge in any new area of scientific interest is laying out the domain for research, such as specifying the boundaries and structures of the entire domain of relevance within which one may wish to conduct research (Runkel and McGrath, 1972). The study of corporate social involvement—i.e., of the relationship between corporate activity and social issues—has received an increasing amount of research attention, reflected in a significant increase in the amount of theoretical and empirical work, over the past decade. With the amount of research interest expanding, and with the amount of research resources (time, manpower, funding, and goodwill of research participants) limited, it is vital that we assess the directions taken by current research and identify priorities for future research efforts.

A review of major corporate social performance and policy issues reveals a wide range of substantive topics addressed, ranging from cor-

Research in Corporate Social Performance and Policy, Vol. 4, pages 35–56
Copyright © 1982 by JAI Press Inc.
All rights of reproduction in any form reserved.
ISBN: 0-89232-259-4

porate governance, employee health and safety, to the involvement of
business firms in public policy controversies surrounding environmental
pollution, urban development, affirmative action, and consumer product
safety (Steiner and Steiner, 1977). The topical choices of business and
society researchers identify important areas of corporate social involvement but provide little guidance to new scholars in their conceptualization
of research problems or in their development of appropriate research
designs.

The present paper is an effort to analyze the strategic choices reflected
in current research on corporate social involvement. Two sets of choices
are explored: (1) those involving *conceptualization* of the corporation-
society relationship; and (2) those involving *design* of the research study.
The analysis does not assume that researchers make their conceptual or
methodological choices on any particular grounds (scientific, opportun-
istic, stylistic or aesthetic), but it does assume that any completed research study has a discernable set of characteristics that can be located
within the choice dimensions of the classification scheme. The discussion
proceeds in four parts: the first describes four dimensions of research
conceptualization and illustrates them with examples from current research. Part two discusses three dominant conceptual frameworks (Business Policy, Pressure/Response, and Public Policy) within the corporate
social involvement organizational literature that represent different patterns of conceptual choice. Part three characterizes some alternatives
in research design and illustrates them by reference to the research
designs used by exponents of the three conceptual frameworks. The final
section identifies three constraints on conceptual and methodological
choices and suggests some ways of overcoming them.

BASIC CONCEPTUAL DIMENSIONS

Four main dimensions are readily observable within current attempts to
conceptualize research on corporate social involvement: Focus of Research, Locus of Control, Standards for Evaluation and Levels of Analysis. Each involves several options; however the options are not mutually
exclusive and a given research study may contain elements of several
options within any conceptual dimension (See Table 1.)

Focus of Research

"Focus of Research" addresses the choice of what aspect of corporate
social involvement to study. Bourgeois (1980) has conceptualized the
business policy literature in terms of "process" vs. "content" ap-

Table 1. Conceptual Dimensions and Alternatives

FOCUS OF RESEARCH

Process	*Content*	*Impact*
Sequence of events: "How does corporate social involvement occur?"	Substantive responses: "What form does cor- porate social involve- ment take?"	Primary (direct); Secondary (indirect): "What effect does cor- porate social involve- ment produce?"

LOCUS OF CONTROL

Internal	*External*	*Interactive*
Organizations: Top management val- ues, social issues spe- cialists, organizational structures, systems of planning, control and reward.	General environmental trends Specific (task environment)	Environment Organization (reciprocal casualty)

CRITERIA FOR APPRAISAL

Internal	*External*
Process	Process
Outcome	Outcome

LEVEL OF ANALYSIS

Micro	*Macro*
Organizational; Intra-organizational: Division Department Group Individual	Inter-organizational: Institution Industry Network Organization set

proaches, and a similar conceptual distinction is apparent in the corporate social involvement literature as well. A "process" approach focuses upon the sequence of events by which a form of social involvement is proposed, decided upon, and implemented. Murray (1976) suggests that social involvement begins with top management recognition of a social issue and its relevance for the organization, commitment to a course of action and communication of top management commitment through policy development. This stage is followed by a process of technical learning during which staff specialists are selected to gather information about the social issue and the organization's current involvement and develop ideas about methods to initiate, plan and control social response action. The stage of administration learning includes the modification of existing planning and control mechanisms, organizational structures, and incentive systems to accomodate corporate social involvement. The institutionalization phase concerns the involvement of operating units in implementing corporate social policies and programs.

The "content" approach to corporate social involvement focuses upon the form, content and occurrences of substantive responses to social issues. Examples of specific substantive responses typically assessed by the "content" approach include advocacy advertising and public relations (Sethi, 1977), lobbying and electoral political involvement (Epstein, 1969, 1976), litigation and other legal-judicial actions (Stone, 1975), research and development on social issue related technologies (McGraw-Hill, 1977), technical-engineering modifications of work place operations (Gricar, 1979), the creation of new positions, committees, departments and other organization structures for social issue involvement (Holmes, 1976), the pronouncements of new corporate policies within annual reports and official policy documents that reflect social involvement (Ernst and Ernst, 1978), establishment of programs with personnel, budget and authority to carry out social involvement activities (Moskowitz, 1974, 1975), and reported corporate compliance with private agency or governmental standards for social performance (Council on Economic Priorities, 1972, Clinard and Yeager, 1979).

A major conceptual effort by students of both the content and process approaches has consisted in the development of typologies for classifying and summarizing different patterns of corporate social involvement. These schemes differ in detail but attempt to classify different firms according to commonalities in the content of their social involvement (Gricar, 1978, Sethi, 1975), the processes of involvement (Ackerman, 1975) or both (Buono and Nichols, 1980).

A third potential focus of research on corporate social involvement assesses the impact of corporate social activity on social issues. Most social impacts induced by corporate activities are the secondary consequences or side-effects of actions taken primarily for economic purposes. Indeed, deliberate corporate social programs may have far fewer and less important social consequences than the unintentional, indirect social impacts of a firm's economic involvement (U.S. Department of Commerce, 1979). Research addressing primary and secondary social impacts has been undertaken by a wide variety of social accountants or auditors: academic social scientists, social issue activists and public interest organizations, the legislative and executive branches of federal, state and local governments and their commissions and regulatory agencies, private consulting firms, and corporate management and corporate staff specialists. Impact assessors may differ in their assessment objectives and informational needs and the resulting assessments of corporate social involvement will reflect these differences (American Institute of Certified Public Accountants, 1977).

Locus of Control

"Locus of Control" involves the researcher's assessment of the extent to which corporate social involvement responses are influenced by internal (organizational) factors or external (environmental) factors. Post (1978) describes three conceptual models that hold different assumptions about locus of control: Business Policy, Pressure/Response, and Public Policy.

Business Policy models of corporate social involvement conceptualize the firm as possessing considerable discretion and autonomy from external pressures in selecting and implementing social policies and programs. The major constraints on management action exist within the firm and include such factors as the values and philosophy of top management, the conflict of authority between staff and line managers, the inadequacy of financial control systems in explaining and evaluating social involvement costs and benefits, and the inability of performance appraisal and compensation systems to either recognize effective social performance or to reward it (Ackerman, 1973). Management process audits attempt to identify and assess internal organizational arrangements for identifying social issues, formulating policy, implementing programs and evaluating, rewarding, and controlling social performance (Bauer, Cauthorn and Warner, 1978; Kelly and McTaggart, 1978).

Pressure/Response models of corporate social involvement view management action as highly constrained by external factors such as legal requirements, stockholder expectations, customer demands, technology trends, economic conditions, political programs, union and supplier contractual obligations, national media (T.V., newspaper) coverage of social issues and pressures for internal reform or external governmental intervention and control by public interest organizations (Vogel, 1978). The model suggests that corporate social involvement consists in an ad hoc series of tactical responses—public relations, legal or bargaining—to immediate social pressures (Sethi and Votaw, 1969). The social response is incremental and social policies and social goals only emerge as a consequence of a precedent setting pattern of tactical commitments to a course of action (Lindblom, 1959).

The Public Policy model differs from the others in its assumption that the organization participates in and helps shape its own external environments, social expectations, and legal requirements. This model emphasizes anticipatory management through early warning assessment and intervention. Environmental assessments utilize a variety of forecasting techniques such as Delphi (Linestone and Turoff, 1975), cross impact analysis (Pfeffer and Salanick, 1978), computer simulation modeling (Forrester, 1969, Meadows, 1972) and scenario creation (O'Toole, 1979) to identify environmental trends and possibilities that warrant corporate social attention and involvement. Firms that fail to forecast adequately their social environment are expected to have fewer social policy options available than firms that engage in long range environmental assessment (Wilson, 1976).

The Public Policy model thus assumes that early awareness of emerging social issues maximizes the firm's opportunity to influence the demands placed upon it and the range of performance options available. A considerable amount of corporate external relations activity is thus devoted to anticipating and influencing legislative and regulatory agency developments potentially affecting a firm or industry's mandated social involvement (Weidenbaum, 1977).

Post (1978) refers to the interpenetration of environmental and organizational boundaries as a defining characteristic of the Public Policy model. To make an analogy from statistics, the three models represent three effects upon corporate social involvement observed in an analysis of variance: the main effect of organizational characteristics (Business Policy model), the main effect of environmental characteristics (Pressure/Response model) and the interaction effect of organization and environment (Public Policy model).

Criteria for Appraisal

"Criteria for Appraisal" refers to the determination by a researcher of the set of performance criteria against which corporate social involvement responses are to be compared and evaluated (Preston, 1978). This dimension is recommended on the grounds that whether one conducts normative research on how corporations should be socially involved or descriptive research on how corporations are socially involved, both research efforts rely upon some "yardstick" for measurement of observed corporate social involvement.

Preston distinguishes among appraisal criteria by whether they are primarily internal or external in their frame of reference and application and primarily outcome or process oriented in the activities they measure. Preston's framework thus suggests four sets of appraisal criteria: Internal process, external process, internal outcome and external outcome. Each set of criteria reflects a different conception of corporate social involvement and suggests a different focus of research and level of analysis.

Internal process criteria attempt to measure the extent to which socially desirable organizational arrangments are present in the observed firm. For example, to what extent is there evidence of top level management concern for a social issue? Does corporate policy exist on the issue? Are staff specialists responsible for managing the issue? (Bauer, Cauthorn and Warner, 1978)? Internal process assessments measure the presence or absence of such arrangements on the presumption that particular organizational arrangements facilitate corporate social involvement (Holmes, 1978).

Internal outcome criteria measure the impact of corporate social involvement activities upon business operations. For example, what is the impact of affirmative action hiring policies and procedures upon the cost of employee recruitment-selection and on the percentage of minority and women employees constituting the firm's work force? Such an assessment may present a comparison of internal costs with internal benefits, or a comparison of the costs and hiring records of firms having affirmative action policies and procedures with firms not having them.

External process criteria assess the types of inter-organizational arrangements existing between a firm and those external groups, organizations and forces which generate demands or pressures for corporate social involvement, for example, the state of relations between a firm and its local community in terms of its sponsorship of community development programs and use of local supplies. Such assessments may reveal whether inter-organizational relations are friendly or antagonistic, stable or unstable, and thus provide clues on future demands and the means by which demands will be articulated.

External outcome criteria evaluate the actual impact of corporate economic and social involvement upon society. For example, what is the impact of an industrial firm's manufacturing activity on levels of environmental pollution? To what extent have the firm's pollution control activities contributed to the reduction in overall pollution in its area? Impact assessments are very difficult to conduct for a single firm or organization because social issues such as pollution reflect the cumulative effects of the actions of a great variety of participants. A firm may be highly "efficient" in removing 98 percent of all particulate matter from its smoke stacks, yet "ineffective" in reducing the overall level of particulate matter in the atmosphere surrounding it. For this reason, appraisals of impact often require aggregation of the behavior of a variety of actors affecting an issue and thus the level of analysis shifts from a single firm (micro) perspective to a more macro analysis of larger aggregates of firms.

Levels of Analysis

"Levels of Analysis" identifies the type of entity whose social involvement activities are assessed. Candidates for corporate involvement research can be hierarchically arranged from small or micro to increasingly large or macro units of analysis: individual, group, department, division, organization, inter-organization (interaction between two organizations), organization set (organizations with whom a firm is in direct contact), network (relation between organizations not necessarily in direct contact), industry, institution (Perrow, 1978).

The selection of boundaries for designating research as either micro or macro is somewhat arbitrary and often reflects disciplinary traditions. In organizational psychology, a macro level study focuses on the department or division; the same research unit is a micro study for organizational sociologists whose definition of macro level research begins with the study of inter-organizations or organization sets. These units are still micro from the vantage point of industrial economists whose own research focuses on industries as their unit for study. Political scientists and historians may view industries as a relatively micro unit in their own research on political systems and economic and social institutions.

Commentators on corporate social involvement generally place the outer limit on micro level research at studies of the firm and its relevant publics (Post, 1978; Preston, 1980). Research at the micro level includes studies focusing on individual attitudes, values, perceptions, beliefs and behavior with respect to social issues (Aldag and Bartol, 1978); studies of group composition, cohesion and normative expectations as determinants of quality of work life (Hackman, 1976); and studies of single firm involvement in social issues (Ackerman, 1975 Murray, 1976). These studies focus on intra-organizational and organizational units for analysis.

Macro studies of corporate social involvement focus on inter-organizational units of analysis and include research on the activities of political action committees in influencing the regulation of business (Epstein, 1979), the collective response by the Tobacco industry to social and regulatory pressures to restrict tobacco use (Miles and Cameron, 1977); the study of regulatory enforcement actions against industries of varying market structure and profitability (Clinard and Yeager, 1979) and research comparing the institutional relations between government and business in the political economies of different countries (Lindblom, 1977).

ALTERNATIVE CONCEPTUAL FRAMEWORKS

The preceeding discussion has examined four conceptual dimensions and alternative choices in each available to researchers. When certain alternatives are very widely used, they become the basis for the development of different conceptual frameworks (Runkel and McGrath, 1972).

Table 2 profiles three alternative conceptual models for the study of corporate social involvement and the conceptual choices involved in each. These three models were initially introduced under the "locus of

Table 2. Profiles of Conceptual Frameworks

Conceptual Dimensions	Business Policy	Pressure/ Response	Public Policy
Mode of Strategy-Making	Entrepeneur	Adaptive	Planning
Focus of Research	Process	Content	Impact
Locus of Control	Internal	External	Interactive
Criteria for Appraisal	Internal Process Internal Outcome	External Process Internal Outcome	External Outcome Internal Outcome
Level of Analysis	Micro: organization division department	Macro: organization set inter-organization	Macro: institutions industries

control'' dimension, to characterize three different views of the relative influence of internal versus external factors on corporate social involvement. The three models bear a striking resemblance to Mintzberg's (1973) description of three modes of strategy-making—Entrepeneurial, Adaptive and Planning—and thus suggest some points of theoretical convergence between the corporate planning and corporate social involvement fields of study.

The Business Policy model reflects an Entrepeneurial strategy mode, with the emphasis placed on managerial commitment and initiative as the starting point for corporate social involvement (Ackerman, 1975; Murray, 1976). The model also focuses on the processes of issue identification, response selection and implementation, and utilizes internal process and outcome criteria in evaluating the influence of organizational arrangements upon social involvement activities and performance. Moreover, the individual firm and its subunits (e.g. divisions, departments) typically constitute the units of analysis for research (Ackerman and Bauer, 1976).

The Pressure/Response model reflects an Adaptive model of strategy making in its emphasis upon incremental, disjointed responses to immediate external pressures (Sethi and Votaw, 1969). The model also focuses on the content of political bargaining, legal maneuvering and public relations posturing with specific external pressure groups. It utilizes external process and internal outcome criteria to evaluate the success of a firm in managing its external relations. Typical units for analysis include the organization and its set of external pressure groups (Sethi, 1979).

The Public Policy model reflects a Planning mode of strategy formation in its emphasis upon an integrated pattern of planned organizational response (Post, 1976). The model focuses upon corporate efforts to achieve substantial impact upon the definition and resolution of social issues and utilizes both internal and external outcome criteria to assess organizational efficiency in satisfying internal demands and organizational effectiveness in shaping and satisfying external societal demands. Typical units for study include industries (Hirsch, 1975) and major institutions of the political-economy (Lindblom, 1977).

Choices in Research Design

The six design features listed in Table 3 provide a basis for describing, classifying and comparing some of the research design strategies employed in empirical studies of corporate social involvement.

Research Purpose

"Research Purpose" assesses whether a research effort is primarily attempting to *build,* or to *test,* theory about the phenomena under investigation. For phenomena about which little is known, much research effort is directed toward identifying and describing phenomena. This *descriptive* phase of research should lead to a *concept development* phase where research attention focuses on the identification of key variables, both those internal to the phenomena and external variables that may affect the phenomena. The next phase is *hypothesis-generation,* where research efforts focus on specifying the relations between and among the variables identified. In the third phase, *internal validation,* hypotheses are tested to see whether they accurately represent the phenomena in question. Those hypotheses surviving the test of internal validation are then subject to *external validation,* in order to determine the degree to which relations originally observed in a limited sample of the phenomena also apply to other samples from the same or different populations (Schendel and Hofer, 1979).

Much research on corporate social involvement has focused on theory building. The preceeding discussion of alternative conceptual frameworks suggests that research efforts have moved beyond description into concept development. The Business Policy approach is perhaps the most theoretically advanced framework and lends itself to the generation of hypotheses for subsequent testing. Thus far, however, research based on this approach has largely consisted of studies which elaborate the original conceptual framework but do not provide an empirical test of specific propositions. The Pressure/Response model is less precise in its specification of relations between variables. Use of this model has gen-

Table 3. Choices in Research Design

RESEARCH PURPOSE (Inductive/Deductive)	*Theory Building* Exploration Description Hypothesis generation Validation	*Theory Testing* Verification Hypothesis testing
EXPERIMENTAL CONTROL (Internal Validity)	*Non-Experimental* Natural setting Learning setting (e.g., classrooms)	*Experimental/ Quasi-experimental* Lab experiments Experimental simulation Field experiments
SAMPLE SCOPE (External Validity)	*Case Study* Single case Multiple (corporation) case	*Comparative* Single population sample Multiple population sample
TIME INTERVAL (Dynamic-Static Relations)	*Longitudinal* Retrospective Prospective	*Cross-sectional*
LEVEL OF DATA (Numeric Measurement and Manipulations)	*Qualitative* Unstructured data collection Non-statistical analysis	*Quantitative* Structured data collection Statistical analysis
RESEARCH PRODUCT	*Verbal Models* Concepts and heuristics	*Mathematical Models* Prediction

erated an increasing variety of concepts and variables to describe the range of corporate response options available; but the work to date fails to specify the conditions under which a particular response pattern is likely.[1]

The Public Policy model, as represented in the research of James Post, has moved beyond description of corporate response patterns to the identification of various environmental conditions (technological, economic, political, cultural) likely to affect the public policy response of a firm or industry. His latest survey of case studies of corporate social policy concludes with a series of general propositions illustrated by the following:

> The stimulus or motivation for change in organizational behavior can derive from the pressure of changed legal rules of the game, pressure from the firm's relevant publics, or from the initiative of management. (Post, 1978, p. 284)

Propositions such as this reflect an early phase of theoretical development. A major theoretical gap is the identification—in testable form—of the specific environmental or internal conditions likely to be associated with various patterns of corporate social involvement. Until such specific hypotheses are developed, one must expect future research in the area to continue to be of an inductive, hypothesis-generating nature.

Experimental Control

"Experimental Control" describes the degree to which a research design allows the investigator to control the variables of interest. Research designs differ in the "experimental control" dimension from almost complete control (the lab experiment) to total absence of control (a natural event). Control is largely determined by the conditions under which data collection occurs. Intermediate controls are obtainable by the use of quasi-experimental and experimental designs in natural settings (Campbell and Stanley, 1963).

Most research on corporate social involvement occurs in natural settings where little or no experimental control exists. The three conceptual frameworks described earlier are based on field research and to date have largely generated additional field research. Some observers suggest that the phenomena subsumed under corporate social involvement research are too complex to be replicated within experimentally controlled settings (Post, 1978; Preston, 1978). Moreover, our review of the three conceptual frameworks suggest that current theory is too imprecise to permit the formulation of hypotheses amenable to experimental assessment.[2]

Sample Scope

"Sample Scope" refers to the degree to which the data used in a study are representative of a larger class of entities (population). This can range from a case study, whose findings permit limited empirical generalization, to large sample studies whose findings are generalizable across a wide range of similar settings.

Research using any of the three conceptual models has consisted largely of case studies. The Business Policy perspective is particularly characterized by single case research. The Conference Board has sponsored several surveys to assess and compare corporate response organizational arrangement across a variety of firms and industries, but such studies have been essentially descriptive and unrelated to any systematic theory of corporate involvement (McGrath, 1976). A growing number of surveys of managerial attitudes and values also exist, but these generally have a limited focus that precludes generalization to the responses of their employing organizations (Aldag and Jackson, 1977; Cavanaugh, 1976). However, some surveys have attempted to link managerial values and attributes to the perceived social performance of their employing firms (Sturdivant and Ginter, 1977). Continued research on links between top management values and corporate response may make it possible to assess key theoretical assumptions (e.g., Entrepeneurial social initiatives) of the Business Policy perspective.

Comparative research based on the Pressure/Response model is beginning to appear. A comparative analysis of the responses by pharmaceutical and food processing firms to criticism of their marketing of infant milk formula in less developed countries suggests hypotheses regarding industry and firm level differences in patterns of both business strategies and social responses (Sethi and Post, 1979). Comparative research using the Public Policy model is limited to cross-cultural comparisons of differences in institutional arrangements between business and government (Lindblom, 1977). Post (1978) has compared case histories compiled from a variety of sources but the absence of systematic data collection and measurement procedures across cases reduces the external validity of his findings.

In summary, research on corporate social involvement is only beginning to move beyond single case studies to comparative studies of a variety of firms in different industries and cultural settings. The current state of research suggests a trend toward comparative case studies in which an attempt is made to retain the conceptual and substantive richness of the case study with the empirical generalizability of the comparative study. Research involving larger sample surveys is frequently limited to non-theoretical, descriptive studies.

Time Interval

"Time Interval" describes whether a research study is based on data covering a single time point (cross sectional) or over some longer period (longitudinal). The time interval dimension refers to the data itself, not to the data collection process. A single data collection effort involving a retrospective assessment of events over a time period constitutes a longitudinal study, as does a prospective design for collecting data at several time points in the future. Prospective studies provide more internal validity for identifying and assessing antecedent conditions and their consequences (Darran, Miles and Snow, 1976).

Most research studies by proponents of the three conceptual models have relied on retrospective studies assessing events occurring over an extended time period; and this emphasis on a longitudinal perspective is not unwarranted. A common theoretical assumption of all three major perspectives is that corporate social involvement activity results from processes which occur over time. Ackerman (1975) and Murray (1976) suggest that the "institutionalization" of corporate social response to a social issue typically takes about eight years. Such long time periods make prospective studies prohibitively time consuming and expensive. However, Preston (1980) has warned that exclusive reliance on longitudinal studies (which are also usually case studies) may retard efforts to collect precise data for detecting specific patterns of corporate social involvement behavior across a wide variety of firms, industries and general social environmental conditions. A recent example of cross-sectional research is Reeder's (1978) doctoral dissertation comparing relations between corporate level policies and plant level programs of social involvement across large, geographically dispersed and small, geographically concentrated firms. A second example is a questionnaire survey of Canadian firms comparing corporate-wide social policies with a firm's stage of involvement in specific social issues (Preston, Dierkes and Rey, 1978). More cross-sectional research focusing on specific external and internal factors associated with corporate social involvement is likely.

Level of Data

"Level of Data" refers to the extent to which methods of data collection and analysis permit quantitative versus qualitative descriptions, comparisons and evaluations. These differences reflect in part the degree to which methods of data collection are structured and methods of data analysis transform raw data into a form suitable for statistical manipulation.

Most research on corporate social involvement relies upon qualitative methods of data collection (unstructured observation, interviews and document reviews) and analysis (clinical insight and inductive categorization). Some of the comparative research has yielded quantitative data on corporate-divisional relations (Reeder, 1978), on the relation between firm size and social involvement (Preston, Diekes and Rey, 1978), and firm profitability and social involvement (Bowman and Haire, 1975; Bragdon and Marlin, 1972; Sturdivant and Ginter, 1977).

To the extent that research on corporate social involvement relies upon qualitative methods of data collection and analysis, the resulting research findings will usually take the form of verbal models of corporate social involvement. Verbal models are most valuable as heuristic devices for demonstrating the richness and complexity of a phenomenon and for inspiring new insights and understanding. However, the informational needs of both business and government require more precise description and estimation of the antecedents and consequences of corporate social involvement which only mathematical models can provide. The formulation and validation of such models requires a substantial increase in both the amount and the quality of quantitative research in this area.

CONSTRAINTS ON CONCEPTUAL-METHODOLOGICAL CHOICES

The preceeding discussion of research conceptualization and design choices suggests that there is a gap between the verbal models and qualitative research methods employed in many studies of corporate social involvement and the mathematical models and quantitative methods that characterize other domains of social science research, and that efforts should be made to increase analytic rigor in both conceptualizing and empirically examining corporate social involvement phenomena. Such a development would appear consistent with the "normal science" paradigm (Kuhn, 1962).

The existence of a conceptual/methodological gap raises two related questions: Why does the gap exist? How can it be reduced?

The first question deserves extended intellectual attention and the present discussion can only offer some hypotheses for further consideration. Three hypotheses are offered here to account for the conceptual and methodological shortcomings cited earlier. These hypotheses suggest that phenomenological, disciplinary, and data access factors have constrained conceptual and methodological choices. Each factor is presented with a discussion of possible correction actions. The discussion concludes with a description of the author's current research which incorporates many of the recommendations discussed earlier.

Phenomenological Complexity

The phenomenological hypothesis holds that phenomena associated with corporate social involvement are so recent, relatively unknown and intrinsically complex that verbal models and qualitative analyses represent appropriate conceptual and methodological strategies. Without challenging the phenomenological premise, which has been argued in a variety of social research domains (Hatten, 1979), one may still question the conclusion that verbal models and qualitative analyses are the only appropriate responses to complex social phenomena. An additional response is to partition a complex phenomenon into more limited domains of inquiry for theoretical and empirical focus. (Merton, 1968). The three conceptual frameworks (Business Policy, Pressure/Response, Public Policy) described earlier represent three broad partitions of scholarly effort within which further subdivisions of theoretical and empirical focus can develop. For example, the Public Policy model offers a rich domain for intensive research focus on corporate involvement and influence upon such substantive policy areas as electorate politics (Epstein, 1979), health (Sethi and Post, 1979) and government regulation (Chatov, 1978). Implementing a limited domain strategy will require a considerable expansion in the amount and variety of scholarly study of corporate social involvement.

Disciplinary Background

A second explanation for the limitations of corporate social involvement research emphasizes the business policy backgrounds of many researchers in this field. Hatten (1979) has characterized business policy scholarship as emphasizing broad verbal models and qualitative case research methods. An emphasis upon case research is reinforced by professional and institutional demands upon business policy faculty to develop teaching cases for classroom use and for distribution by the Intercollegiate Case Clearing House. One remedy would be to encourage research contributions from representatives of a variety of disciplines. No single discipline can encompass the complexities inherent in corporate social involvement phenomena but different disciplines offer unique perspectives on selected aspects of the research domain. Economics, political science, and sociology offer a rich array of conceptual and methodological tools for constructive application to the study of corporate social involvement. Increased understanding of corporate social involvement phenomena will most rapidly develop if contributors with different disciplinary backgrounds employ their specialized skills to enrich the conceptual and research base already established.

Data Access

A third explanation for the preponderance of case study and descriptive research activity lies in the perceived barriers to developing data bases amenable to explanatory model building and quantitative assessment. Corporations are alleged to be highly secretive about their efforts to influence social issues and public policy (Stephenson, 1973). Moreover, the expense of obtaining data from corporate sources has limited the scope of most research efforts. One remedy to these difficulties may be to look to publicly available information on corporate behavior. Numerous departments of the federal government compile data on business activity and access to much of this data is available under the Freedom of Information Act. Moreover, federal data on corporate activity provides a convenient access point for comparative assessments of a large number of business organizations across a wide range of issues and forms of social involvement. Implementation of a government data access strategy will require that business and society scholars develop greater familiarity with government data archives and procedures for their access. Data archives are also available at state and local government agencies.

IMPLEMENTING ANALYTIC RESEARCH STRATEGIES

To illustrate how more analytically-oriented conceptual and methodological strategies may be employed in corporate social involvement research I will describe briefly my own ongoing study of constituency (interest group) influence on regulatory agency decision making. (DeFillippi, 1981) The conceptual framework selected for assessing business and non-business interest group impacts on regulatory decisions was the Public Policy model, where a research focus on business impacts on the social (in this case regulatory) environment is directly applicable.

Employing the public policy conceptual framework directed me to a consideration of the interpentration of constituency and regulatory agency boundaries and thus the interaction between business policy and public policy. Moreover, the public policy framework suggested that research attention be directed toward an appraisal of the impact of business and other constituency efforts on the definition of social issues (in my study, the regulatory agency's agenda) and their resolution (agency decision making on agenda items). Finally, the public policy framework suggested a macro-level analysis including trade associations and coalitions of organizations representing industry and non-industry constituencies.

A review of the research literature on business-government relations revealed a variety of case studies of business efforts to influence specific issues in specific government agencies, but very little empirical research that systematically compared the success of different constituencies and their influence tactics across a range of issues. Available literature also suggested a variety of influences on agency decision behavior, including characteristics of the constituency, the nature of constituency demands, the variety and intensity of influence behavior, and the issue context in which constituency influence behavior occurs. These variables and the working hypotheses concerning their impact upon agency decision making represent vital conceptual and hypothesis generation contributions of qualitative case research.

In developing a research strategy for modelling and assessing the impact of these factors on agency decision making, I elected to employ data available from the Consumer Product Safety Commission on two hundred business and consumer organizations and individuals petitioning the agency for rule making action between 1973 and 1980. The selection of a federal agency was more than a data access tactic. The choice also limited the scope of my research to a specific policy arena (consumer product safety) and a specific public policy mechanism for constituency influence (the petitions process). Thus my data access choices also limited my domain of inquiry to an area sufficiently narrow to permit analytic model development and quantitative assessment.

Before implementing an analytic research strategy one should be aware of potential risks arising from its misuse. One risk is that data availability may replace theoretical or policy relevance as the criterion for selection of research projects. The issues requiring scholarly attention are too important to be subordinated to data access opportunities; data access choices must be subordinated to problem identification.

A second risk is the overinterpretation of research findings. For example, my data base on constituency influence behavior is limited to "public behavior" documented in agency records. A review of literature on constituency-regulatory agency relations suggests that a considerable amount of constituency influence occurs informally and in private settings (Nader and Serber, 1976). Results from a study based solely on *public* behavior by constituencies and agency officials must qualify and delineate its findings to that domain.

A final risk is that of assuming that any single research strategy is sufficient to analyze the complexities of corporate social policy and performance. The complex and multifaceted phenomena to be addressed in this area provide abundant opportunities for both independent and coordinated research efforts employing a variety of conceptual and methodological approaches. Each approach has its strengths and limitations, but the employment of multiple approaches increases the cumulative knowledge gained and provides an empirical basis for validating our concepts and increasing our confidence in the results generated by each research strategy.

SUMMARY

This paper has examined the conceptual and methodological choices reflected in current research on corporate social involvement. Most research in the field reflects a descriptive level of conceptual development in contrast to the explanatory models common in the basic social science disciplines. Qualitative case studies and descriptive surveys are the dominant research methods in contrast to the social science trend toward quantitative assessment and modelling of complex phenomena.

Explanations for the gap between corporate social involvement research and social science disciplinary research include the inherent complexity of corporate social involvement phenomena, the limited number of researchers active in the field, the institutional and professional role demands upon faculty to devote research time to the development of teaching cases and the difficulties and expense in accessing data from business sources.

Recommendations for overcoming constraints on corporate social involvement research include the employment of limited domain strategies for theoretical and research focus, an increase of research involvement by scholars from a variety of disciplinary backgrounds, and greater reliance on governmental sources for data access. An example of an analytic study that attempts to overcome some of these conceptual and methodological limitations is presented.

ACKNOWLEDGMENTS

The author thanks Barbara Grey Gricar of Pennsylvania State University for comments on an early version of this paper presented on May 5, 1980 at the Joint National Meeting of the Institute of Management and the Operations Research Society of America.

NOTES

1. Sethi (1975) has compared corporate response patterns of Japanese and American firms and has thus begun to develop and examine broad hypotheses on the relation between cultural differences as a moderator of the impact of social pressures on corporate response patterns.

2. Hegarty and Sims (1976) have employed experimental methods to assess the impact of heightened competition on unethical decisions by individuals.

REFERENCES

Ackerman, R., *The Social Challenge to Business*. Cambridge: Harvard University Press, 1975.

Ackerman, R., and R. Bauer, *Corporate Social Responsiveness: The Modern Dilemma*. Reston: Reston Publishing Co., 1976.

Aldag, R., and K. Bartol, "Empirical Studies of Corporate Social Performance and Policy: A Survey of Problems and Results." In L. Preston (ed.), *Research in Corporate Social Performance and Policy*, vol. 1. Greenwich: JAI Press, 1978, pp. 165–200.

Aldag, R., and D. Jackson, "Assessment of Attitudes Toward Social Responsibilities." *Journal of Business Administration* 8 2(1977):65–80.

American Institute of Certified Public Accountants, *The Measurement of Corporate Social Performance*. New York: AICPA, 1977.

Bauer, R., L. Cauthorn, and R. P. Warner, "The Management Process Audit Manual." In L. Preston (ed.), *Research in Corporate Social Performance and Policy*, vol. 1. Greenwich: JAI Press, 1978, pp. 265–278.

Bourgeois, L. J., "Strategy and Environment: A Conceptual Integration." *Academy of Management Review* 5 1(1980):25–39.

Bowman, E. M., and M. Haire, "A Strategic Posture Toward Corporate Social Reporting." *California Management Review* 18 2(1975):49–58.

Bragdon, J. H., and J. T. Marlin, "Is Pollution Profitable?" *Risk Management* 19 4(1972):8.

Buono, L., and L. Nichols, "Researching Corporate Responsiveness: From Conceptualization to Data Collection." Paper presented at TIMS/ORSA Joint National Meeting, Washington, D.C. (May 5):1980.

Campbell, D. T., and J. C. Stanley, *Experimental and Quasi-Experimental Designs for Research.* Chicago: Rand McNally, 1963.

Cavanaugh, G. F., *American Business Values in Transition.* Englewood Cliffs, N.J.: Prentice-Hall, 1976.

Chatov, Robert, "Government Regulation: Process and Substantive Impacts." In L. Preston (ed.), *Corporate Social Performance and Policy,* vol. 1., 1978, pp. 223–54.

Clinard, M., and P. Yeager, et al., *Illegal Corporate Behavior.* Washington, D.C.: U.S. Department of Justice, Law Enforcement Assistance Administration, 1979.

Council on Economic Priorities, *Paper Profits.* Cambridge, Mass.: MIT Press, 1972.

Darran, D., R. Miles, and C. Snow, "Organizational Adjustment to the Environment: A Review." Paper presented at the Annual Meeting of the American Institute for Decision Sciences, Washington, D.C., 1975.

DeFillippi, R., "Constituency Influences On Regulatory Decisions: A Multivariate Model". Dissertation Proposal. Yale University, 1981.

Epstein, E., "The Emergence of Political Action Committees." In H. E. Alexander (ed.), *Political Finance.* Beverly Hills, CA: Sage Publications, 1979.

———, "Corporations and Labor Unions in Electoral Politics." *Annals of the American Academy of Political and Social Science,* 1976.

———, *The Corporation in Americal Politics.* Englewood Cliffs, N.J.; Prentice Hall, 1969.

Ernst and Ernst, *Social Responsibility Disclosure Survey of Fortune 500 Annual Reports.* Cleveland, Ohio: Ernst and Ernst, 1978.

Forrester, J. W., *Urban Dynamics.* Cambridge, Mass.: M.I.T., 1969.

Gricar, B. G., *The Environmental Imperative Created by Government Regulation: Predicting Organizational Response.* Ph.D. Dissertation, Case Western Reserve University (August):1979.

Hackman, R. J., "Group Influence on Individuals." In M. D. Dunnette (ed.), *Handbook of Industrial and Organizational Psychology,* Chicago: Rand McNally, 1976.

Hatten, K. J., "Quantitative Research Methods in Strategic Management." In D. E. Schendel, and C. W. Hofer (Eds.), *Strategic Management,* Boston: Little, Brown and Company, 1979.

Hegarty, W. H., and H. P. Sims, Jr., "The reinforcement of unethical decision behavior: An experiment." Proceedings of the Eighth Annual Conference of the American Institute for Decision Sciences, pp. 250–252, 1976.

Hirsch, P. M., "Organizational Effectiveness and the Institutional Environment." *Administrative Science Quarterly* 20(1975):327–344.

Holmes, S., "Adopting Corporate Structures for Social Responsiveness." *California Management Review* 21 1(1978):47–54.

———, "Executive Perceptions of Corporate Social Responsibility." Business Horizons 19(1976):34–40.

Kelly, D. W., and R. T. McTaggart, "Guidelines for Social Performance Case Studies." In L. E. Preston (ed.), *Research in Corporate Social Performance and Policy,* vol. 1. Greenwich, Conn.: JAI Press, 1978, pp. 287–291.

Kuhn, T., *The Structure of Scientific Revolutions.* Chicago: University of Chicago Press, 1962.

Lindblom, C. E., *Politics and Markets.* New York: Basic Books, 1977.

———, "The Science of Muddling Through." *Public Administration Review (Spring):1959.*

Linstone, H. A., and M. Turoff, *The Delphi Method: Techniques and Application.* Reading, Mass.: Addison-Wesley, 1975.

McGrath, J. E., "A Multi-facet approach to classification of individual, group, and organizational concepts." In B. Indik, and K. Berrien (eds.), *People, Groups, and Organizations: An Effective Integration,* New York: Teachers College Press, 1967, pp. 191–215.

McGrath, Phyllis, *Managing Corporate External Relations.* Report #679. New York: The Conference Board, 1976.

McGraw-Hill, *Economics Department Survey of Preliminary Plans for Capital Spending.* New York: McGraw-Hill Publications Co., 1977.

Meadows, D. et al., *The Limits to Growth.* New York: Universe Books, 1972.

Merton, R. K., *Social Theory and Social Structure.* New York: The Free Press, 1968.

Miles, R. H., and K. Cameron, "Coffin Nails and Corporate Strategies: A Quarter Century View of Organizational Adaptation to Environment in the U.S. Tobacco Industry." Working Paper No. 3. Research Program on Government-Business Relations. New Haven: Yale School of Organization and Management, 1977.

Mintzberg, H., "Policy as a Field of Management Theory." *Academy of Management Review* 2 1(1977):88–103.

——, "Strategy-Making in Three Modes." *California Management Review* 16 2(1973):44–53.

Moskowitz, M., "Profiles in Corporate Responsibility." *Business and Society Review.* 13(1975):28–42.

——, "46 Socially Responsible Corporations." *Business and Society* 7 8(1974).

Murray, E. A., "The Social Response Process in Commercial Banks: An Empirical Investigation." *Academy of Management Review* 1 3(1976):5–15.

O'Toole, J., "What's ahead for the Business-Government Relationship." *Harvard Business Review* (March-April):1979.

Perrow, C., *Complex Organizations: A Critical Essay.* Glenview, Illinois: Scott, Foresman & Co., 1978.

Pfeffer, J., and G. Salancik, *External Control of Organizations.* New York: Harper and Row, 1978.

Post, J., *Corporate Behavior and Social Change.* Reston, Va.: Reston Publishing Co., 1978.

——, *Risk and Response.* Lexington, Mass.: D. C. Heath, 1976.

Preston, L. E., "Business, Society and Public Policy: Current Research and Research Approaches." In L. E. Preston (ed.), *Business Environment/Public Policy: 1979 Conference Papers,* St. Louis: AACSB, 1980.

——, "Corporate Social Performance and Policy: A Synthetic Framework for Research and Analysis." In L. E. Preston (ed.), *Corporate Social Performance and Policy,* vol. 1. Greenwich, Conn.: JAI Press, Inc., 1978.

Preston, L. E., M. Dierkes, and F. Rey, "Comparing Corporate Social Performance: An Analysis of Recent Studies in Germany, France, and Canada, and Comparison with U.S. Experience." *California Management Review,* 1978.

Reeder, J., "Corporate Social Involvement at the Local Level." *Proceedings of the 38th Annual Meeting of the Academy of Management,* pp. 356–59, 1978.

Runkel, P. J., and J. E. McGrath, *Research on Human Behavior.* New York: Holt, Rinehart and Winston, Inc., 1972.

Schendel, D. C., and W. C. Hofer (eds.), *Strategic Management: A New View of Business Policy and Planning.* Boston: Little, Brown and Company, 1979.

Sethi, S. P., "A Conceptual Framework for Environmental Analysis of Social Issues and Evaluation of Business Response Patterns." *Academy of Management Review* 4(1979):63–74.

——, *Advocacy Advertising and Large Corporations.* Lexington, Mass.: D. C. Heath, 1977.

———, *Japanese Business and Social Conflict: An Analysis of Response Patterns with American Business*. Cambridge, Mass.: Ballinger Press, 1975.

———, "Dimensions of Corporate Social Performance: An Analytic Framework." *California Management Review* 7 3(1975):58–65.

Sethi, S. P., and J. Post, "Public Consequences of Private Action: Marketing of Infant Formula in Less Developed Countries." *California Management Review* 21 4(1979):36–48.

Sethi, S. P., and D. Votaw, "Do We Need a New Corporate Response to a Changing Social Environment?" Part II, *California Management Review* 12 1(1969):17–31.

Steiner, G. A., and J. Steiner, *Issues in Business and Society*. New York: Random House, 1977.

Stephenson, L., "Prying Open Corporations: Tighter than Clams." *Business and Society Review* 8(Winter 1973):42.

Stone, C. D., *Where the Law Ends*. New York: Harper & Row, 1975.

Sturdivant, F. D., and J. L. Ginter, "Corporate Social Responsiveness: Management Attitudes and Economic Performance." *California Managment Review* 19 3(1977):30–39.

U. S. Department of Commerce, *Corporate Social Reporting in the United States and Western Europe: Report of the Task Force on Corporate Social Performance*. Washington, D.C., 1979.

Vogel, D., *Lobbying the Corporation: Citizen Challenges to Business Authority*. New York: Basic Books, 1978.

Weidenbaum, M., *Business, Government and the Public*. Englewood Cliffs, N.Y.: Prentice-Hall, 1977.

Wilson, I., *Corporate Environments of the Future*. New York: The President's Association, Special Study #61, 1976.

THE THOMPSON-PAGE
CONTRIBUTION TO SOCIAL
ISSUES RESEARCH

John F. Mahon

James D. Thompson, who died in 1973, was a recognized leader in management thought. Robert Avery in his eulogy for Thompson noted that:

> Students of organization and administration will be reaping dividends for a long time from Jim Thompson's investment in ideas. (1974:4)

Thompson's ideas are often cited in the leading texts of both organizational behavior and management policy (Pfeffer and Salancik, 1978; Galbraith and Nathanson, 1978). It is a tribute to his brilliance and foresight that *Organizations in Action*, a thin volume, 177 pages, has served as such a rich and varied source of new concepts and research ideas. Researchers in the social issues arena, however, have apparently felt that Thompson provides little stimulus for theoretical or empirical

Research in Corporate Social Performance and Policy, Vol. 4, pages 57–76 research relevant to corporate social responsiveness. The "empirical" criticism has often been made of Thompson's work. It is argued that the level of abstraction is such as to make empirically-based investigations difficult, if not impossible, to perform.

It now appears that Thompson was well aware of this problem with his work and that he undertook some action to resolve it. The resolution involved Thompson's sponsoring doctoral dissertation work along empirical lines to extend and/or modify his theoretical contributions. One such thesis, undertaken by Robert R. Page, with Thompson as chairman, was completed in 1971. Page died shortly thereafter, and the thesis was never published, Page's thesis is clearly an extension of Thompson's work, and it serves as a linking pin between Thompson's contributions and the more recent research literature in corporate response to non-market aspects of the environment.

The purpose of this paper is to illuminate the intellectual roots of social issues research in the Thompson-Page collaboration and the substantive work of Page. It is clear that when Thompson finished *Organizations in Action* he began to refocus his energies and talents on broader organization-environment relationships. His writings and research took him away from economic considerations of the firm to an analysis of the role of business in a larger social framework. The titles of some of his last works are indicative of this shift: "The Regeneration of Social Organizations" (1971); "Society's Frontiers for Organizing Activities" (1973); "Social Interdependence, The Polity, and Public Administration" (1974)' and "Technology, Polity, and Societal Development" (1974).

THE THOMPSON-PAGE LEGACY

Organizations in Action was Thompson's attempt to address what he saw as the critical organizational problem: coping with uncertainty. His analysis of this issue laid the early framework and conceptual foundation for the pattern of response literature and the research in corporate involvement in public policy that was to follow. Although Thompson confined himself primarily to economic and technical issues, his emphasis on response patterns was extended by Page to include corporate response to social issues and changing public policy agendas.

Thompson notes that organizations act in certain ways because they must. Organizations are expected to produce results, and that requires them to act in a rational manner. Yet, any uncertainty threatens their capability to do so. For Thompson, the central problem for complex organizations is dealing with uncertainty which arises from technology and the environment. This thesis allows Thompson to make a creative leap in theory building. If the afore-mentioned concepts and relationships hold true, then ". . . organizations with similar technological and environmental problems should exhibit similar behavior; *patterns should appear.*" (1967: 1, 2, emphasis added)

In order to investigate these relationships, Thompson frames the argument in an open/closed system perspective drawing heavily on the works of Weber (1947), March and Simon (1958), and Parsons (1960). He analyzes the tension that exists in an organization seeking certainty but constantly faced with uncertainty, and parallels that argument with the dynamics of open and closed systems operations. The pressure of the dynamic interactions between certainty and uncertainty requires the organization to act and to organize (or structure) itself in order to survive and operate.

The action response of the organization is characterized by "homeostasis," a process of self-stabilization where the organization spontaneously balances and alters the relationships among the parts and activities (both internal and external) to insure organizational survival when faced with uncertainties generated in the environment. This process alone is not sufficient to ensure corporate survival when the environment becomes more complex.

The structural response is oriented to controlling uncertainties in the environment while simultaneously providing some measure of control over technological uncertainties. The foundation of this analysis is Parsons' (1960) distinction among technical, managerial, and institutional sub-systems within the organization. The technical sub-system is concerned with the technical tasks of the enterprise (e.g. underwriting in insurances, assembly line production in automobile manufacturing). The other two sub-systems, according to Thompson, protect and insulate this technical sub-system (Thompson uses the term "technical core") from uncertainties. The managerial sub-system serves as the link between the technical and institutional sub-systems, and it provides direction and control for the organization. The institutional sub-system is the linking pin between the overall organization and its environment. This system is concerned with the maintenance of organizational legitimacy and the enterprise's interaction with other institutions and agencies of the community.

Although recognizing the importance of the institutional sub-system in the management or organization-environment relationships, Thompson did not explore its full potential. Corporations, because of their intimate familiarity with economic planning and technical management, have often ignored the challenges posed by changing public policy agendas and the increased interest in the social responsibility of the firm. This area of interaction involves the greatest uncertainty for the firm and receives the least treatment in *Organizations in Action.*

Page's thesis, *Organizational Response to Social Challenge: Theory and Evidence for Two Industries,* was an attempt to take Thompson's theory into the social arena. He observed that organizations seem to move only when pushed. Even when it is quite obvious that an issue is building and must be confronted, the firm cannot be expected to adapt or change automatically unless forced to do so. In a clear link with the notion of interpenetrating systems (Preston and Post, 1975), Page observes that:

> Organizations are slow to adapt to environmental pressures, and if they are powerful enough, they don't adapt. The society in which they are situated has to. (1971:241)

Six Areas of Conceptual Development

Thompson and Page's work was instrumental in the genesis and development of six distinct lines of inquiry. These research paths are being pursued by researchers in social issues in management, organizational behavior, and strategic planning. They are:

- Thompson's recognition of the interdependency between the organization and the environment was a clear signal to researchers. He was one of the first supporters of the necessity for research that would simultaneously analyze the corporate and societal response mechanisms and their interdependencies with one another. Preston and Post (1975) picked up on this notion, and applying systems theory as a conceptual filter, developed the interpenetrating systems model. This approach recognizes the interdependent relationship between actors, but notes that they can influence one another *both* directly and indirectly.
- Thompson provides further support for this interpenetration between the organization and society when he addresses *domain and domain consensus.* Domain, in its essence, is the expectation that actors in the corporate-environment relationship hold concerning corporate behavior. This expectation involves both traditional economic issues (e.g., provide jobs, good products at reasonable prices, etc.) and social issues (e.g., product safety, concern for the environment and the local community, etc.). It is his analysis of this relationship that serves as the basis for several strands of current research in business and society and in strategic planning.
- The expectations concerning economic and social issues, when linked with the concept of *domain* consensus, forms a basis for the current *effectiveness/effficiency distinction* in the strategic planning literature. Pfeffer and Salancik (1978) and Hofer and Schendel (1978) explore this relationship in great detail.

- Thompson also makes it quite clear that there is a difference between subjectively determined organizational goals and operative policies which can be objectively verified. The former category is the articulation of goals made by the organization. The latter category, operative policies, requires us to analyze the interaction between the organization and the environment. Post's (1976) articulation of the reactive, proactive, and interactive modes of corporate response is a clear example of what Thompson meant by operative policies. In analyzing corporate societal relationships, a reliance on the statement of organizational goals by the firm is clearly insufficient. We must look at these operative goals as well.
- Thompson appears to place great faith in organizational boundary spanning activities as providing a solution to the uncertainty problem that the organization faces. Thompson's faith in this area has been supported by the growing research into boundary spanning activities (Adams, 1976; Aldrich and Herker, 1977; Miles, 1975, 1980).
- Page's work, largely unrecognized, moved Thompson's theoretical approach clearly into the social issues arena with an empirical focus. Page's thesis in 1971 addressed the trade association as a political actor in the public policy process, and offered some early ideas on stakeholder analysis. In addition, Page may have been one of the first researchers to investigate corporate response patterns to social issues.

THOMPSON-PAGE AND SOCIAL ISSUES RESEARCH

In order to demonstrate the relevance of the Thompson-Page contribution to social issues research, I have selected three issues of current research activity for more detailed discussion: (1) corporate involvement in the public policy process and business-government interaction in the political arena; (2) corporate responses to social issues; and (3) stakeholder analysis.

Corporate Involvement in the Public Policy Process and the Political Arena

This area of study has been investigated by a number of researchers (Bauer, Pool, and Dexter, 1964; Epstein, 1969, 1973, 1974, 1980, 1980a; Lindblom, 1968, 1977; Post, 1976, 1978, 1978a; and Preston and Post, 1975). Page's study was an extension of the previously existing works on this subject.

The central concept in Page's thesis was:

. . . that when an organization is challenged by a serious threat to its operations,
it responds by resisting the demanded change, and the resistance takes the form
of a *patterned sequence of actions* to restore compatability with the environment.
(1971: *x, emphasis added*)

Page was concerned with the broad issue of the relationship of the
organization to its environment. He wanted to examine ". . . how certain
business firms maintain viability over a period of time when confronted
by a challenge from the environment that creates uncertainties about
relationships vital to their functioning." (1971:2)

Page accepts from Thompson that the motive for corporate action is
the alleviation of uncertainty. In its simplest form, Page's theory is that
challenge threatens the ability of the firm to function, which in turn
creates considerable uncertainty. Uncertainty often arises out of social
and political (non-market) forces, but a significant challenge has to come
from a vital element in the firm's environment. A vital element is an
external actor or force whose role relationships with the organization are
essential to the organization's present method of operating. For example,
for many large organizations, the federal government is a vital element
of the environment.

Page's analysis, although controversial and exploratory in nature, was
firmly grounded in theory and empirically verifiable. He pursued this
work through an in-depth analysis of two unrelated environmental/cor-
porate situations: (1) The issue of automobile safety, particularly during
the period 1956-1966; and (2) the controversy surrounding the drug industry and the promotion of ethical drugs during 1956-1962. The situations were similar in that each involved the federal government as the
challenger; and both were concerned with social issues important enough
to involve vital elements in the organization's environment, thereby ensuring a good test of Page's postulated corporate response patterns. A
secondary reason for this choice was the availability of information on
the situations; since both issues involved the federal government, and
they both received a great deal of publicity.

Page used publicly available documents and the practitioner's literature
(*Fortune, Wall Street Journal, Business Week,* and so forth) to construct
a chronological record of organizational and governmental actions. The
main interest of the study was in the *response patterns* of the organizations involved. This longitudinal research allowed Page to determine
if there were sequential changes in organizational responses to the challenges as time progressed, and thereby confirm or deny the existence
of the hypothesized patterns.

It is important to note that the level of analysis in this study was the
industry, not the individual firm. The automotive analysis was focused

on the actions of the Automobile Manufacturers Association, and in the drug investigations he used the Pharmaceutical Manufacturers Association. Page's study is therefore, first of all, a record of the participation of these industry groups in the public policy process.

Corporate Ressponse to Social Issues

Page described his study as ". . . a report of *how* organizations respond. . . . The test is whether complex business organizations exhibit the postulated pattern in their responses to challenges." (1971:51)

Research in this area has proceeded along two distinct, yet related paths. Bauer (1978), Ackerman and Bauer (1976), and Murray (1974) working at Harvard, and Sethi (1971, 1973, 1975, 1978) as well as others have attempted to analyze corporate response from an *internal* perspective, focusing on the process of internal adaptation to social issues and demands. The other path has analyzed the relationship of the corporation with the environment from an *external* perspective (e.g., Galbraith, 1967; Lindblom, 1968, 1977), where the research begins from the societal or public policy viewpoint. Post (1976, 1978, 1978a, 1980) has also viewed corporate response to social issues from an external viewpoint but at a more micro level, including an analysis of the response patterns of individual firms within the same industry to a common problem (the infant formula controversy, Post & Baer, 1980). Page took an external perspective, with the trade association as the focal organization. This use of the trade association as the "organization" was unique and advanced for the time.

Page notes that there are a limited number of options available to the organization to resolve environmental uncertainty. These options fall into five broad response patterns (or strategies):

1. Total Resistance—The organization refuses to change, repulses the challenge, and/or forces the environment to adapt to the organization.
2. Bargaining—The organization bargains or compromises so that adjustment on both sides is required.
3. Capitulation—The organization adapts or gives in to the environment's demands.
4. Termination—The organization may end the relationship with the challenger, seek a replacement or change its environment.
5. Cessation of activity—The organization may be unwilling or unable to adapt or make the demanded changes, and therefore disbands. (Page, 1971:36-53)

The response patterns involve different levels of costs to the organizations, and also demand different amounts of coordination of organizational elements and sub-systems.

These responses are undertaken because any disruptions or disturbance in the "role-set agreement" between the organization and its environment threatens corporate goals, stability and viability. The concept of "role-set agreement" refers to the set of reciprocal expectancies or exchanges that govern the relationship between the organization and any element of the external environment. A particular role relationship includes bundles of rights and responsibilities. Rights are things of value or privilege gained by one actor in the process, while responsibilities are the duties or obligations offered in exchange for these rights. As a consequence, both the product and process of these role agreements are essential to organizational continuity and success. This approach clearly reflects the key aspects of Preston and Post's (1975) notion of interpenetrating systems, whereby actors influence one another directly and indirectly through an interaction process.

The response strategies noted above are very broad, but a variety of specific tactics may be associated with each (See Figure 1). If the firm elects to resist the change (the first strategy), it can either ignore the challenge (give no outward response) or engage in persuasion or propaganda. The organization can try to discredit the issue, or deny its existence or legitimacy, by acclaiming the legitimacy of present organizational behavior. The firm could also attempt to discredit those promoting the issue, acclaim the organization's social responsibility by emphasizing what the firm is doing in this area or in other areas, or has done in the past. The enterprise can also issue countercharges of irresponsible behavior directed toward the challengers. If all these tactics fail, the organization can engage in diversionary tactics; that is, the existence of the issue is admitted, but responsibility or legitimacy for dealing with the problem is disclaimed.[1] If the challenge can be resolved by these tactics, no changes in exchange agreements are necessary; and the organization can continue on with little or no changes in actual operations. Page notes that the organization would logically act only when the cost of inaction is higher than the cost of action (assuming both are known or estimated).

If resistance proves futile, the firm will seek out compromises (the second strategy). This is more threatening to the firm than resistance as it involves the renegotiation of role relationships and exchange agreements. Again, there is a patterned sequence of responses. The first tactic the enterprise can pursue is to offer positive inducements, in essence an attempt is made to buy off the challenger. If this is ineffective, negative inducements can be applied (for example, threats, warnings, sanctions,

Figure 1. Page's Response Patterns/Strategies

RESISTANCE	BARGAINING	CAPITULATION	TERMINATION	CESSATION
Ignore	Positive inducements	Concede	Cease relationship with the challenger	Dissolve the organization
Persuasion/ Propaganda ● discredit ● deny ● question legitimacy ● acclaim organization's social re- sponsibility ● counter charges	Negative inducements	Seek best solution for firm		
	Expand the conflict (build coaltions)	Seek exoneration ● promote social responsibility ● enchance prestige		
Diversionary Tactics				

TACTICS

65

and so forth). There is a danger here in that this tactic could result in adverse reactions from the challenger and other environmental elements.[2] The firm could also expose the conflict to other members of the role set, thereby gaining sympathetic allies as well as preparing them to accept changes in their role agreements with the organization with less resistance if the firm loses the challenge. This a dangerous tactic because it brings into question the ability of the firm to cope with challenges. The strength and stability of the enterprise is questioned and other members of the role set may themselves seek new exchange arrangements.

If these two general strategies fail, the organization can capitulate on the issue. Basically the organization concedes to the challenger on the major point of controversy. As a consequence the exchange agreements with the challenger change, and some or all other exchange agreements of the organization will have to be renegotiated. Although the organization gives-in, it will seek the best arrangements for its interests in the new exchange agreements. In addition it will seek exoneration by promoting an image of social responsibility in an attempt to enhance its prestige and perhaps receive some payoff from the concession. It is entirely possible that capitulation may be one of the first tactics used by the firm, if the costs of giving in are not too great, or the gain in prestige or image offsets them.

Two other general strategies are available to the firm. One would be for the enterprise to terminate the relationship with the challenging elements. This may be the first choice of the organization in responding to the challenge if the challenger's role is unimportant. The final strategy would be for the firm to dissolve itself, to cease to exist. If all other strategies and tactics are unsuccessful, this is the final and most drastic option available. All roles and relationships end with this response.

Pfeffer and Salancik offer response strategies and tactics consistent with those developed by Page. In addition, Pfeffer and Salancik note the importance of trade association activity as a method of limiting the demands of the environment on an organization; and observe that "In spite of the pervasiveness of trade and industry associations, there is remarkably little literature about them" (1978:179). Richards, writing on organizational goal structures, addresses the issue of organization responses to external demands within a strategic management framework. He notes that the initial response to external change by the corporation is resistance or divestment where possible. In addition the firm can use rhetorical support, tactical diversions, environmental co-optation, compliance, proaction, and advocacy (1978:78–82). All of these responses appear consonant with Page's typology.

In addition, Page's response patterns, and interactions between the organization and the government, parallel Preston and Post's notion of interpenetrating systems, where the interpenetrating systems model emphasizes that the various systems are related and that they interact in a variety of ways and processes that the systems themselves shape (1975, Chapter 2). In essence the elements in the system shape their relationships and the process that those relationships will follow.

Finally, the research of Kenneth Thomas (1976) and Gladwin and Walter (1980) on responses and modes of conflict resolution reflect the earlier developments of Thompson and Page. These authors note that management can attempt to overcome the opposition, try to avoid conflict, or accommodate the opposition. The firm can also attempt to collaborate with its opponents or attempt to reach a compromise. Thomas was one of the first researchers to lay out these various options in a managerially useful framework, and many of the tactics and strategies he offers are consistent with Page's developments. Post (1978a) utilized Thomas' model in a comparative analysis of five firms and their approaches to coping with social conflict (the infant formula controversy).

Page's first proposition is of relevance to this area of research, and is well supported in his analysis.

> The resistance of an organization to challenge will take the form of a *patterned behavior sequence* until some sort of compatibility with the environment is restored. The pattern is based on actions that create the least uncertainty for the organization. (1971: 37).

Stakeholder Analysis

Research in the area of stakeholder analysis and management has grown in recent years. Ansoff (1965), Dill (1976), MacMillan (1978), Rothschild (1976), and Freeman (1980) have all attempted to address the importance of various publics (''stakeholders'') on managerial action and discretion. Thompson and Page also worked on this issue. Thompson addressed the stakeholder problem through his analysis of the use of boundary spanning structures, organizational domains, and the assessment criteria used by environmental elements in evaluating organization action (1967:Chapters 3, 6, 7).

Page observed, following Thompson et al. (1959), that business firms are administered organizations and that they exist within and related to an environment. Page builds on the open systems framework of Thompson, noting that the firm has to convert inputs from the environment into outputs. A key factor in this process for Page is the notion of exchange—including exchange with both internal and external elements—to provide support for the organization. In order for these exchanges to take place, there has to be an exchange agreement between the elements. According to Page, this agreement involves what is to be given and received by each participant, both in substantive terms and in behavioral expectations.[3] Page defines these agreements as "roles." Although Thompson does not use the term "role," the essence of this exchange agreement notion is contained in his discussion of domain, dependence, and environment (1967:25–29). Page argues that the organization's behavior in one of its roles can be challenged by a dissatisfied element (or stakeholder) in the environment. This vital element may demand that the organization take on new responsibilities or obligations toward that element, or that the organization give up previous rights. Such a challenge may present a serious threat by being potentially disruptive not only of one role (or exchange agreement) but of other roles as well. To capture this relationship, Page offers a proposition for further study:

> When the demand concerns a social issue, resistance comes about, not particularly because social responsibility as such is resisted or the aims of business are evil by design, but because some, and perhaps all, of the interrelated roles in the role set will have to be readjusted and defined.[5] (1971:27)

This leads to a consideration of how roles become redefined as a result of these challenges. There are four methods by which a redefinition of roles could come about:

1. Relationships may change gradually by changes in the accepted norms and values of individuals comprising the related groups (e.g., change in mandatory retirement age to 70);
2. A particular exchange agreement could be redefined over a significant time period by small issues slowly eroding away a set position and effecting change in perceived privileges and obligations (e.g., women in business);
3. The organization could grow more powerful in relation to an environmental element and force a more advantageous bargain for itself (e.g., growth of General Motors and its relationship to suppliers);
4. From some element or combination of elements in the environment an issue could arise that threatens the continued functioning of the organization (e.g., Chrysler's situation). (Page, 1971:20–21)

Conceptually, this relationship is shown in Figure 2. Page is developing a composite picture of the business organization. Individuals occupying positions interrelated to other positions by means of roles form sub-units. The interconnection of all these subunits forms the total system (organization). This relationship is dynamic, and is depicted in three "frames" representing the organization's position at sequential points in time in

Figure 2. Dynamic Relationship between the Organization and its External Role Set

FRAME ONE	*FRAME TWO*	*FRAME THREE*
Visible roles set in place.	The role set is disturbed.	Adjustments are made in the role set.
Relationship understood and clear and satisfied.	Exchange agreements no longer satisfactory	New exchange agreements entered into with other roles.
Support from internal and external elements obtained and secure.	A challenge is posed for the organization to respond to.	The challenge is dealt with in a satisfactory manner.
	Requires the organization to act in order to restore equilibrium (i.e., get back to frame one situation).	Equilibrium is restored and support assured.

TIME →

69

Figure 2. Page is concerned with the processes involved in making the adjustments between frames two and three. How does the firm adapt to challenges that upset exchange agreements already in force? This problem is particularly acute when we consider the multiplicity of exchange agreements an organization has with internal and external elements.

Simply put, Page makes the point that resistance to social issues arises out of corporate concern that its relationship with one or more key stakeholders in its domain will have to be renegotiated in a lengthy, time consuming process. As noted, once the firm engages in this process with one stakeholder, other agreements with other stakeholders may have to be renegotiated as well, and so on in a continuous bargaining process since all the stakeholders are interrelated.

RECENT CORPORATE RESPONSES
TO SOCIAL ISSUES

Gatewood and Carroll (1981) have investigated the response of three corporations to three very difficult issues with large social impact. The three firms and issues are Procter and Gamble, and Rely Tampons; Firestone and the 500 series of steel-belted tires; and Ford and the Pinto. My own investigation of the chemical industry's response to recent superfund legislation (Mahon, 1981) provides an additional example of recent corporate action for study in the light of the analytical scheme set forth here.

The superfund legislation that became public law in 1980 was subjected to intense debate starting in January 1979. The legislation was designed to provide a fund ($2.6 billion) to pay for the clean up of hazardous waste sites. The monies for the fund were to be raised from taxes on the chemical and petroleum industries, with the bulk of the funds coming from the chemical industry. The chemical industry's initial response to proposed superfund legislation was that the hazardous waste problem was not severe and that the scope of the problem was not well known. In addition, they argued that the problem was really the result of behavior of unconscionable midnight haulers and other unscrupulous people and efforts should be made to punish the guilty parties. As Robert Roland (1979), president of the Chemical Manufacturers Association, noted:

> One of the things that we must all realize in discussing the solid-waste disposal problem, including toxic or hazardous wastes, is that it is not just the problem of the chemical industry. It is a result of society's advanced technology and pursuit of an increasingly complex lifestyle.

Later, Roland was even more specific.

> The administration's bill unfairly singles out the chemical and related industries to bear a disproportionate burden of clean-up costs. In doing so, it fails to adequately reflect the society's responsibility for resolving a problem which everyone has helped create and for whose solution everyone should help pay. (*Chemical and Engineering News,* June 25, 1979)

The chemical industry attempted to deflect criticism and to deny the necessity of this type of legislation arguing that current laws were sufficient and that any large superfund would cause severe economic damage to the industry and to individual firms. The industry group also advocated different (and less expensive) legislation focused on the problems of *abandoned* waste sites.

> Robert A. Roland, CMA President, said the association considers the superfund approach to be a "one-shot panacea which unwisely imposes economic burdens on companies that did not create the problems which superfund attempts to address". And he stressed that the industry is "on record" in favor of a new law specifically dealing with abandoned dumpsites. (*Chemical Week,* September 5, 1979:19)

In addition to these public statements, the chemical industry launched a $6 million public relations campaign to point out the positive side of the chemical industry. All this was in vain, as Congress eventually passed superfund into law. After the passage of the bill, the CMA noted that they would do their best to make it work and that it reflected the intense work that the CMA put into this legislation.

The Gatewood and Carroll (1981) piece provides similar patterns involving three different firms in three different industries. Their analysis of the Proctor and Gamble handling of Rely shows that the firm first argued that there was no correlation between toxic shock and their tampon, and that their in-house tests supported this conclusion. When the Center for Disease Control announced publicly that Rely was a major element in toxic shock, the firm argued that the information and data was too limited and fragmentary for any conclusions to be drawn. In addition, Procter and Gamble protested that exhaustive coverage in the news media biased the results, that the data were inaccurate and the interviewing techniques suspect.

However, Procter and Gamble halted production of Rely and eventually withdrew the product from the market. But this did not occur until after Harness, the chairman and executive noted that he was:

> . . . determined to fight for a brand, to keep an important brand from being hurt by insufficient data in the hands of a bureaucracy. (Rotbart and Prestbo, 1980:21)

When Procter and Gamble did withdraw the product, Harness observed that:

This is being done despite the fact that we know of no defect in Rely tampons and despite evidence that the withdraw of Rely won't eliminate the occurrence of toxic shock syndrome. (Procter and Gamble News Release, September 22, 1980)

Firestone's handling of the 500 series tire is very similar. Firestone's initial arguments were that there was nothing wrong with the tire and that any problems were caused by customer abuse. The firm constantly tried to block investigations of its tire and publicly questioned the motives of the investigators. The organization deflected requests for more detailed information on the grounds that it would cost a great deal of money and require a large amount of time and effort. Eventually, Firestone was compelled to initiate what was to become one of the largest recalls in history.*

Ford's response to the investigation surrounding the Pinto was also similar, but far more sophisticated. Ford lobbied against federal standards which would have forced the redesign of the Pinto gas tank for over eight years. Their tactics involved offering arguments successively that could only be worked on one at a time, arguing that the problem was the people not cars and ". . . accompanying each argument, no matter how ridiculous, with thousands of pages of highly technical assertions that would take the government months or, preferably, years to treat." (Gatewood and Carroll, 1981:14)

Even after the Federal Government proved that auto fires were a real and growing problem, Ford countered with a new position: There were auto fires, but rear end collisions rarely happen. Later Ford would argue that regardless of fire, people would have died anyway from the force of the impact. In the later stages of the disagreement, Henry Ford warned, "If we can't meet the standards when they are published, we will have to close down," for example, adopt Page's ultimate strategy. (Dowei, 1977:54)

CONCLUSIONS

The four incidents reviewed here amply demonstrate that Page's strategies and tactics are relevant to an analysis of the business-government relationships that exist today. The chemical industry at first resisted, using tactics shown in Figure 1, then began to bargain and finally capitulated. This pattern is repeated in the Procter and Gamble, Firestone, and Ford situations. It does seem true that firms will move only when pushed. This "pushing" may, as these short cases demonstrate, involve time and constant pressure on the firm to obtain some movement.

*See additional analysis of the Firestone 500 experience in the essay by Elliot Zashin in this volume. Ed.

From a managerial perspective, all of these firms, with the exception of Procter and Gamble, incurred some additional negative costs. Although these costs in some instances are difficult to measure, they are nonetheless real. The chemical industry's actions severely damaged their political image in Congress and publicly embarrassed their supporters. We can only speculate, but it seems logical to assume that their credibility will be lowered as Congress begins debates this year on Clean Air and Clean Water Act amendments.

Firestone is still suffering from the court cases, congressional hearings and bad press over the 500 tire issue. Their share of the market has fallen by one-half of one percent, a loss that amounts to millions of dollars (Louis, 1978:45). Ford has discontinued the Pinto line and announced last year a major loss in North American sales which they attributed to the publicity surrounding the Pinto case.

The only firm to realize any positive gain from a publicly embarrassing situation was Procter and Gamble. They realized an increase in favorable public attitude following the removal of Rely from the market (Rotbart and Prestbo, 1980:21). These gains came as they proceeded through Page's response patterns. After Procter and Gamble admitted that there might be a problem, they followed up with positive action. They pledged research expertise to investigate toxic shock, financed and directed an education program about the disease and issued a warning to women not to use Rely. Thus, instead of merely claiming that they were good citizens, they backed up their position with concrete action. They capitulated, it is true, but they also sought exoneration through enhancing their prestige and promoting their own social responsibility.

The Thompson-Page research into social issues has gone largely unnoticed. Their analysis is important to several current areas of inquiry and it demonstrates that Thompson's theoretical contributions could be useful in empirical studies. The Thompson-Page research should thus be in the mainstream of current investigations in the social issues in management areas.

ACKNOWLEDGMENT

The author wishes to thank Professor Paul J. Gordon of Indiana University for bringing Page's work to his attention.

NOTES

1. J.P. Stevens' battle with unionization attempts may be a classic example of a firm following a long pattern of resistance to challenges from the environment. This particular example may also demonstrate the futility of a strategy of resistance in the face of committed opponents prepared to wage a lengthy battle.

2. See Post and Mahon (1980) for an analysis of a situation where an industry made threats that resulted in extremely adverse reactions by other elements in the environment.

3. This link between behavioral expectations and organizational performance aligns closely with Post's (1978b) model of Status—Behavior—Performance.

4. Post and Mellis's (1978) investigation of Polaroid's response to the women's movement is another excellent example of the dynamics of Page's proposition.

REFERENCES

Ackerman, R. W., *The Social Challenge To Business*. Cambridge, MA: Harvard University Press, 1975.

Ackerman, R. W., and R. Bauer, *Corporate Social Responsiveness: The Modern Dilemma*. Reston, VA: Reston Publishing, 1976.

Adams, J. S., "The Structures and Dynamics of Behavior in Organizational Boundary Roles." In M. Dunnette (ed.), *Handbook of Organizational and Industrial Psychology*, Chicago: Rand McNally, 1976.

Aldrich, L., and D. Herker, "Boundary Spanning Roles and Organizational Structure." *Academy of Management Review* 2(1977):217–230.

Ansoff, H. I., *Corporate Strategy*. New York: McGraw-Hill, 1965.

Avery, R. W., "James D. Thompson: A Memorial." *Administrative Science Quarterly* 19(1974):3–4.

Bauer, R., "The Corporate Response Process." In L. Preston (ed.), *Research in Corporate Social Performance and Policy*, vol. 1. Greenwich, CT: JAI Press, 1978; pp. 99–122.

Bauer, R., I. Pool, and L. Dexter, *American Business and Public Policy: The Politics of Foreign Trade*. New York: Atherton Press, 1964.

Chemical, and Engineering News, "Bill Proposes Hazardous Waste Cleanup Fund." (June 25, 1979):27.

Chemical Week, "CMA Blasts Superfund Plan on Dump Cleanups." (September 5, 1979):19.

Dill, W., "Strategic Management in Kibitzer's World." In H. Ansoff, R. Declerck, and R. Hayes (eds.), *From Strategic Planning to Strategic Management*, New York: Wiley, 1976.

Dowei, M., "How Ford Put two Million Firetraps on Wheels," *Business and Society Review* 23(Fall 1977):26–55.

Emshoff, J., and R. Freeman, "Who's Butting Into Your Business." *The Wharton Magazine* 4(1979):44–48ff.

Epstein, E., *The Corporation in American Politics*. Englewood Cliffs: Prentice-Hall, 1969.

———, "The Dimensions of Corporate Power." Part 1, *California* Management Review 16(1973):9–23.

———, "The Dimensions of Corporate Power." Part 2, *California Management Review* 16(1974):32–47.

———, "Firm Size and Structure, Market Power and Business Political Influence: A Review of the Literature." Paper presented at the Bureau of Economics of the Federal Trade Commission Conference on the Economics of Firm Size, Market Structure and Social Performance. Rosslyn, VA:(January 17–18, 1980).

———, "Business Political Activity: Research Approaches and Analytical Issues." In L. Preston (ed.), *Research in Corporate Social Performance and Policy*, vol. 2, Greenwich, CT: JAI Press, 1980; 1–56.

Freeman, E., "Stakeholder Theory and Strategic Management." Paper presented at the Academy of Management Meeting. Detroit: (August, 1980).

Galbraith, J. K., *The New Industrial State*. Boston: Houghton Mifflin, 1967.

Galbraith, J. K., and D. Nathanson, *Strategy Implementation: The Role of Structure and Process.* New York: West, 1978.

Gatewood E., and A. Carroll, "The Anatomy of Corporate Social Response: The Rely, Firestone 500, and Pinto Cases." *Business Horizons 24(1981):9–16.*

Gladwin, T., and I. Walter, "How Multinationals Can Manage Social and Political Forces." *The Journal of Business Strategy* 1(1980):54–68.

Hofer, C., and D. Schendel, *Strategy Formulation: Analytical Concepts.* New York: West, 1978.

Lindblom, C., *The Policy Making Process.* Englewood Cliffs, NJ: Prentice-Hall, 1968.

———, *Politics and Markets: The World's Political-Economic System.* New York: Basic Books, 1977.

Louis, A., "Lessons From the Firestone Fracas." *Fortune* (August 28, 1978):45.

MacMillan, I., *Strategy Formulation: Political Concepts.* New York: West, 1978.

Mahon, J. F., *The Corporate Public Affairs Office: Structure, Process and Impact.* Doctoral Dissertation. Boston University, 1981.

McNeil, K., and J. Thompson, "The Regeneration of Social Organizations." *American Sociological Review* 36(1971):624–637.

Miles, R., "Role Conflict in Boundary and Internal Organizational Roles." Unpublished manuscript, Yale University, 1975.

———, "Organizational Boundary Roles." In G. Cooper, and R. Payne (eds.), *Current Concerns in Occupational Stress,* London: Wiley, 1980.

Murray, E., *The Implementation of Social Policies in Commercial Banks.* Doctoral Dissertation. Harvard University, 1974.

Page, R., *Organizational Response to Social Challenge: Theory and Evidence for Two Industries.* Doctoral dissertation. Indiana University, 1971.

Pfeffer, J., and G. Salancik, *The External Control of Organizations.* New York: Harper and Row, 1978.

Post, J., *Risk and Response: Management and Social Change in the American Insurance Industry.* Lexington, MA: D.C. Heath, 1976.

———, *Corporate Behavior and Social Change.* Reston, VA: Reston, 1978.

———, "Research on Patterns of Corporate Response to Social Change." In L. Preston (ed.), *Research in Corporate Social Performance and Policy,* vol. 1. Greenwich, CT: JAI Press, 1978; pp. 55–78.

Post, J., and M. Mellis, "Corporate Responsiveness and Organizational Learning." *California Management Review* 20(1978):57–63.

Post, J., and E. Baer, "Analyzing Complex Policy Problems: The Social Performance of the International Infant Formula Industry." In L. Preston (ed.), *Research in Corporate Social Performance and Policy,* vol. 2. Greenwich, CT: JAI Press, 1980; 157–196.

Post, J., and J. Mahon, "Articulated Turbulence: The Effect of Regulatory Agencies on Corporate Response to Social Change." *Academy of Management Review* 5(1980):399–407.

Preston, L., "Corporation and Society: The Search for a Paradigm." *Journal of Economic Literature* 13(1975):434–453.

———, "Corporate Social Performance and Policy: A Synthetic Framework for Research and Analysis." In L. Preston (ed.), *Research in Corporate Social Performance and Policy,* vol. 1. Greenwich, CT: JAI Press, 1978; pp. 1–26.

Preston, L., and J. Post, *Private Management and Public Policy.* Englewood Cliffs, NJ: Prentice-Hall, 1975.

Richards, M., *Organizational Goal Structures.* New York: West, 1978.

Roland, R., "Toxic Scapegoats." *Washington Post* (April 2, 1979):15.

Rotbart, D., and J. Prestbo, "Killing a Product." *Wall Street Journal* (November 3, 1980):21.

Rothschild, W., *Putting It All Together.* New York: AMACOM, 1976.

Sethi, S., *Up Against the Corporate Wall: Modern Corporations and Social Issues of the Seventies.* Englewood Cliffs, NJ: Prentice-Hall, 1971.

———, "Corporate Social Audit: An Emerging Trend in Measuring Corporate Social Performance." In D. Votaw, and S. Sethi (eds.), *The Corporate Dilemma: Traditional Values Versus Contemporary Problems,* Englewood Cliffs, NJ: Prentice-Hall, 1973.

———, "Dimensions of Corporate Social Performance: An Analytical Framework for Measurement and Evolution." *California Management Review* 17(1975):58–64.

———, "An Analytical Framework for Making Cross-Cultural Comparisons of Business Responses to Social Pressures: The Case of Japan and the United States." In L. Preston (ed.), *Research in Corporate Social Performance and Policy,* vol. 1. Greenwich, CT: JAI Press, 1978:pp. 27–54.

Taylor, B., "Managing the Process of Corporate Development." In B. Taylor, and J. Sparkes (eds.), *Corporate Strategy and Planning,* New York: Wiley, 1977.

Thomas, K., "Conflict and Conflict Management." In M. Dunnette (ed.), *Handbook of Industrial and Organizational Psychology,* Chicago: Rand McNally, 1976.

Thompson, J., *Organizations In Action.* New York: McGraw-Hill, 1967.

———, "Society's Frontiers for Organizing Activities." *Public Administration Review* 33(1973):327–335.

———, "Social Interdependence, The Polity and Public Administration." *Administration and Society* 6(1974):3–20.

———, "Technology, Polity, and Societal Development." *Administrative Science Quarterly* 19(1974):6–21.

Thompson, J., P. Hammond, R. Hawkes, B. Junker, and A. Tuden, *Comparative Studies in Administration.* Pittsburgh: University of Pittsburgh Press, 1959.

STRATEGIC PLANNING SYSTEMS FOR A POLITICIZED ENVIRONMENT

Duane Windsor and George Greanias

The external environment of the corporation has been substantially restructured by the increasing *politicization* of market relationships. By politicization, we mean that the roles of stakeholder interests, business-government relations, and corporate social impact or responsibility have become more important in strategic management relative to economic performance. Corporate social policy and performance is thus one aspect of a much broader transformation of the corporate environment.

We argue that fundamental conditions and trends (in the economy, society, culture, environment, science, natural resources, industrial structure, and so on) have substantially altered the type and number of stakeholders, constituencies, or clienteles affected by and interested in corporate decisions. Corporations are key components of the economic system and as such have great economic, stakeholder, and social impact.

Research in Corporate Social Performance and Policy, Vol. 4, pages 77–104
Copyright © 1982 by JAI Press Inc.
All rights of reproduction in any form reserved.
ISBN: 0-89232-259-4

Politicization involves the intervention of a wider range of stakeholders in corporate decisionmaking through governmental processes and legal and social relationships which ultimately control market interactions and corporate governance.

Such politicization of the corporate environment implies significant, even dramatic, consequences for strategy formulation and strategic planning systems. On the basis of the arguments presented in this paper, we reach the following conclusions. First, enterprise-level strategy formulation assumes greater relative importance in a politicized environment. Second, enterprise missions and performance evaluations expand to incorporate clientele satisfaction and social impact as well as market performance in the traditional sense. Third, enterprise strategy formulation must be based on some system of environmental scanning and sociopolitical forecasting that apprehends the effects of politicization. Finally, such a strategic planning system should serve as a basis for political and legal, as well as market, strategy formulation.

Traditional corporate planning procedures have focused on growth and financial goals developed largely within the context of market and technological conditions. Politicization of the corporate environment therefore creates serious difficulties for existing approaches to strategic planning. Wilson has argued that an essential prerequisite for the formulation and implementation of an operational corporate social policy is a fundamental reform of the strategic planning process so as to integrate social and business needs (1974b, p. 2). In other words, social responsibility and economic performance must become equal values in corporate strategy and must be fully coordinated in corporate decisionmaking. The need for such reform results directly from politicization of the corporate environment. Wilson concluded that strategic planning systems must be redesigned and expanded to handle environmental scanning and sociopolitical forecasting of a sophisticated character. In this manner, social responsibility can be made a central consideration in corporate planning and performance.

The objective here is *not* to propose a specific strategic planning system or particular procedures for environmental scanning and socio-political forecasting. The very thrust of our argument, indeed, is that the internal state, external environment, and management style of each company will vary. As a result, there are a wide variety of corporate planning systems in use and there is no comprehensive theory of strategic planning. Extant systems focus on the critical contingencies in the firm's environment as perceived by top management. What we are arguing is that politicization of the environment is changing managerial perception of critical contingencies. "Social responsibility" is not a voluntary goal of the modern corporation. It is a response to the stakeholder, business-government relations, and legal consequences of the politicization of the corporate environment.

Our objective therefore is to address the question of how to design and evaluate strategic planning systems which confront the environmental scanning, socio-political forecasting, and strategy formulation requirements of the corporation operating in a politicized environment. We suggest that a conceptual understanding of the nature of politicization and strategic planning is essential to developing corporate social policy. It is fair to suggest that we have only scratched the surface of the problem. Environmental scanning, socio-political forecasting, and corporate social policy as active components of strategic planning are literally in their infancy.

Strategic management can be viewed generally as occurring at four levels of strategy formulation arranged hierarchically (Schendel and Hofer 1979). As a result of the increasing politicization of the corporate environment, what Schendel and Hofer term enterprise-level strategy has become more important relative to the corporate-portfolio, business-unit, and functional levels of strategy. Every firm, diversified or not, must select one or more industries in which to compete. The modern multidivisional corporation in particular is a diversified firm operating as a portfolio of product-market segments requiring a differentiated management. The corporate-portfolio level of strategy formulation is concerned with selecting the set of industries (that is, product-market segments) in which to operate.[1] Within each industry, a different business-unit strategy for market competition must be formulated. The business unit is that part of the corporation operating in a specific product-market segment. Finally, the business unit, in addition to its competitive strategy, will develop plans and strategies for the conduct and coordination of its various functional activities (production, marketing, finance, research and development, human resources, and so on). The hierarchy of strategy formulation thus reaches from the selection of industries in which to operate and the design of competitive policies for each product-market segment to the integration of functional activities. Traditional growth and financial goals are the guiding principles for these three levels.

Strategic management also includes what Schendel and Hofer term enterprise-level strategy. This level of strategy formulation is inherently less susceptible to conceptual treatment in principle and inherently more difficult to handle in practice. Enterprise-level strategy deals with the socio-political and legal environment of the entire firm (the whole portfolio of business) in terms of its impact on long-run growth, goals and objectives, and corporate missions. The broader environment beyond markets and technology is the special responsibility of enterprise-level strategy. At this level of strategy formulation, clientele satisfaction and social impact must be combined with market performance within the context of governmental processes and legal relationships. Enterprise-level strategy is concerned with achieving long-term survival and growth through organization-environment fit in a changing economy, polity, and society. We see the firm as interacting with its entire environment through a wide variety of constituencies, clienteles, or stakeholders. Politicization of this corporate environment is making enterprise-level strategy increasingly important with consequent implications for strategic planning systems.

This level of strategy formulation deals with issues of stockholder and constituency expectations (forming together with management the immediate "stakeholders" of the firm), business-government relations, ethical conduct, the social responsibilities (if any) of the firm, and so on— as components of the corporate mission and performance criteria. It is within this overall enterprise framework that corporate-portfolio, business-unit, and functional plans are ultimately developed and coordinated. The broadly defined socio-political and legal environment of the firm is the predominant consideration at the enterprise level of strategy formulation.

The paper first argues that strategic planning is ultimately an articulation of the total enterprise with its politicized environment in order to promote long-term growth, given multiple (and potentially conflicting) objectives of market performance, social impact, and clientele satisfaction. This view of strategic management is developed into a prescriptive model of the strategic planning system as a guide for designing and evaluating procedures at the enterprise, corporate-portfolio, and business-unit levels of strategy formulation. Next we present a detailed explication of the modern corporate environment as a basis for conceptualizing the strategic planning problem and to explain how and why politicization of that environment occurs. Special attention is paid to business-government relations and the legal system as intermediaries in the interaction among markets, stakeholders, and companies. We introduce and explain what we call the "law of government control" as a way of explicating the changing legal environment of business. This particular approach is taken because of the illumination it casts on the requirements of strategic planning systems which can cope with socio-political and legal issues at the enterprise-level of strategy formulation.

In the third section, we examine the issue of designing and evaluating a strategic planning system to handle a politicized environment. Such an environment is characterized by great strategic complexity and rapid change. As a direct result, "The analysis of the firm's environment becomes a critical part of . . . strategic planning" (Whittaker 1978, p. 19). We seek to determine the information required and strategic decisions to be made by such a planning system so as to promote the company's long-term growth. At the end of the section, we relate strategic planning to the formulation of political, as well as market and legal, strategies as a basis for enterprise involvement in governmental processes and handling of stakeholder relations.

Finally, we examine and evaluate several existing environmental scanning or socio-political forecasting systems in use at companies like Monsanto, General Electric, Southern California Edison, and Sears, Roebuck which have been described in the literature. The sophistication of existing systems must be considered in light of the very early stage at which scanning and modeling of a complex and increasingly politicized environment are presently occurring.

STRATEGIC PLANNING AS ENVIRONMENTAL FIT

Business strategy or strategic management is widely conceived of as the acquisition and allocation of enterprise resources (programming) and funds (budgeting) to courses of action (strategies) which are intended to achieve basic goals and objectives in fulfillment of some more fundamental enterprise mission or missions. Planning is the process of determining those missions, goals, and strategies. In Chandler's pithy and now classic explication, "Strategy can be defined as the determination of the basic long-term goals and objectives of an enterprise and the adoption of courses of action and the allocation of resources necessary for carrying out these goals" (1962, p. 13). Strategic planning is thus "The art and science of influencing the long-term growth of a company" (Berg 1965, p. 79).

The dominant model of the business strategy literature emphasizes a view of strategic planning as environmental fit or articulation (Bourgeois 1980). This approach is most systematically explained in Whittaker (1978, chs. 1, 3-4). In the long run, the organization and its environment *must* be adapted to each other—either by the organization changing itself and its strategies, or by the organization changing the environment through its strategies. Thus, "Strategy can be viewed as a pattern or positioning of resources of the firm relative to its environment, all to achieve desired performance outcomes" (Schendel and Patton 1978, p. 1611). Hence, "The essence of formulating competitive strategy is relating a company to its environment" (Porter 1979, p. 1). This conception of strategic planning as a process of organization-environment articulation is ". . . heavily emphasized in both the business policy and organization theory literature" (Bourgeois 1980, p. 25).

The concept of strategic planning as environmental fit can be expanded into a prescriptive model for strategy formulation (Wilson 1980, p. 162).

A strategic profile can be constructed from the resource audit (internal strengths and weaknesses) and environmental assessment (external threats and opportunities) as the basis for an analysis of strategic issues and problems.[2] That analysis will inevitably be shaped by managerial philosophy, values, desires, and assumptions which we can term the business strategy concept. The enterprise's mission, objectives, and goals are defined by this organizational process of strategic assessment. Competitive strategies and organizational policies are planned as the framework for the development of specific capital and operating plans, programs, and budgets. In principle, it is possible and desirable to conduct contingency analyses of alternative scenarios to be prepared for possible changes in operations. Both the strategic profile and business performance concept are presumably reevaluated periodically based on performance.

This analysis of strategic management as environmental fit has important implications for the information requirements of a strategic planning process. It should be evident that, in addition to standard accounting and financial data, a corporate information system must identify and record resource, environmental, and performance information of a broader character. The resource audit, environmental assessment, and performance evaluation components point out these information needs. In a narrower context (the accounting information system), Gordon and Miller (1976) view the design of information systems as a function of the organization's attributes, its environment, and its management's decisionmaking style. From this perspective, the design and evaluation of information systems ought to consider the organization's specific needs as shaped by its attributes, environment and managerial style. Environmental dynamism and hostility are hypothesized by Gordon and Miller to increase the corporation's need for forecasted nonfinancial information. Under such conditions, a strategic planning system must be oriented toward identification of contingencies.

Planning attention is typically focused on the most critical contingencies in the firm's environment and is related directly to the complexity of that environment. The perceived need for planning is increased by organizational complexity, environmental instability (particularly in markets, technologies, and distribution channels), competitive stress, and sub-unit interdependency (Saunders and Tuggle 1977, p. 21). Stated more simply, "Companies have initiated planning systems because of the increasing complexity of their organizations and the increasing complexity in which they operate" (Moskow 1978, p. 1).

Strategic planning systems have been most thoroughly developed at the corporate-portfolio, business-unit, and functional levels of strategy formulation. A standard product-market matrix (i.e., strategy space) lays out the basic strategic alternatives for the firm. Within each industry (or product-market segment), there is a comparison of industry attractiveness and the firm's relative competitiveness. This comparison is the basis for selecting the corporation's portfolio of businesses. Within each product-market segment, the business unit's competitive strategy is a positioning of the company so as to match its critical strengths and weaknesses to the threats and opportunities posed by the basic economic structure of the industry (Porter 1980, chs. 1 and 2; Porter 1979). Key structural forces determine the intensity of competitive forces and hence the relative profitability of the industry.[3]

We deliberately skip over the functional level of strategy formulation for two reasons. First, each functional area is different and involves highly specific types of policy decisions. Second, functional strategies are essentially an implementation of the firm's business-unit strategy for market competition within an industry. The basic strategic issue is coordination of functional activities. Nevertheless in a politicized environment functional strategies are guided by and coordinated with the enterprise-level overall strategy. Production is subject to environmental, safety, and liability constraints. Marketing involves various legal considerations. Human resources management touches on equal opportunity. The functional plans are hardly isolated from politicization of the corporate environment. Indeed the failure of functional planning will ultimately cause the failure of enterprise strategy.[4]

In our view, the basic foci of enterprise-level strategy can be broken into market performance, social impact, and clientele satisfaction. The firm must be profitable in the long run; companies with negative present value are unlikely to survive over time. It has long been postulated that profitability underlies both management values and stockholder expectations. The Chandler thesis (1962) argues that business strategy and structure have been shaped historically by market demand and technological forces, with relatively limited influence from other environmental variables in the United States. Market performance drives the corporate-portfolio, business-unit, and functional levels of strategy. But the firm can also have a variety of constituencies, clienteles, or stakeholders with other than a profit orientation. Some constituencies may desire or accept a reduction in profit maximization in order to accomplish other purposes: management to preserve organizational slack and enjoy perquisites; environmentalists to secure clean air, water, and so on; consumers to obtain higher quality commodities. Investors and stockholders may exhibit an interest in ethical conduct and social responsibility. Part of enterprise-level strategy is to accommodate these constituencies. The social impact of firm activities can also be important because of their implications. In determining a hierarchy of missions, objectives, and goals, it is important to differentiate among, and coordinate the market performance, social impact, and clientele satisfaction dimensions for which performance evaluation criteria must be developed.

POLITICIZATION OF THE CORPORATE ENVIRONMENT

By *politicization* of the corporate environment we mean that social, political, and legal developments are assuming greater strategic importance relative to market competition and technology. In the view of Reginald Jones, Chairman of General Electric Company, "It is no exaggeration to say that for most managers, their main problems—the main obstacles to achieving their business objectives—are external to the company . . . the main problems of business these days are . . . determined in the arena of public policy" (Watson 1980, p. 60). The implication is that planning at the level of enterprise strategy is increasingly important relative to the corporate-portfolio, business-unit, and functional levels. It has been estimated that top executives of major companies spend as much as half their time on external relations, especially with governments and constituencies (Bok 1979; Child 1979). Jones reported he was spending one working day in five in Washington, D.C. It appears that ". . . planners will be increasingly confronted with ill-structured problems . . ." (Ansoff and Brandenburg 1967, p. B-231) presented by the non-economic factors of clientele satisfaction and social impact, together with greater government control over corporate governance, clientele relations, and market performance. The politicized environment thus involves a relative shift in environmental forces from market and technological to political and legal factors. The problem imposed on strategic planning is that ". . . environmental analysis is not an activity which has been formalized, systematized, or proceduralized to any significant degree in business" (Thomas 1974, p. 37).

Udell, Laczniak, and Lusch (1976) surveyed high level executives in the Fortune 500 industrial corporations in order to forecast the business environment of 1985. Their published results are based on questionnaires from 147 firms. The respondents indicated that:

1. Social responsibility issues will continue to be important, with consumerism becoming an even stronger pressure;
2. Environmental protection will continue to be a significant policy issue;
3. Natural resource prices will be somewhat higher due to scarcities limiting the rate of economic growth;
4. Technological developments are not expected to solve these problems;

5. The regulatory environment will grow increasingly complex; and
6. Inflation will continue and economic growth will be slow, placing some additional pressures on marketing to maintain adequate earnings.

In our view, there are two basic forces driving environmental politicization in the United States. First, government regulation—transforming into a law of government control—is increasingly aimed at social impact and corporate governance processes. Second, stakeholders are increasingly seeking means of obtaining legal rights to participation in corporate decisionmaking. Examples are the ethical investor movement, public interest groups, consumerism, and environmental protection. The increasing attention of top executives to explicitly legal, government control, and stakeholder issues augurs a fundamental change in strategic planning systems toward enterprise-level issues.

An Example

It will be easier to grasp the nature of the politicized environment if we examine a particular instance. The legal relationships within which corporations operate are becoming increasingly dominated by the rapid development of what we term the "law of governmental control." Analysis of the Airline Deregulation Act of 1978 illustrates how this law of government control functions and has evolved (Greanias 1980). The Airline Deregulation Act has been hailed as the first major change in government policy on airlines since the Civil Aeronautics Act of 1938, and also as the first time in decades that the federal government has withdrawn from involvement in an entire industry. At the time of its passage, the Act was considered a major step towards decreasing government interventions in the airline industry; control over fares and routes would gradually be phased out, and the Civil Aeronautics Board would be dismantled.

The impression of government withdrawal from the industry was, however, illusory. While the Civil Aeronautics Board was on its way to oblivion, the overall ability of the government to intervene in the airline industry remained as great as ever. The Securities and Exchange Commission still affected the industry through the securities laws and relatively new internal accounting controls and bookkeeping provisions of the Foreign Corrupt Practices Act. The National Labor Relations Board dealt with labor-management relations. The Federal Aviation Authority still had primary responsibility for airline safety. The Antitrust Division of the Justice Department kept a watchful eye on the mergers and acquisitions that took place during the period of consolidation that followed passage of the Act. Other agencies affected the industry directly. The Environmental Protection Agency was concerned with air and noise pollution generated by airplanes. The Equal Employment Opportunity Commission set requirements for hiring to be followed in recruiting and promoting minority personnel. The conceptual error was in assuming that the interventions of government in the airline industry could be summed up as a direct relationship with a single federal agency, and that if only the CAB were dissolved and its functions allowed to atrophy, the airlines would be free of government entanglements.

In fact, however, this conceptualization—and the conclusions drawn from it—were largely wrong, for both the conceptualization and the conclusions were oversimplifications of the diversity of government involvement in the airline industry. Government intervention in the airline industry involves multiple federal, state, and local agencies. At the federal level there are both the direct interventions of the Federal Aviation Agency and the less direct effects of Executive Orders. In addition, there are other government and "quasi-government" interventions affecting the airline industry which act partly through and partly outside of federal channels: specifically, the actions of individual states, as well as numerous private or public interest groups, ranging from shareholders and employees to "stakeholders" such as communities which have or desire to obtain air transportation service.

Failure to understand the real implications of the Airline Deregulation Act—and thus hailing it as a major reduction in government involvement in the airline industry, when in fact it was something much more marginal—is a direct reflection of the absence of comprehensive notions of government control, of the full range of rationales for government action, of the rights government claims, and of the tools employed by government to act upon those rights pursuant to those rationales. The view that the Airline Deregulation Act involved a general reduction of government's role in the airline industry is wrong because it ignores the many levers of government power that affect the operations of the airlines.

POLITICIZATION MORE THAN REGULATION

It is not surprising that, with regard to government interventions in the private sector, most of the interest in the past few years has centered on regulation. But this approach obscures as much as it illuminates. The tendency to lump whatever is happening under the heading of "government regulation" obscures the depth and breadth of the government's activities, some of which have nothing to do with *regulation* as such, and in some of which the government is a secondary rather than a primary actor (e.g., private or public interest actions under public laws or government-sponsored programs). Politicization embraces government actions across this full spectrum of activity.

There is a good deal of overlap in government; different agencies have responsibility for different laws that pursue the same policy. The environment is not just the concern of the EPA; the Departments of Agriculture, Interior, State, Energy, Housing and Urban Development, Justice, Health and Welfare, Commerce, and Transportation, as well as the President's Council on Environmental Quality and the Smithsonian Institution are also mandated by law to deal with environmental problems. Sometimes several agencies have responsibility for enforcing the same law, as in the case of the antitrust laws with the Antitrust Division of the Justice Department and the Federal Trade Commission.

Looking at only one law or one agency to deduce a policy is likely to be misleading. An analysis of management-labor relations that adopts the traditional focus of the National Labor Relations Act misses the full complexity of the contemporary management-labor relationship, and crystallizes the failure of "regulation" to describe the nature of contemporary government interventions in the private sector. The labor market is not simply regulated by the National Labor Relations Board; it is studied by the Wage and Hour Division, protected by the Unemployment Insurance Program, affected directly by the Pension and Welfare Plans Division of the Labor Department, and altered in its composition by a variety of emergency, employment training, and incentive programs.

Regulation not only obscures this breadth of approaches to the private sector; it also minimizes the panoply of tools available to the government. The courts, for example, have been prime movers in fixing manufacturer liability for defective products. Statutes and ordinances, whether or not administered by an agency, are another tool of control; the choice of a site for a corporate headquarters or a new plant will partly depend on whether the local government has zoned the property commercial, residential or industrial. One of the most common functions of government is to grant franchises, licenses, and certificates; everyone and everything from doctors and lawyers to public utilities needs this permission from the government to operate. Taxes and subsidies are another engine for government action, not all of it directed primarily at economic activities; the charitable contributions deduction is allowed in order to stimulate private giving to nonprofit institutions. Government contracts come replete with requirements which the contractor must meet. Even industry self-government, as in the securities field, has often been the product of a government policy, and has usually included government involvement.

Another tool often overlooked is the investigation, whether by Congress, presidential commission or independent agency. The result of such an investigation may not be legislation, but the publicity alone may be enough to change a corporation's course of action. Emergency controls are another government tool; though not regularly used, they may actually be more powerful in contemplation than in application. Finally, government ownership and operation can have a major effect on the private sector. The Tennessee Valley Authority impinges directly on the business of many utilities in its area. The National Passenger Rail Corporation affects tourism, local business, and alternative transportation forms, such as airlines and buses.

A MODEL OF GOVERNMENT CONTROL

Today, government interventions for economic purposes (antitrust and regulation strictly defined) share precedence with interventions for non-economic goals, such as equalization of employment opportunities, elimination of risks in the marketplace and workplace, fair disclosure to investors of corporate information pertinent to their investment decisions, oversight of the corporate governance process, protection of the consumer, and assurances of due process in everything from hiring and firing practices to the obtaining of credit. Given the breadth of these government involvements, the term regulation, even in the loosest sense, no longer applies. Government intervenes for more than economic purposes, and employs a variety of methods that run well beyond the regulatory agency.

Moreover, not all public interventions in the private sector come directly from government. Gradually at first, then with increasing rapidity, we have legitimized interventions by an ever-widening spectrum of stakeholders in private-sector processes. The Securities and Exchange Commission operates directly under the 1933 and 1934 Securities Acts; but in so doing also opens up the entire corporate process to increasing scrutiny by shareholders and others. Private citizens and interest groups concerned with the environment are invited through the National Environmental Policy Act to involve themselves in the siting and relocation of plants. While the Federal Trade Commission and the Antitrust Division of the Justice Department seek out monopolists, competitors are also encouraged to monitor each other's marketing techniques and overall strategy for violations of the Sherman and Clayton Acts. Every finding of the Federal Drug Administration that a particular item must be removed from the market as harmful to the public health brings with it private lawsuits stimulated by the federal claim. In each instance, government is at best a supporting actor for others who have served as the primary forces of public intervention. Yet in each instance the result is an intervention into the private sector encouraged by, and backed by the full sanctions of, the government.

Given this more complex environment, our concept of *government control* or *impact* must include any policy adopted by government which directly or indirectly causes private actions to differ materially from those that might otherwise be pursued. A successful model of government control cannot merely group activities on some administrative basis, but should be organized in terms of *rationales* for government intervention.

Our model establishes the following basic rationales for government intervention to serve as the categories for grouping government activity for analytical purposes:

1. To establish efficient and fair rules for participants in the market system;
2. To define and enforce standards of fairness and ethical behavior in both labor and product markets;
3. To act where private market participants fail to take into account the important external consequences of their actions;
4. To pay directly for public goods;
5. To guarantee availability of certain goods and services;
6. To set standards for common references;
7. To eliminate risks for which no form of insurance is otherwise available;
8. To coordinate domestic and foreign policies; and
9. To encourage citizen activism and ability to intervene.

Each rationale, of course, requires enrichment and elaboration, specification of appropriate sub-categories and of the policies, laws, and agencies intended to implement the rationale. One example will suffice. The "establishment of efficient and fair rules for participants in the market system" subdivides into several categories, including but not necessarily limited to: (i) protecting against collusive or predatory actions to restrict competition, (ii) protecting against "unfair" or "unacceptable" restrictions of competition, (iii) recognizing and protecting property rights, (iv) enforcing contract rights, (v) establishing standards of social impact, and (vi) maintaining adequate information for sellers and buyers. The policies and laws involved include the Sherman Act, the Federal Trade Commission Act, the Federal Reserve Act, the Securities Act of 1933, the Securities Exchange Act of 1934, the Interstate Commerce Act, and the National Gas Policy Act, as well as various state laws. As for agencies, these would include the Federal Trade Commission, the Antitrust Division of the Justice Department, the Federal Reserve Board, the Federal Deposit Insurance Corporation, the Securities and Exchange Commission, state insurance commissions, the Federal Communications Commission, the Interstate Commerce Commission, and so on.

The purpose of listing in this example so many laws and agencies is not to overwhelm the reader, but to demonstrate the approach and show how it brings together seemingly disparate government activities and agencies under a single common denominator. The principal point is that this model of government control is far more comprehensive—and as a portrayal of the reality of government activity, far more accurate—than other descriptions in common use today.

A STRATEGIC PLANNING SYSTEM FOR A POLITICIZED ENVIRONMENT

The critical task is to design a strategic planning system at the enterprise level of strategy formulation with the capability to handle environmental scanning and socio-political forecasting in a politicized environment. Such a strategic planning system must fundamentally address the formulation of political and legal, as well as market, strategies as a basis for company handling of constituency relations and involvement in governmental processes. Political strategy concerns clientele satisfaction and social impact. Legal strategy is more narrowly focused on compliance with specified obligations (statutory, regulatory, and common law).

The literature of strategic planning provides little in the way of definitive guidance for the design and use of specific analytical, forecasting, and planning procedures within a given firm. "No . . . comprehensive, effective theory [of strategic planning] is currently available. . . " (Saunders and Tuggle 1977, p. 23). The reason is that planning procedures depend fundamentally on the particular company) (its internal strengths and weaknesses), industry (markets and technologies), and situation (the threats and opportunities of the particular environment). These circumstances will vary across companies, and still more across industries and countries (Whittaker 1978, ch. 2). It is therefore difficult to be highly specific about procedures, methods, and techniques as distinct from general approach. "No single corporate planning model is commonly accepted in major companies in the United States. Instead, corporate planning varies widely among companies depending on the industry, mix of products, degree of decentralization, organizational structure, and management style of . . . top management officials . . . in general, planning systems are tailored to the unique characteristics of the organization and the top management" (Moskov 1978, p. 37).

In a politicized environment, strategy formulation must be expanded to handle systematically business-government relations, legal problems, clientele satisfaction, and social impact as well as market performance (the focus of corporate-portfolio and business-unit strategy). MacMillan (1978) has argued that an analysis of environmental threats and opportunities must underlie the development of a political strategy which has as its focus: the identification of key actors, analysis of the power and influence of the firm as a negotiating base for dealing with both allies and opponents, and the formulation of contingency strategies in light of opponents' potential counter-responses.

Corporate strategy results from an interaction of external stakeholders and internal interest groups with the corporate governance process, which ultimately focuses on board-management relations (Greanias and Windsor 1982). Internal interest groups are created in part by the functional responsibilities and organizational structure of the firm. Stakeholders are created by fundamental conditions and trends outside the firm in the society, economy, science and technology, culture, environment, natural resources, industrial structure, and so on. These stakeholders may include shareholders, employees, investors, consumers, the media, environmentalists, competitors, suppliers, schools, and others. A stakeholder is anyone who is affected by or perceives an interest in the activities and decisions of a company. A stakeholder becomes a clientele or constituency when that effect or interest is taken into account or perceived as important by the company in its decision making.

Politicization of the corporate environment means that the influence of stakeholders is actively or latently directed through political and legal relationships which ultimately control or regulate markets and corporate governance processes. Relationships within society are channeled through legal instruments: contracts, statutes, licenses, regulations, patents, and so on. We argue that it is difficult to think of a business activity (at the enterprise, corporate-portfolio, business-unit, or functional level) which is not legally regulated. These legal relationships arise out of and are affected by governmental processes, in which stakeholders are involved by fundamental conditions and trends. It is this set of factors that must be modeled and forecasted by a strategic planning system in a politicized environment.[5] With politicization, the external environment of the corporation becomes more complicated and turbulent.

We hypothesize that politicization of the corporate environment implies three basic constraints on strategic planning:

First, longer time horizons for planning will be needed. Since decisions will take longer to make and implement with stakeholder intervention and governmental regulation, and will involve complicated multidimensional assessment, the time frame for strategic planning will have to be adjusted. For example, the Storm King Mountain project of Consolidated Edison was delayed for two decades by environmentalists before finally being killed (Thompson and Strickland 1978). A proposed Sohio pipeline project involved more than 700 permits from a large number of agencies.

As a result, financial planning and research and development for new products and processes in particular must adjust to these longer lead times. The basic corporate cycle may well have to be adjusted to deal with longer time horizons, complexity of issues, and increasing stakeholder involvement.

Second, more contingency analysis will be required due to the greater involvement of multiple stakeholders, often acting through governmental agencies and legal instrumentalities. As a result, there will have to be broader-based company participation in the strategic planning process for acquisition of more information about issues, involvement of internal interest groups, and integration of corporate-portfolio, business-unit and functional plans with enterprise-level planning.

Third, strategy formulation will have to be more oriented toward political activity, legal relationships, handling public opinion, media relations and public agencies, and required earlier disclosure of corporate plans and actions.

ENVIRONMENTAL SCANNING SYSTEMS

We now turn to an examination of some existing strategic planning systems which already incorporate some form of environmental scanning or socio-political forecasting component. The purpose of this examination is to judge the adequacy of these systems, necessarily bearing in mind the very early stage of development of such systems at present. There is information in the literature about systems used at Monsanto, General Electric, Southern California Edison, and Sears.

The central problem in strategic management involves identifying the dominant features of the external environment and determining their potential impact on the corporation as a basis for deciding how and when to respond to trends, events, and issues. Probably the most difficult aspect of this problem is to determine the cross-impacts of external conditions and how combinations of such conditions will interact with the internal state of the enterprise (Brown 1979, p. 9).

Figure 1 shows schematically the logical relationship of the three basic stages in the strategic planning process. Under the impact of politicization, environmental scanning and socio-political forecasting are critical components of enterprise-level strategy formulation. By environmental scanning, we mean a search of the external environment for pertinent events, issues, and trends that may affect the corporation. Socio-political forecasting is the projection of such factors to the appropriate planning horizon in terms of probability of occurrence, impact on the company, and cross-impact of factors. Strategy formulation at the enterprise level

Figure 1. Elements of Strategic Management in a Politicized Environment

Stage	Object	Information	Conceptual Format	Company	Program
I. Environmental Scanning	A. Trends, Issues, Events	Background Information and Data		Monsanto	"Issues Management System"
	B. Demands, Threats, Opportunities	Critical Indicators	Activity Matrix	Southern California Edison	Assumptions for 25-Year Planning Horizon
				Sears	"Strategic Trend Information System"
				General Electric	"Public Issues Management"
II. Socio-Political Forecasting	Probability and Impact	Forecasts	Probability-Impact Matrix	General Electric	"Business Environment Studies Program"
III. Strategy Formulation	Response	Contingencies	Alternative Scenarios	General Electric	"Business Environment Studies Program"

should build on these other two procedures. Strategic management is the direction of the firm's resource allocation process in light of its environment. Logically these three stages of the strategic planning process should follow one another sequentially in the same order: environmental scanning forms the basis for socio-political forecasting, which in turn underlies strategy formulation.

Environmental scanning attempts to identify trends, issues, and events that may potentially affect the enterprise in some fashion. These external conditions may constitute demands on, threats to, or even opportunities for the firm. Scanning is the acquisition of background information and data from a variety of sources that may lead to the development of critical indicators for demands, threats, and opportunities. An activity matrix which shows the relationship of trends to company areas or functions is conceptually one way of doing so. Socio-political forecasting attempts to turn these critical indicators into specific forecasts of probability, impact, and cross-impact. Probability-impact matrices are conceptually a way of doing so. Strategy formulation for corporate response in terms of resource allocation is increasingly apt to be based on alternative scenarios as a form of contingency planning.

One approach to environmental scanning and socio-political forecasting can be characterized as issues management. In a politicized environment, public policy issues are more numerous, complex, turbulent, and subject to rapid change. "An issue is a condition or pressure, either internal or external to an organization, that, if it continues, will have a significant effect on the functioning of the organization or its future interests" (Brown 1979, p. 1). This definition can be compared to Wilson (1980, p. 161, n.*): "A 'strategic issue' can be defined as a major opportunity or threat which could critically affect the long-term future of the business." Molitor (1977; 1980) argues that it is feasible to forecast public policy changes in legislation and regulation. In his view, both issues and trends follow a kind of life cycle which can be predicted. Government intervention in social problems is an evolutionary process. "Public policy change—new legislation and regulation—can be forecasted with great accuracy . . . as long as 10 years ahead of occurrence for almost any issue. . . " (Molitor 1980, p. 139). Forecasting is achieved by identifying and tracking what Molitor calls leading events, authorities and advocates, literature, organizations, and political jurisdictions. Among the latter he includes Sweden, Denmark, West Germany, New York State, Massachusetts, New York City, and Dade County (Miami). About a decade is required for the cycle of issue development.

Monsanto

Environmental scanning at the Monsanto Company is built on an "issues management system" which attempts to collect both information and data from a wide variety of sources about issues which may potentially affect the firm (Stroup 1980). The Monsanto system assumes that the life cycle of an issue can be characterized as an "issue curve" which begins with a few people and publications and then expands to many, resulting in an organized reaction which leads eventually to government action (such as the National Environmental Policy Act) or establishment of a social phenomenon (such as two-professional families). These issue life cycles can be identified well ahead of time by a monitoring procedure. The objective is to identify issues affecting the company and then position its response at an appropriate time in the issue life cycle. The standard used to determine the appropriate time is when flexibility and variety of response are still possible (Stroup 1980, p. 147).

Monsanto's system is operated by two management committees. The monitoring staff provides information and data to an Issue Identification Committee, consisting of line managers who are expected to become vice presidents in a decade. This committee decides which issues are high priority for response by Monsanto. The options for corporate response to such issues are then formulated by a Social Responsibility Committee, consisting of eight vice presidents. This committee functions as a subcommittee of the top-level Corporate Administrative Committee of 18 vice presidents who report to the company's chief executive officer. The Corporate Administrative Committee makes decisions on company policy. Information and data are developed by the monitoring staff from five basic sources: (1) the "Corporate Priorities" national poll of public and government leaders on issues in business-government relations conducted by Yankelovich, Skelly and White; (2) the "Stakeholder Outlook" prepared by the Human Resources Network of Philadelphia; (3) contacts with knowledgeable academics; (4) contacts with company employees; and (5) printed matter (publications scanning).

Sears

Sears, Roebuck and Company operates a complex environmental scanning program entitled the Strategic Trend Information System (Ashley 1980; Barmeier 1980). Contrary to the Monsanto approach, Sears operates on the assumption that the future is essentially unpredictable. Consequently, environmental scanning seeks to monitor specific trends and events which may present future threats and opportunities to corporate strategy. A wide net is cast to secure external information. Monitoring occurs for some 130 external and 190 internal factors. The latter are grouped into eleven major categories.

The external factors are grouped into eight major categories:

1. *demographics* (population, employment, income, spending, housing);
2. *values and life-styles;*

3. *resources* (energy supply and demand, mineral and chemical supply, agriculture, water availability, strategic depletion or shortage, land);
4. *technology* (research and development expenditures, alternate energy resources, plastics, communications, transportation, manufacturing techniques, product development);
5. *public attitudes* (consumer confidence, attitudes toward specific trends, public interest groups, consumerism);
6. *government* (operations, regulations, legislation, employment, economic controls, environment, consumer credit, physical distribution, privacy, products, communication with customers, service, health care, postal service, taxes);
7. *international* (world population, resources, trade, developing nations, technology transfer, economic indicators);
8. *economics* (a variety of measures of macroeconomic activity).[6]

The general procedure for developing areas to be reviewed is to determine the appropriate areas internally with subsequent external review by experts. About 60 periodic publications and research reports are monitored; research associations and specialists are consulted..

This environmental scanning system is one part of the long-range planning procedures at Sears which include five other components. Scanning seeks to monitor and forecast the internal state and external environment for a period out to five or ten years. The other components of long-range planning are sightsetting (specific quantitative goals for five years), strategy (how to achieve those goals), structure (organization, reporting responsibilities, and accountabilities to implement the selected strategy), scorekeeping (measures of success as a basis for employee rewards), and synchronization (administrative coordination of company segments). The long-range planning procedures are focused on setting and meeting quantitative sales and earnings goals. Therefore attention is directed to what businesses the company should be in, the mix of products to be sold, markets, customers, geographic areas, selling methods, and basic policies toward stakeholders (customers, employees, shareholders, governments, and financial community).

The monitoring system tries to identify through analysis of trends the main supports for the business in its environment and the threats affecting each support, including probability of occurrence, impact, and cross-impacts. Sears is interested in the vulnerabilities of its main supports. The strategic plan sees as main supports at present the economy, population characteristics, single-family housing, auto transportation, postal service, credit, manufacturing sources, and labor. The company must define strategic issues and a hierarchy of priorities for dealing with them.

The environmental scanning system leads to a trend summary as a guide to determining areas for strategy formulation. Barmeier reports that the public issues agenda at Sears is divided into four priorities. The first three priorities categorize issues regarded as having direct impact on the company; the fourth priority is those issues seen as having indirect impact on Sears. First priority issues included equal employment opportunity, social security, minimum wage, employee health care, credit, Federal Trade Commission requirements, product liability, and warranty requirements.[7] By contrast, equal pay was accorded second priority, flame retardency third priority, and water conservation fourth priority.

Environmental scanning was started at Sears in 1973 when a Central Planning Office reporting to the chairman of the board was first established. An environmental forecasting unit was included. In 1974, a Directors' Committee on Public Issues of four outside directors and a senior vice president was formed. Subsequently the environmental forecasting unit was transferred from Corporate Planning to the newly formed (1979) Public Affairs Department under a senior vice president, public affairs, to whom a vice president of public relations and a vice president of governmental affairs report. To provide linkage to other departments, there is a Public Affairs Committee composed of senior executives from 22 corporate headquarters departments.

Southern California Edison

Southern California Edison Company, a major public utility serving the area between Los Angeles and San Diego, does not develop an overall corporate plan (although initially tried, such strategic planning was dropped). Since 1971, the objective of the Management Committee (renamed in 1973 from the Corporate Planning Committee established in 1967) and the Corporate Planning Staff (formed 1968) has been the coordination of corporate planning, budgeting, and operations. "Southern California Edison has no formally stated corporate objectives. Top management sees no clear purpose in making a long list of corporate goals that would have little meaning. They prefer to have more specific goals stated in the major organizational units. Objectives are developed within the program, resource, and organization plans so that SCE has multiple objectives which are very specific, and often quantitative. What the company does not have is one major list of general goals called the corporate objectives" (Whittaker 1978, p. 101). A ten-year master plan for system expansion is developed annually with physical, operational, and financial components. This master plan incorporates forecasts, assumptions, problems, policies, and objectives. These components are developed, however, in a variety of resource, program, and organization plans with a five-year planning horizon. Resource plans cover finances, fuel, power generation, materials, land, and electric facilities. Program plans cover electronic data processing, public relations, research and development, materials management, buildings and structures. Organization plans are for finances, personnel and administration, operations and maintenance, corporate systems and planning, engineering and construction, customer service, marketing and public relations.

Assumptions about the external environment up to 25 years are developed as the planning horizon. These assumptions cover economic, political, technological, social, and ecological trends. Southern California Edison's Corporate Planning Staff looks in detail at social attitudes and values, political trends, human resources, economic and business conditions, technological change, electric system growth, and fuel resources. For example, Southern Edison anticipates increased criticism and distrust of business, greater public demands for regulation of rates, non-economic impacts and pollution, public opposition to nuclear hazards and advertising. At the same time, political trends will be toward limiting facility expansion to socially and environmentally acceptable areas, increased public involvement, and more stringent controls on land use. Constraints imply higher fuel costs, supply dislocations, and lags in facility expansion.

General Electric

General Electric also approaches environmental scanning as "public issues management" (Wilson 1974a; 1974b; 1980). In 1971, environmental scanning of this type was made a major component of a new strategic planning system. Then in 1972, the company established five new board committees chaired by outside directors, one of which deals with public issues. The objective of monitoring, forecasting, and tracking trends is to identify and prioritize key issues potentially affecting the company's competitive position. A 1972 priority analysis for the board-level Public Issues Committee identified six areas of challenge for General Electric: (1) constraints on corporate growth; (2) corporate governance issues; (3) work force management; (4) external constraints on employee relations; (5) problems and opportunities in business-government partnership; and (6) the politicization of corporate decision-making resulting from increasing government and stakeholder involvement in a variety of issues. General Electric handles issue analysis on an ad hoc basis with staff drawn from its economics, employee relations, tax accounting, and public relations sections. The latter includes a Public Issues Research unit which initially identifies a list of priority issues for detailed analysis, which is then assigned to a functional section in order to obtain a more balanced corporate view of the issue area.

Socio-political forecasting at General Electric developed out of the Business Environment Studies Program established in 1967 for the analysis of long-term social and political trends. It was this experience which led to the public issues approach adopted in the early 1970s. That program attempted to interpret the history of the decade 1960–1970 and forecast the decade 1970–1980 in a variety of areas as a means of developing a strategic planning system based on socio-political forecasting. This analysis identified some 75 major trends and events affecting the economic, technological, and socio-political environments of General Electric. The social forecast covered areas such as changing values, life-styles, and demographics; the political forecast pressure groups, legislation, and business-government relations; the technological forecast the state of the art, research and development; the economic forecast markets, energy, materials, GNP, consumer spending, and business investment. Major social changes anticipated for the decade 1970–1980 included increasing affluence, economic stabilization, education, pluralism and individualism, urban and minority problems, and institutional interdependence, together with changing attitudes toward work and leisure, and movement toward a "post-industrial society." A cross-impact analysis of the 75 trends and events on these eight social changes was used as the basis (through a probability-impact assessment) for the development of four alternative scenarios of social evolution. These scenarios were intended to serve as contingent socio-political forecasts for strategic planning by General Electric.

Summary

We may summarize this section by reference to Figure 1. The Monsanto "Issues Management System" is a form of environmental scanning focused on the acquisition of background information and data about trends, issues, and events. As a result it casts a wide net in an effort to identify anything of consequence that might affect the company. The Sears "Strategic Trend Information System" is somewhat more sophisticated in the sense that it moves beyond acquisition of background information and data to the identification of specific demands, threats, and opportunities. External factors are grouped into major categories expected to have significant impact on the firm. The environmental scanning system is one component of a full-scale long-range planning cycle. Probability of occurrence, impact, and cross-impacts are estimated as a basis for strategic decision-making. Southern California Edison lies roughly between Monsanto and Sears in sophistication. It does not develop an overall corporate plan. But it does conduct environmental scanning out to a 25-year planning horizon, looking at economic, political, technological, social, and ecological trends expected to affect the company significantly. These trends are treated as planning assumptions. Demands, threats, and opportunities are identified. The General Electric approach moves beyond environmental scanning to detailed socio-political forecasting. Its "Public Issues Management" program resembles the environmental scanning activities of the other companies. Its "Business Environment Studies Program" looks at probability, impact, and cross-impact of 75 trends and events in relationship to eight major social changes anticipated by the firm. This analysis is used as the basis for developing four alternative scenarios of social evolution which are intended to serve as contingent socio-political forecasts for strategic planning by General Electric.

CONCLUSION

This paper has discussed why and how corporations should design and evaluate strategic planning systems that are suitable for use at the enterprise level of strategy formulation in a politicized environment. We argue that the external environment of the corporation has been substantially restructured by the increasing politicization of market relationships. Corporate social performance and policy have become an important issue because of this politicization, in which stakeholder interests, business-government relations, and the social impact of corporate activities have become more important relative to economic performance. The type and number of stakeholders affected by and interested in corporate decisions have been substantially altered. Politicization is the increased intervention of such stakeholders in corporate strategic management through governmental processes and legal relationships.

This process of politicization imposes additional burdens on strategy formulation and strategic planning systems. The enterprise level of strategy formulation assumes greater importance relative to the corporate-portfolio, business-unit, and functional levels. Enterprise-level strategy must combine market performance, clientele satisfaction, and social impact. Strategic planning systems must incorporate environmental scanning and socio-political forecasting; and must serve as a basis for political and legal, as well as market, strategy formulation. Wilson (1974b) argues that an essential prerequisite for the formulation and implementation of an operational corporate social policy is a fundamental reform of the strategic planning process so as to integrate social responsibility and economic performance. Our analysis of the environmental scanning or socio-political forecasting systems in use at Monsanto, General Electric, Southern California Edison, and Sears indicates that this process of change is underway.

NOTES

1. This approach developed out of the "strategic business unit" (SBU) concept originally formulated at General Electric in the 1970s (Cox 1975; Cox 1977; Hall 1978).

2. A detailed explication of this strategic profile approach is available in Windsor and Tuggle (1980a; 1980b).

3. Porter (1979; 1980) identifies five basic competitive forces which must be considered in the design of business-level strategy: (1) the type and degree of rivalry among existing firms (which depend on their number and relative size, their diversity, industry growth and profitability, exit barriers, and other conditions); (2) the threat of new entrants (which depends on entry barriers and the likely reaction from existing firms); (3) the bargaining power of suppliers; (4) the bargaining power of buyers; and (5) the threat of substitute commodities. Generally speaking the company's strategy will seek to acquire a position of cost leadership, product differentiation, or focus on some particular market segment.

4. Consider for example the problem of planning for product recall, which must inherently be on a contingency basis. It has been reported that, in 1974, one quarter of the consumer goods companies listed in the Fortune 500 had product recalls, and that some 25 million units are recalled annually (Kerin and Harvey 1975, p. 5). The Consumer Product Safety Commission has ordered the recall of over 245 products as hazardous (Chandran and Linneman 1978, p. 332). Companies are by law subject to product liability, which is the legal obligation of the manufacturer or vendor to indemnify users for bodily injury or property damage resulting from defective production or misrepresentation, including negligence. Politicization of the corporate environment has involved as one aspect greater government, consumer, and public-interest group litigations over product liability (McGuire 1976; Rados 1969). Chandran and Linneman conclude that these conditions present corporations with the need for designing and implementing a comprehensive program for product liability prevention planning (see also Fisk and Chandran 1975; McGuire 1974; 1975). The components of such a program would include: (1) a product safety committee of company executives under a product safety coordinator; (2) periodic safety audits and tests, including an early warning system for product performance; and (3) contingency planning for product recall. Rather than ignoring or evading legal responsibility for product liability, corporations should adopt comprehensive plans for minimizing and handling product recall.

5. For other views of the political process, see Preston and Post (1975) and Wilson (1974a; 1974b; 1980). Wilson views strategic management as encompassing a "four-sided" framework of economic, technological, political, and social environments. Wilson's political environment is divisible into what we distinguish as governmental processes and legal relationships.

6. An analysis of each of the subcategories can be more detailed. The employment subcategory of demographics covers growth rate, size and characteristics (full time versus part time, sex, working wives, occupation), regional distribution, labor union membership, hours, and benefits. A detailed exposition of the external factors is available in Brown (1979, p. 11). A somewhat similar system is operated by New York Telephone Company. Their major categories are the demographic environment, the work environment, the governmental environment, the economic environment, and the societal environment. See Brown (1979, p. 13), for a full listing. Each company will see its environment differently. The societal environment perceived by New York Telephone includes growth limits, ideology, power shifts, the litigious society, attitudes toward business, social responsibility, consumerism, privacy, the environmental movement, land use, exclusionary zoning, lifestyles, the leisure ethic, living arrangements, housing, and time.

7. A complete listing is available in Barmeier (1980, p. 158).

REFERENCES

Aguilar, Francis J., *Scanning the Business Environment.* New York: Macmillan, 1967.

Ansoff, H. Igor, and Richard C. Brandenburg, "A Program of Research in Business Planning." *Management Science* 13 B(February 1967):B-219/B-239.

Aplin, John C., and W. Harvey Hegarty, "Political Influence: Strategies Employed by Organizations to Impact Legislation in Business and Economic Matters." *Academy of Management Journal* 23(September 1980):438–450.

Ashley, William C., "Strategic Planning: Impact of Public Policy and Environment." In Rogene A. Buchholz (ed.), *Public Policy and the Business Firm,* St. Louis, Mo.: Center for the Study of American Business, Washington University, 1980, pp. 123–130.

Barmeier, Robert E., "The Role of Environmental Forecasting and Public Issues Analysis in Corporate Planning." In Lee E. Preston (ed.), *Business Environment/Public Policy: 1979 Conference Papers,* St. Louis, Mo.: American Assembly of Collegiate Schools of Business, 1980, pp. 152–158.

Berg, Norman A., "Strategic Planning in Conglomerate Companies." *Harvard Business Review* 43(May–June 1965):79–92.

Blank, Stephen et al., *Assessing the Political Environment: An Emerging Function in International Companies.* New York: The Conference Board, Report No. 794, 1980.

Bok, Derek C., "The President's Report, 1977–1978." Cambridge, Mass.: Harvard University, 1979.

Bourgeois, L. J., "Strategy and Environment: A Conceptual Integration." *Academy of Management Review* 5(January 1980):25–39.

Brown, James K., *This Business of Issues: Coping with the Company's Environments.* New York: The Conference Board, Report No. 758, 1979.

Chandler, Alfred D., Jr., *Strategy and Structure: Chapters in the History of the Industrial Enterprise.* Cambridge, Mass.: M.I.T. Press, 1962.

Chandran, Rajan, and Robert Linneman, "Planning to Minimize Product Liability." *Sloan Management Review* 20(Fall 1978):33–46.

Child, John, "Commentary." In Dan E. Schendel and Charles W. Hofer (eds.), *Strategic Management: A New View of Business Policy and Planning,* Boston: Little, Brown, 1979, pp. 172–179.

Cox, William E., Jr., "Product Portfolio Strategy: A Review of the Boston Consulting Group Approach to Marketing Strategy." In R. Curhan (ed.), *Marketing's Contribution to the Firm and to Society,* Chicago: American Marketing Association, 1975, pp. 465–470.

———, "Product Portfolio Strategy, Market Structure, and Performance." In Hans B. Thorelli (ed.), *Strategy + Structure = Performance: The Strategic Planning Imperative,* Bloomington: Indiana University Press, 1977, pp. 83–102.

Curtiss, Ellen T., "Introduction: The Key Issues Confronting Business." In Ellen T. Curtiss and Philip A. Untersee (eds.), *Corporate Responsibilities and Opportunities to 1990,* Lexington, Mass.: Lexington Books, 1979, pp. 1–8.

Fahey, Liam, and William R. King, "Environmental Scanning for Corporate Planning." *Business Horizons* 20(August 1977):61–71.

Fisk, G., and Rajan Chandran, "How to Trace and Recall Products." *Harvard Business Review* 53(November-December 1975):90–96.

Gabriel, Peter, "Managing Corporate Strategy to Cope With Change." *Conference Board Record* 12(March 1975):57–60.

Gordon, Lawrence A., and Danny Miller, "A Contingency Framework for the Design of Accounting Information Systems." *Accounting, Organizations and Society* 1(June 1976):59–69.

Greanias, George, "Improving Our Model of Government Control: A First Cut." Houston,

Texas: Jesse H. Jones Graduate School of Administration, Rice University (November): Working Paper No. 3, 1980.

Greanias, George, and Duane Windsor, "Beyond Entrepreneurship and Competition: Business Strategies for the New Corporate Environment." *Current Business Perspectives* 1(April 1981):3–10.

Hall, William K., "SBUs: Hot, New Topic in the Management of Diversification." *Business Horizons* 21(Feburary 1978):17–25.

Hanley, John W., "Monsanto's 'Early Warning' System." *Harvard Business Review* 59 (November-December 1981):107–122.

Keim, Gerald D., "Foundations of a Political Strategy for Business." *California Management Review* 23(Spring 1981):41–48.

Kerin, Roger A., and Michael Harvey, "Contingency Planning for Product Recall." *MSU Business Topics* 23(Summer 1975):5–12.

Lindsay, William M., and Leslie W. Rue, "Impact of the Organization Environment on the Long-Range Planning Process: A Contingency View." *Academy of Management Journal* 23(September 1980):385–404.

MacMillan, Ian C., *Strategy Formulation: Political Concepts*. St. Paul, Minn.: West, 1978.

McGuire, E. P. (ed.), *Managing Product Recalls*. New York: The Conference Board, 1974.

McGuire, E. P., "Product Recall and the Facts of Business Life." *Conference Board Record* 12(February 1975):13–15.

———, "What Is Ahead in Product Safety." *Conference Board Record* 13(August 1976):33–34.

Molitor, Graham T. T., "How to Anticipate Public-Policy Changes." *S.A.M. Advanced Management Journal* 42(Summer 1977):4–13.

———, "Environmental Forecasting: Public Policy Forecasting." In Lee E. Preston (ed.), *Business Environment/Public Policy: 1979 Conference Papers*, St. Louis, Mo.: American Assembly of Collegiate Schools of Business, 1980, pp. 139–151.

Moskow, Michael H., *Strategic Planning in Business and Government*. New York: Committee for Economic Development, 1978.

O'Toole, James, "What's Ahead for the Business-Government Relationship." *Harvard Business Review* 57(March-April 1979):94–105.

Porter, Michael E., "Note on the Structural Analysis of Industries" (1975, revised 1979), Boston-Harvard Business School, ICCH 9-376-054.

———, *Competitive Strategy: Techniques for Analyzing Industries and Competitors*. New York: Free Press, 1980.

Post, James E., "The Challenge of Managing Under Social Uncertainty." *Business Horizons* 20(August 1977):51–60.

———, "The Corporation in the Public Policy Process: A View Toward the 1980's." *Sloan Management Review* 21(Fall 1979):45–52.

Preston, Lee E., "Corporation and Society: The Search for a Paradigm." *Journal of Economic Literature* 13(June 1975):434–453.

———, "Strategy-Structure-Performance: A Framework for Organization/Environment Analysis." In Hans B. Thorelli (ed.), *Strategy + Structure = Performance: The Strategic Planning Imperative*, Bloomington: Indiana University Press, 1977, pp. 30–49.

Preston, Lee E., and James E. Post, "The Public Policy Process." Ch. 5 in *Private Management and Public Policy: The Principle of Public Responsibility*. Englewood Cliffs, NJ: Prentice-Hall, 1975, pp. 55–74.

Rumelt, Richard P., *Strategy, Structure and Economic Performance*. Boston, Mass.: Graduate School of Business Administration, Harvard University, 1974.

Salamon, Lester M., and John J. Siegfried, "Economic Power and Political Influence: The

Impact of Industry Structure on Public Policy." *American Political Science Review* 71(September 1977):1026–1053.

Saunders, Charles B., and Francis D. Tuggle, "Why Planners Don't." *Long Range Planning* 10(June 1977):pp. 19–24.

Schendel, Dan E., and G. Richard Patton, "A Simultaneous Equation Model of Corporate Strategy." *Management Science* 24(November 1978):1611–1621.

Schendel, Dan E., and Charles W. Hofer (eds.), *Strategic Management: A New View of Business Policy and Planning.* Boston, Mass.: Little, Brown, 1979.

Segev, Eli, "How to Use Environmental Analysis in Strategy Making." *Management Review* 66(March 1977):4–13.

Smith, Clifford N., "Predicting the Political Environment of International Business." *Long Range Planning* 4(September 1971):7–14.

Stevenson, Howard H., "Defining Corporate Strengths and Weaknesses." *Sloan Management Review* 17(Spring 1976):51–68.

Stroup, Margaret, "Issues Management." In Rogene A. Buchholz (ed.), *Public Policy and the Business Firm,* St. Louis, Mo.: Center for the Study of American Business, Washington University, 1980, pp. 143–152.

Thomas, Philip S., "Environmental Analysis for Corporate Planning." *Business Horizons* 17(October 1974):27–38.

Tipgos, Manual A., "Integrating Social Goals into Corporate Strategic Planning." *Managerial Planning* 25(March/April 1977):26–30.

Thorelli, Hans B., "Organizational Theory: An Ecological View." In Hans B. Thorelli (ed.), *Strategy + Structure = Performance: The Strategic Planning Imperative,* Bloomington: Indiana University Press, 1977, pp. 277–301.

Thompson, Arthur A., Jr., and A. J. Strickland (eds.), "Consolidated Edison Company." *Strategy and Policy: Concepts and Cases,* Dallas, Texas: Business Publications, 1978, pp. 857–884.

Udell, Jon G., Gene R. Laczniak, and Robert F. Lusch, "The Business Environment of 1985." *Business Horizons* 19(June 1976):45–54.

Watson, D. J., "The New Political Role of Business." In Lee E. Preston (ed.), *Business Environment/Public Policy: 1979 Conference Papers,* St. Louis, Mo.: American Assembly of Collegiate Schools of Business, 1980, pp. 60–68.

Whittaker, James B., *Strategic Planning in a Rapidly Changing Environment.* Lexington, Mass.: Lexington Books, 1978.

Williams, Richard, "Strategic Implications of Environmental Regulations." In Ellen T. Curtiss and Philip A. Untersee (eds.), *Corporate Responsibilities and Opportunities to 1990,* Lexington, Mass.: Lexington Books, 1979, pp. 275–280.

Wilson, Ian H., "Socio-Political Forecasting: A New Dimension to Strategic Planning." *Michigan Business Review* 26(July 1974):pp. 15–25.

———, "Reforming the Strategic Planning Process: Integration of Social and Business Needs." *Long Range Planning* 7(October 1974):2–6.

———, "Environmental Scanning and Strategic Planning." In Lee E. Preston (ed.), *Business Environment/Public Policy: 1979 Conference Papers,* St. Louis, Mo.: American Assembly of Collegiate Schools of Business, 1980, pp. 159–163.

Windsor, Duane, and George Greanias, "Long-Range Planning in a Politicized Environment." *Long Range Planning,* forthcoming.

Windsor, Duane, and Francis D. Tuggle, "Organizational Needs as a Framework for Policy Research." In *Proceedings of the Southern Management Association* (November 1980):22–24.

———, "Toward a Theory of Organizational Needs." In *Proceedings of the American Institute of Decision Sciences* (November 1980):436–438.

STRUCTURE, CULTURE AND PERFORMANCE IN PUBLIC AFFAIRS:

A STUDY OF THE FOREST PRODUCTS INDUSTRY

Jeffrey A. Sonnenfeld

The response of business firms to the great increase in the number and importance of public affairs pressures over the past two decades has generated substantial organizational change. New job titles have proliferated, and new responsibilities have been added to existing positions. However, there has been little attention paid to the way in which these changes in organizational structure actually affect the operation and behavior of organizations. Most of the business and society literature reflects an external perspective, with little attention to internal variables; and much of it is anecdotal or deals with only a single case. By contrast,

Research in Corporate Social Performance and Policy, Vol. 4, pages 105–127
Copyright © 1982 by JAI Press Inc.
All rights of reproduction in any form reserved.
ISBN: 0-89232-259-4

the literature on organization-environment adaptation has focused a great deal more on internal firm structure and has employed more systematic research methods and data. However, this literature has virtually ignored the important changes that have taken place with respect to public affairs management in recent years. The present research is intended to fill this gap by focusing specifically on the relationship between a company's internal structure and its responsiveness to public affairs issues. Responsiveness is appraised both by direct evidence and by reference to the perceptions of external publics.

The conceptual model guiding this research suggests that the public affairs responsiveness of large corporations can be understood by analogy to the structure and functioning of the human sensory mechanism. In this mechanism, information acquired through diverse receptors (for example, eyes, ears, and on.) is collected, transmitted inward, and coordinated. This information flow affects both the richness of internal perceptions of the outside environment and the responsiveness of behavior to it. The application of this model to the corporation suggested that specialized departments (for example, corporate counsel, public relations, and government affairs) and senior management can use their respective competences to collect perceptions of the business environment. These perceptions, however, are derived from biased vantage points, and must be balanced internally through transmission and coordination. The companies with more *receptive* information-gathering units, better *transmission,* and better *coordination* were hypothesized to be more responsive to public affairs issues than those which were weaker in these three dimensions.

This hypothesis was explained by a comparative study of several companies that face the same complex environment. A group of companies in the forest products industry, where firms have faced a long history of wide-ranging public affairs concerns, were chosen for detailed investigation. The industry's public affairs experience was initially examined through a wide-ranging review of secondary materials, where the need for company-specific information was clearly revealed. Six of the ten largest companies in the industry were then studied through extensive interviews and questionnaire surveys of senior executives and public affairs specialists in each company. In addition, company responsiveness was evaluated by a questionnaire survey of 75 officials of outside stakeholder groups that closely interact with this industry.

LITERATURE AND MODEL

Discussions about the characteristics of the business environment have identified dimensions such as scarcity, turbulence, complexity, and perceived uncertainty (Tung, 1979; Miles and Snow, 1978; Pfeffer and Salancik, 1978; Downey, Hellriegel, and Slocum, 1975; Duncan, 1972; Lawrence and Lorsch, 1967; Thompson, 1967; Emery and Trist, 1965). An important feature shared by most of this research on organization-environment relations is the failure to consider aspects of the business environment other than market and technological factors. With the notable exception of inspirational, but brief, treatments of the "institutional level struggle for organizational legitimacy" (Parsons, 1960; Thompson, 1967) prominent organization theorists have not given significant attention to the public affairs environment. Business and society analysts, however, have pointed out that public affairs has become at least as complex and turbulent an area of concern as the traditionally recognized components of the business environment (Manne and Wallich, 1972; Steiner, 1974; Hargreaves and Dauman, 1975; Preston and Post, 1975; Post, 1978; Sethi, 1977, Carroll, 1978). These writers have also demonstrated the compelling nature and strategic importance of problems at the corporate-public interface.

Other research has implied that a firm's internal characteristics may have much to do with its external social performance. In particular, questions about the relevance of the inner chemistry of the firm have been raised in literature on changing public opinions (Brenner, 1979; O'Toole, 1979; Hacker, 1978; Lodge, 1976), government regulation (Kasper, 1978; Leone, 1977; Chandler, 1979; Fenn, 1979), community relations (Schmenner, 1979), labor relations and human resources (Mills, 1979; Perry and Angle, 1979; Burak and Gutteridge, 1979; Sonnenfeld, 1978; Glueck, 1974; Stagner and Rosen, 1965) or investor relations (Chatlus, 1974). In considering these various areas in the aggregate, it is evident that large corporations may exacerbate problems on many fronts simultaneously because their internal structures are poorly designed to receive and process external signals. In particular, reliance on trade associations for information and action is insufficient when geographic and competitive differences require different firm-level responses. Yet little research has been done to see how internal structures can be altered to facilitate greater responsiveness to public concerns.

A related limitation of much of the existing literature on organization-environment relations is the rarity of research and conceptual work which addresses the process by which the organization specifically reads and interprets its environment (Starbuck, 1976). Analysts belonging to the "evolutionary" school of adaptation theory (e.g., Aldrich, 1979; Hannan and Freeman, 1977; Weick, 1969; Stinchcombe, 1965) and the "strategic choice" school (e.g., Child, 1972; Pfeffer and Salancik, 1978) take different stances on environmental determinism, but share a disinterest in analysing the way a company comes to learn about its environment, which it either reacts to or attempts to alter. Distorted perceptions due to executive role bias as illustrated in the laboratory (Dearborn and Simon, 1958) or in the field (Sonnenfeld, 1981b) are not considered by these researchers.

Researchers from the "business policy" and "contingency school" traditions, however, give far more attention to internal firm chemistry. In the business policy area, field investigation seems to have moved from a posture which glorified the role of the chief executive as the primary institutional actor (e.g., Selznick, 1957; Andrews, 1971; Ackerman and Bauer, 1976) to one which describes the broader delegation of functions throughout the organization (Aguilar, 1967; Votaw and Sethi, 1973; McGrath, 1976, 1979; Newgren, 1977; Holmes, 1978; Fleming, 1979). However, this literature, although featuring the growth of new structural configurations (for example, new departments, task forces, steering committees, specialized futurists and regulatory experts, etc.), does not provide an organization-wide systemic map of the appropriate degree of specialization and coordination involved in these new structural innovations. In addition, the description of these new organizational forms is rarely linked with any measure of their effectiveness.

On the other hand, contingency school theorists (for example, Burns and Stalker, 1971; Thompson, 1967; Lawrence and Lorsch, 1967; and Duncan, 1973) encouraged the study of differentiated boundary spanning units and inter-unit coordinating structures which reflected the uncertainty of the business environment and the interdependence of the units. More recent writers have added an emphasis on the need to consider the acquisition and maintenance of power by these boundary spanning units and integrating structures (Miles, 1980; Jemison, 1979; Speckman, 1978; Pettigrew, 1975; Patchen, 1974). Thus we might add "influence" to the important conceptual terms "differentiation" and "integration" commonly used in structural analysis.

While contingency theorists have not directly considered the specific demands of the public affairs environment, their concepts can provide a helpful framework for designing structures to better manage public affairs issues. Since the public affairs environment is complex and volatile, differentiated boundary spanning units are required to keep the organization adaptive in advance of crisis. The difficulty of establishing organizational influence for these differentiated boundary spanning units presents an important responsibility for top management. In addition, integrating mechanisms are needed to combat the tendency for isolated specialists to transmit conflicting, confusing, and irrelevant information.

As with the human sensory mechanism, correct perception requires the integration of various sensory receptors carrying different messages about the environment. Accordingly, any organization whose environmental perception is overly influenced by its chief executive, government lobbyist, lawyers, public relations officials, operating executives, human resource experts, or engineers, and so on, will have a less accurate vision of the outside than that which would come from more balanced participation among these internal actors. Like human sensory receptions, these actors have information-gathering biases (for example, different time orientations, professional languages, networks, and so on). Companies can strengthen the *receptivity* of these units, enhance the *transmission* of their receptions, and *coordinate* or *integrate* their fragmentary views into a coherent environmental profile. It was theorized that such changes would affect both a company's overall perceptions of its environment and its subsequent performance or responsiveness.

RESEARCH METHODS

This research explored the usefulness of this model by studying the multiple public affairs pressures faced by a single industry, forest products. This industry provides examples of many of the types of public affairs exposure that American industry in general is beginning to face. Forest products is a nation-wide industry; it is fairly unconcentrated and not subject to any special revolutions in its technological or market environment. It is not the principal client or target of any specialized government regulatory agency.

A company in the forest products industry strongly affects the lives and well-being of those who live in the small towns around its mills. Critical mill openings and mill closings have become very troublesome events. Logging and sawing as well as lumber and paper production processes are very hazardous. Labor relations are notoriously poor, as evidenced by a seven-month strike in West Coast paper mills in 1977. Serious environmental controversies surround the intense struggles over increased cutting on public forest lands, air and water pollution from mills, aerial spray of dangerous herbicides and pesticides, and solid waste issues. Many of these environmental concerns as well as land taxation issues and labor issues have both local and natonal aspects. Companies differ sharply among themselves on each of these issues, and also about international trade problems. Dramatic antitrust prosecutions for price fixing in folding cartons, fine papers, corrugated containers, and plywood have recently cost the industry several hundred millions of dollars in penalties, plus executive jail sentences, morale loss, and recruitment problems. Finally, with an undervalued asset base (the forest), these companies are frequent takeover targets; thus, shareholder relations have become critical.

Each of the six companies included in the study has a national base of commercial activity. Three have headquarters in the West, two in the Midwest, and two in the East. Each employs more than 30,000 workers and each has sales from multiple product lines exceeding $3 billion per year.

After an extensive review of the major social issues facing the industry, the author interviewed the chief executive of each compnay, the top vice presidents of line operations and public affairs units, and their staffs, roughly 15–20 people per company. The interviews probed the allocation of responsibility for public affairs management and for the perception of public affairs issues. Then a questionnaire was designed for uniform measurement across companies. This questionnaire was returned by 141 of the 180 executives who received it (75 per cent). Finally, interviews with outside industry experts led to the creation of a 75-person panel comprised of journalists, environmentalsts, congressional staff members, regulators, investment community spokesmen and trade association officials. Their function was to provide an external appraisal of the responsiveness of the participating companies.

The four specific study objectives were as follows:

1. An improved understanding of how managers can design their organizations to become and remain responsive to public affairs issues.
2. An expansion of theories of organization adaptation to include the public affairs environments.
3. A demonstration of structural bias in the perception of an organization's environment.
4. A comparison of internal measures of company structure in the external performance ratings.

THE INFLUENCE OF PUBLIC AFFAIRS IN THE INDUSTRY

The first premise of this research is that the institutional role of a business in society is important to a firm's success. Public affairs issues are neither peripheral to the corporation, nor are they merely isolated questions of conscience. These issues fundamentally affect all the traditional business functions such as operations, marketing, and finance. Forest products are directly involved in the operations of virtually every U.S. industry, from construction and shipping to publishing and health care. This is evident when we consider the complex network of wood-based sub-industries, producing such products as wood fuel, timber, lumber, flooring, furniture, tableware, plywood, chipboard, paperboard, container-board, folding cartons, corrugated containers, bags, packaging paper, printing paper, writing paper, newsprint, tissue paper, duplicating paper, computer paper, bandages, and dinnerware (napkins, cups, and plates).

During the 1970s forest products industries involved with intermediate and consumer products, its market situation is dynamic by virtue of three factors: (1) the close relationship of lumber and paper demand to the business cycles; (2) the evolution of new technologies of forest management; and (3) the discovery of new paper products and paper substitutes.

The non-market environment of the forest products industry is unique. Forest products producers face a particularly crowded and active collection of stakeholders in the world outside the marketplace. The growth of the industry has not only led to greater contributions to society, but has also meant greater consumption of society's resources. Accordingly, each firm has had to become responsive not only to market and technological events, but also to societal objectives. These companies simultaneously face powerful pressures from community, labor, legislators, litigators, and shareholders. A recent trade journal survey of forest products executives showed that such non-market pressures produce much greater worry than do marketplace issues.

The technological market, and instituttional aspects of the business environment have each had a pronounced influence on the development and contribution of forest products companies. This industry, however, does not face the technological turbulence of many other industries such as communications, electronics, or transportation, nor does it have to deal with the marketplace uncertainty of agriculture, retailing, or banking. For forest products companies, much of the real drama arises from public affairs issues that these companies, as major social institutions, must manage.

A glance at the industry's technological characteristics helps explain its size, location, and company structure. The readily transferable skills of timber-cutting and papermaking, along with plentiful raw materials (trees and water), encouraged geographic spread. Technological advancements joined together the two great sections of this industry, wood products and paper products. The link between timber and paper eventually led to vertical integration in large companies. Technological advances in one sub-industry dramatically affect events in another. The shift in timber supply from the Northeast, to the Northcentral, to the Northwest, and now to the South greatly affected the economics and location of paper mills. New pulping technologies and use of wood residuals in papermaking have changed the use of various tree species. Improved genetic strains of trees and improved forest management practices have further affected the planning and location of these sub-industries.

In the marketplace, competition across companies has been quite intense. There are several thousand companies on the lumber and timber side of the business and several hundred on the paper and packaging side. Most of the top twenty firms have fully integrated across the industry, and they are in intense competition with one another. The production of certain items, particularly in packaging, has shown a tendency towards overcapacity. Instead of being overtaken by substitute materials, the industry has succeeded in developing paper products which use new synthetic materials, and has improved its own position in the process. One of the many challenges in the future will be the structure of demand for fine paper after the advent of the long-heralded "paperless office."

In neither of these two environments were the major events sudden and surprising. The fundamental technologies of Leif Erickson's loggers and Paul Bunyan, and of the ancient Chinese and Arab papermakers, have been dramatically improved, but the changes have been gradual and the process stages have been remarkably stable. New products have appeared, and substitute construction and packaging products have become widely used. Through acquisition-based growth and substantial transportation improvements, the industry structure is becoming more national and international. Yet, all these changes have been gradual and the GNP remains a powerful predictor of demand.

With respect to public affairs, however, the environment of the industry is characterized by rapid change and uncertainty. In each of the fundamental areas of the forest products business, companies must reckon with a complex and volatile scenario. Corporatre actions involving raw materials (timber supply), production (primary and secondary conversion), financial affairs, and marketing directly or indirectly affect many segments of the larger community. These community segments are represented by various public interest and environmentalist groups, shareowners, employees, plant communities, labor unions, municipal and state governments, federal agencies, and the judiciary. These groups are the forces which confer social legitimacy on a corporation. While their expectations may be, at times, unreasonable or contradictory, they have at least as much power as management in determining the continued life of the enterprise. Their expectations therefore must, at a minimum, be acknowledged and addressed.

Looking briefly at each of the functional areas, the supply of *raw materials* is affected by: (1) the release of public (national and state) forest land for commercial use; (2) legislation, such as taxation and zoning, which affects the commercial forest potential of private land; and (3) regulation of forest management practices (including the size of clear-cutting logs, monoculture, soil conservation, fire control, wildlife management, and herbicide and insecticide spraying). Environmental issues also surface as constraints on *production*. Production-related public affairs issues thus include (1) air and stream pollution; (2) brittle labor relations related to hazardous working conditions, wages, and mill closings; (3) energy policy; and (4) transportation. *Financial* matters are affected by taxation (of forest land, plant, and capital equipment), reporting (disclosure requirements, and complex non-financial reporting on land use and employment practices), and intense merger threats (due to greatly undervalued stocks). Finally, company *marketing* activities are restrained by limits on log exports, possible product standardization, and strict price-fixing penalties.

As a result of this wide-ranging and complex exposure to external pressures, the forest products industry has developed an outstanding degree of sophistication in managing public affairs. The three major trade associations—the American Forest Institute (public relations activities), the National Forest Products Association (general representative of lumber and wood products companies), and the American Paper Institute (general representative of paper and packaging companies)—have shown sensitivity to environmental and other issues for over 40 years. Both the NFPA and API have economists, policy analysts, and lobbyists working on a wide range of subjects. Joint committees meet regularly and frequently to coordinate a single industry voice on certain issues. These organizations communicate with the member companies through company representatives on committees, rotating officers from the companies, and various newsletters and bulletins. The API's 300-page *Public Affairs Leadership Manual* stands out as a unique and impressive trade group effort to educate and assist its members in developing their own public affairs programs.

Although the industry has a good sense of its public image, it has a fair amount of room for improvement. A recent survey conducted by Yankelovich, Shelley, and White for the American Forest Institute found that the public's perception of the forest products industry as socially responsible has seriously eroded. In 1978, 29 percent of the public felt that the industry has done a "good job" of behaving in a socially responsible manner; in 1979, this figure dropped to 21 percent. The industry slipped from the top to the middle of a group of twenty leading industries, in which broadcasting companies, banks, telephone companies, airlines, food companies, and drug companies were seen as superior performers (Yankelovich, 1979).

This study also found a sharp reversal in the upward trend in the public's perception of the industry as a conserver of natural resources: It's "good job" rating plunged from 34 to 26 percent. In fact, 46 percent of the public thinks that both forest products and oil have done a "poor job" in conserving natural resources. Both government officials (61 percent) and the media (48 percent) see the industry as exerting "undue influence" on government—a rating equaled only by the oil industry.

Eighty percent of the public disagree with industry perceptions, believing that the primary purpose of national forests is to provide habitat for wildlife. Eighty percent of the public also felt that the federal government has allowed too much harvesting. Almost half of the government officials surveyed believed that clear-cutting forests is subject to widespread abuse. The industry is generally seen as complying fairly well with pollution laws, but the public has maintained a strong interest in control of litter, ranking it right in behind inflation, energy, and pollution, and along with taxes, on a list of domestic issues for which corrective action was suggested.

Thus, substantial gaps between the view of the public and the interests of industry remain. A survey focused on various interest groups and agencies might well suggest an even wider gap in expectations. Even more important are industry-level actions and the aggregate image of the industry in the quality of the relationship between individual firms and their particular stakeholder groups. While many of the public affairs issues facing forest products companies are common to firms across the industry, many public affairs issues exist at the firm level: Regulatory agencies take enforcement action against individual firms. Individual mills or firms must deal with local taxation and licensing authorities. The union locals in the industry are far more powerful than the national leadership in the resolution of labor disputes. Although company holdings are distributed unevenly across the states, the dramatic growth in regulation thrusts its enormous impact on the internal operation of each of the plants and mills with equal vigor. Thus, company-specific pressures are quite evident.

Furthermore, even the industry-wide issues affect individual firms differently. Interest in log exports or land taxation depends on a particular company's land ownership profile. Similarly, forest product companies find different sorts of energy legislation attractive, depending on their biomass fuel potential, their generation of steam, and the oil reserve, gas reserve, and hydro-power potential of their properties. Even the effects of air and water pollution control regulation can depend on a company's product line, location, effluent systems, and antitrust compliance. Lastly, shareholder loyalty can be realistically nurtured only at the firm level, rather than on an industry level.

As the forest products industry has grown from fragmented regional clusters into a well-integrated national system, the latitude of management discretion has become tempered by the increasing influence of public agents on the use of public resources. Market growth, technological development, and changing public expectations over the past century have caused corporate social behavior to shift through three phases. The original policy of unbridled resource exploitation shifted to a policy of prudent resource management, and now to a policy of mediation of business and public interests. Accordingly, management prerogative has been eroded in each of the functional areas of the enterprise. The nature of these institutional responsibilities also cuts vertically through industry posture, company strategy, and daily plant-level activities. Successful negotiation of management's interests and public's interests requires both attentive listening and appropriate responses at each of these levels and across each of the functional areas. Public affairs issues are intimately intertwined with business priorities.

PUBLIC AFFAIRS ACTIVITY

Given the importance of public affairs issues to the forest products industry, this study examined the way in which public affairs activities were conducted in the sample companies. An initial question was the extent to which such activities were handled by specialized public affairs departments (government affairs, public affairs, legal and public relations), and/or by other departmental units (general management, human resources, engineering, and finance). For each firm and department studied, data were gathered on:

1. Time spent in contact with outsiders;
2. Breadth of contact with different outsiders;
3. Appreciation of outsiders as information sources;
4. Departmental boundary spanning efforts: (a) overall conscious attention to outside factors, and (b) readiness to listen to outside signals.

The results highlighted certain general characteristics of stakeholder contact and information sources across the departmental level of the sample. Great time was spent by most departments on trade association activities and with legislators, while state regulators, unions, and professional associations were given relatively little time. The departmental analysis also revealed a strong preference for impersonal information sources (see Table 1). Public affairs activities were far from incidental to any of the departments studied. No department allotted less than 25 percent of the average work week to stakeholder interactions. Each department maintained contact with at least seven stakeholder groups. Finally, every department reported that it recognized more than a fair amount of responsibility for public affairs boundary spanning activities.

There were, however, substantial differences between public affairs departments and the other departments studied. Public affairs executives tended to spend far more time in interactions with outside stakeholder

Table 1.   Rank Order of Value of Information Sources

Rank Order	Information Sources	Average Rating*
1.	Within the Company	4.021
2.	Trade Associations	3.246
3.	*Wall Street Journal*	3.207
4.	Trade Contacts	2.761
5.	*Business Week*	2.619
6.	Professional Press	2.556
7.	Broadcasting	2.546
8.	Government Contacts	2.526
9.	Popular Press	2.481
10.	Business Research Organization	2.478
11.	Books	2.256
12.	*Fortune*	2.234
13.	Government Publications	2.328
14.	Trade Press	2.321
15.	*Forbes*	2.210
16.	Consultants	2.197
17.	*New York Times*	2.09
18.	*Duns*	2.007
19.	Public Interest Groups	1.985
20.	Environmentalist Publications	1.978
21.	*Harvard Business Review*	1.884
22.	Investor Community	1.733
23.	Environmental Contacts	1.706
24.	Labor Contacts	1.453
25.	Labor Publications	1.380

Note:
* 1 = low, 5 = high

groups, and maintained contact with many more outside constituents. Furthermore, public affairs executives recognized a greater responsibility for public affairs boundary spanning activities. Non-public affairs executives were more issue—specific in their stakeholder interactions. For example, financial executives spent more time on investor relations, and human resource executives spent more time on labor relations. They also tended to be more likely to acquire information from their outside contacts. (See Table 2)

In summary, public affairs executives tended to 1) spend more time in contact with outside stakeholders, 2) maintain contact with a broader array of outside stakeholders, and 3) recognize a greater formal obligation to watch over public affairs activities. Non-public affairs executives tended to be more issue-specific in their stakeholder interactions, more respectful of outsiders as information sources, and more interested in listening to outsiders than expounding their own views.

Table 2. Stakeholder Interaction Time for Public Affairs
and Other Departments

Stakeholder Group	Public Affairs[1] Departments	Other Departments[2]
(Rank ordered by Public Affairs Interaction Time)	(Hours/Week)	(Hours/Week)
Industry Associations	6.18*	2.95
State Legislators	4.95*	.62
U.S. Congress	3.45*	.63
Environmentalists	2.68*	1.15
Press	2.33*	.49
Other (local, civic, etc.)	2.07	1.23
Federal Regulators	1.98	1.26
Investment Community	1.57	1.41
State Regulators	1.12	.56
Advisors (consultants, institutes)	1.02*	1.62
Professional Associations	.62	.22
Labor	.13	1.09
TOTAL	28.07*	12.67
	N = 60	N = 81

Notes:
1 = legal, public relations, government affairs, public affairs
2 = general management, line operations, financial, planning, engineering, human resources
* Statistically significant differences

PUBLIC AFFAIRS SENSITIVITY
AND RESPONSIVENESS

Company-wide *receptivity* to public affairs issues—as indicated by the breadth of outside contacts, ability to appreciate the information value of stakeholder interactions, amount of attention directed toward public affairs, readiness to listen to outsiders, and depth of involvement in issues—varied significantly across the companies studied. And these variations were associated with differences in internal coordination (*integration*) of public affairs information and in the *influence* of public affairs information in company decisions (see Table 3). These three company traits—receptivity, integration and influence—are considered distinct dimensions of the public affairs sensitivity of the firm. It was hypothesized that companies with higher levels of sensitivity, as measured along these dimensions, would also be perceived as more socially responsive by external stakeholders.

After interviews with industry executives and a number of knowledgeable outside parties, a sample of 150 external stakeholders for the

Table 3. Overall Company Sensitivity to Public Affairs

Company[a]	RECEPTIVITY MEASURES[b]					INTEGRATION[c]	INFLUENCE[d]
	Breadth	Appreciation	Attention	Listenership	Depth		
Pacific Timber	hi	hi	hi	hi	hi	hi	hi
New York Paper	lo	hi	lo	lo	lo	hi	lo
Central Paper	lo	lo	lo	lo	lo	lo	lo
Northwest Forests	hi	lo	med	hi	lo	lo	lo
American Forests	lo	hi	med	hi	med	lo	hi
U.S. Paper	hi	lo	hi	lo	hi	hi	hi

Notes:
a. Company names disguised.
b. Measured by individual statistical indicators.
c. Indicated by use of task forces and steering committees.
d. Measured by total of objective and subjective indicators.

forest products industry was constructed. This group included investment analysts, trade union members, environmentalist, state regulators, federal regulators, congressional staffers, trade association officials and academicians. It was presumed that these types of people might have different perspectives on industry and company performance. Mail questionnaires were sent to the selected respondents, and 50 percent (75) were returned.

The questionnaire asked for assessments of both the social responsibility (ethics) and social responsiveness (alertness) of the forest products industry as compared to 11 other important industry groups, and of each of the 20 largest forest products firms. In addition, respondents were asked to rate the seven individually studied companies according to a number of more precise performance dimensions and to predict the top three major public affairs issues that the industry was likely to confront in the next year.

The stakeholder panel rated the forest products industry as just slightly better than average in their public affairs posture. Five industries (petroleum, steel, chemicals, tobacco and mining) were seen as substantially less responsive, and four (insurance, drugs, consumer products, and banking) as roughly comparable. The broadcasting and airlines industries were considered more socially responsive than forest products. These findings exactly parallel those of a similar survey of the general public (Yankelovich, 1979).

Having anchored the forest products industry relative to other major industries, we can look at the responses of the panel of judges in more detail. These seemed to vary markedly along stakeholder lines, descending in order of favorability to the industry from industry trade association officials, investment community representatives, local regulators, academicians, journalists, federal regulators, to environmentalists. The more favorable stakeholder groups tended to have a somewhat broader multi-issue interaction with forest products companies, while the less favorable groups have more issue-specific interactions.

While responsibility and responsiveness were strongly correlated in the overall ratings of the companies (see Table 4), a closer look at the six companies visited for the intensive interviews can help to distinguish these similar terms. Looking first at social responsibility, it appears that three companies (Pacific Timber, Central Paper, and New York Paper) were above the industry average. Although these six companies were not significantly different from each other in this collective stakeholder rating, Pacific Timber, the highest rated, and Northwest Forests, the lowest rated, were very different from each other. Results for the other companies were not significantly different on responsibility, and their rankings relative to each other reversed on responsiveness.

Table 4.   Company Social Performance Ratings

Company*	Responsibility	Responsiveness
Pacific Timber	3.88	4.26
New York Paper	3.26	3.21
Central Paper	3.36	3.13
Northwest Forests	2.53	3.08
American Forests	3.10	3.32
U. S. Paper	3.11	3.30

Notes:
Responsibility, Average = 3.10
Responsiveness (overall), Average = 3.17
* Company names disguised.

It is interesting to note that executive ratings of their own company's social performance did not correspond to these outside stakeholder ratings in even a general way. Executives were asked to rate their company's public affairs performance relative to other companies in several areas. In no case did company executives locate their own organization relative to the other companies in the same order as the stakeholder ratings. Even rough high-low comparisons do not generally correspond. Thus, there is reason to suspect a significant gap in perceptions of the industry from the inside and the outside.

CORPORATE STRUCTURE AND SOCIAL PERFORMANCE

The hypothesized relationship between organizational structure and social performance was central to this study and was broadly supported by the data. (See Figure 1.) The most structurally sensitive company— Pacific Timber was rated as most responsive to public affairs by the sample of stakeholders. Conversely, Northwest Forests, rated least responsive to public affairs by stakeholders, also displayed low internal indicators of sensitivity. While the stakeholder groups differed among themselves in their appraisal of the industry, a rough rank-listing of company responsiveness was remarkably consistent across the groups. Companies that were seen as socially alert by more than one set of outside constituents were usually seen that way by all their constituencies. But actual company ratings were very different among groups. For example, some companies received their highest ratings from federal regulators. Such differences may be explained by company differences in internal emphasis on external matters. Similarly, the investment community's more favorable ratings of some companies, relative to those

Figure 1. Summary of Company Performance

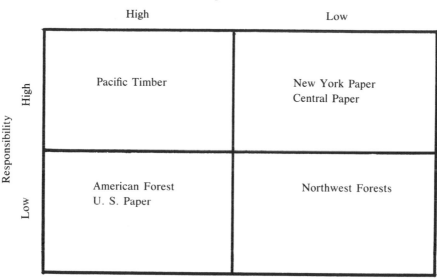

Responsiveness

	High	Low
High	Pacific Timber	New York Paper Central Paper
Low	American Forest U. S. Paper	Northwest Forests

Responsibility

of other stakeholder groups, may have been an indication of differences of focus in this area.

Reference to individual company history is required to explain some of the more detailed results. Three companies—Pacific Timber, New York Paper, and Central Paper—were older companies with far more stable market and financial histories. These companies had long-standing, well-articulated codes of business conduct, longer traditions of community awareness, and less disruptive executive succession. These companies were also enthusiastic about this research project, despite a feeling that their own performance was uneven. Finally, the distinct quality which distinguished these three companies was their curiosity about stakeholder interests. The other three companies were somewhat younger and far more volatile in their market and financial histories. They lacked strong traditions of public concern; and each had suffered volatile executive transitions. The atmosphere which emerged from these settings was one of suspicion rather than curiosity. While many executives in these less sensitive companies were socially conscious individuals, the overall goal of their corporate approach to public affairs seemed to be directed toward *persuasion* rather than toward *understanding*.

These differences in the cultural patterns were reflected in company perceptions of public affairs issues. Company backgrounds helped to explain issue priority and company posture. For example, log exporting companies were naturally more conerned about proposed log export restrictions; large land-owning companies were more concerned about land taxation and timber harvesting issues, and paper products-oriented companies were more concerned about pollution control. Cultural differences among the companies also seemed to correspond with perceptual openness (tolerance) towards outside stakeholders. Furthermore, the more sensitive companies displayed a greater degree of internal agreement about the company posture on issues and about the priorities facing the company. This greater internal sharing of values would probably mean less dysfunctional internal squabbling over limited resources as well as a more consistent set of external actions.

CONCLUSIONS

The importance of these historical and cultural factors in explaining our results suggests that we should revise the original model of this research. The thesis underlying this model was that the company needs to have both the equipment in place to receive information from the outside and the internal capacity to understand what has been gathered. This model was insufficient because it proposed a mechanical sensory system without allowing for the non-rational context within which the system operates. There is an analogy with the mistake of studying human perceptions and behavior based strictly in terms of physiological structures. To understand the human character, we must supplement our knowledge of the sensory organs with insight into individual personality and setting. Perceptual blockages occur as readily through personality features, such as expectations and fears, as through faulty receptors. We should expect at least as much complexity when we consider the social character of a large corporation.

Selznick (1957) labeled this notion of organizational character the "institutional embodiment of purpose" (p. 134). Using a metaphor similar to that developed above, Selznick elaborated:

> The study of institutions is in some ways comparable to the clinical study of personality. It requires a genetic and developmental approach, an emphasis on historical origin and growth stages (p. 141).

Only one company in the study, Pacific Timber, had institutionalized the structural and cultural aspects of its character. At the same time, only one company, Northwest Forests, was relatively poorly developed in both of these dimensions. The other four companies were at different stages of development in these areas. It is not surprising, then, that

Pacific Timber and Northwest Forest were polar opposites in perception and performance in all dimensions, while the other companies alternated in assessments of strengths.

The major academic implication of this study is its call for more internal study of organizations with respect to public affairs and social performance. Recent trends in organizational behavior studies highlight evolutionary explanations of company existence and stress the analysis of company actions as a series of strategies chosen to control external resource dependence. These studies remind us to consider the immediate and long term potency of environmental threats. Certainly the inability of organizations to adapt to environmental change inevitably leads to their demise.

Similarly, it cannot be denied that there is great value of studying organization efforts to: 1) coopt challenges, 2) form alliances with outside enterprises and 3) diversify operations away from settings where they are too much at the mercy of external forces. However, an over-emphasis on these perspectives can leave the analyst strictly on the outside of the organization. Prior research has discussed "proactive" and "reactive" behavior without effectively explaining how or why these occur.

Organizational analysis must therefore not lose sight of the internal workings of companies. The dynamics of the institutional battleground is important but not novel. Political science has properly studied company activities from the outside. Organizational behavior studies can contribute by analyzing the internal dynamics that lead to external actions. Given the identical external circumstances, different companies will perceive and act differently. This study has suggested that company structure and culture may help explain some of that variation.

In addition, this research has called for an extension of our definition of the organizational environment to include the public affairs arena as well as the marketplace. Organization theory has treated the non-market environment far too lightly. Some leading theorists have even suggested that organizational attention to this sector through scanning and monitoring is possibly harmful. Through the present study of a leading U.S. industry, we have found that major corporations do, in fact, encounter environmental forces which may threaten their survival as powerfully as does the marketplace. All the functional areas of this industry were influenced by public affairs.

We have also found that the companies studied differed in their success in managing relations with this environment. This success seemed to relate to the structure of the company, in particular its structure for receiving and dealing with stimuli from its environment. In this respect, contrary to arguments of strict process-oriented schools of thought, structure may precede strategy.

Both structure and strategy can be anticipatory or reactive. The attempt to explore the sources of company perceptions best illustrates the excessive simplicity of most "process" versus "structure" debates. The cultural values, historical experience, and previous organizational arrangements may contribute as much to company perceptions as current structures or processes. This effort to move beyond phrases such as the "enacted environment" and probe the determinants and dimensions of organization-level perceptions deserves further attention. Gricar's (1980) work on the relevance of management ideology to regulatory compliance is a valuable step in this direction. Consideration of a structure-culture model is not novel, but the conception itself is underdeveloped.

Additionally, far more work in measuring social performance is needed. This study has shown some differences between perceptions of social responsibility (ethics) and those of social responsiveness (alertness). The components of each of these must be better developed. The strength of various aspects of social responsiveness were emphasized here. These need to be refined, and parallel definitions and systematic evaluation of responsibility dimensions is warranted.

The methodology of this study also has implications for future research in this area. Important attempts to further our understanding of business-society relations have all too often included large-scale surveys of many firms on scattered issues. Such endeavors ignore what has been learned about the inner complexity of organization life. Typically, such studies rely on a single questionnaire from a single company official to represent that organization's perspective. It is probable that such data tell us more about that individual official than about the company itself. To study a company, it is essential to take multiple readings. Many different executives in different departments and at different hierarchical levels must be contacted to discover the overall posture of the company. Similarly, companies are not well understood by tracing individual actions or isolated issues. To understand how organizations adapt to their environment, researchers must forego the convenience of creating an artificial and simplistic view of the environment in place of the overlapping complex conditions which companies actually face. The quality of a company's environmental response can only be appreciated through the recognition of its total set of concerns and pressures.

Furthermore, multiple types are essential in this sort of research. For example, corporate environmental behavior should be studied by both external and internal assessments. Organization self-concepts vary greatly from external views. Outsiders are not fully aware of what was intended, and insiders are not fully aware of what was achieved. In fact, mixed data sources are valuable even within companies. Analysis of corporate publications and on-site interviews led to the discovery of unsuspected "cultural" variables. For these reasons it may be advisable to encourage small sample studies where we learn a lot about a few organizations, as opposed to very little about many.

From its history and breadth of public affairs exposure, the forest products industry has learned a great deal about the management of public affairs. However, as one regulator commented in this study,

> Environmental problems occur in the best managed companies. The key is the way they each respond. Some of these forest products companies have fought regulations on environmental protection or employee safety before they understood them. If we'd worked together, they could have had both better rulings and equipment purchased at a lower price. Further, when a company develops a nasty reputation with us and with the community, politicians are less likely to come to their defense. In that situation, where regulatory agencies have a chip on their shoulder, that company is in real trouble.

Each company acts on the basis of its own social character and unique frame of reference. The extent to which a company shapes its ability to seek an understanding of its major stakeholders will determine its success in developing a partnership with the public for mutual benefit.

NOTE

This paper is based on the author's doctoral dissertation which received the annual prize awarded by the Social Issues Division, Academy of Management, for 1981 and has subsequently been published in full (Sonnenfeld 1981a).

REFERENCES

Ackerman, R., and R. Bauer, *Corporate Social Responsiveness: The Modern Dilemma.* Reston, VA: Reston Publishing, 1976.

Aguilar, F. J., *Scanning the Business Environment.* New York: Macmillan, 1967.

Aldrich, H. E., *Organization and Environments.* Englewood Cliffs, NJ: Prentice-Hall, 1979.

Andrews, K. R., *The Concept of Corporate Strategy.* Homewood, IL: Irwin, 1971.

Brenner, S. N., "Business and Politics: An Update." *Harvard Business Review* 57 6(Nov.-Dec. 1979):149–163.

Brown, J. K., *This Business of Issues: Coping with the Company's Environment.* New York: The Conference Board, 758, 1979.

Burack, E. M., and T. G. Gutteredge, "Institutional Manpower Planning: Rhetoric versus Reality." *California Management Review* 20 (Spring, 1978): 13–22.

Burns, T., and G. M. Stalker, *The Management of Innovation.* London: Tavistock, 1961.

Chandler, A. D., *The Visible Hand.* Boston: Belknap, 1977.

Chatlos, W., "What is Investor Relations?" In A. R. Rochman (ed.), *Investor Relations,* New York: Amacon, 1974, pp. 3–19.

Child, J. "Organizational Structures, Environment and Performance: The Role of Strategic Choice." *Sociology* 6(1972):1–22.

Dearborn, D. C., and H. A. Simon, "Selective Perception: A Note on The Identification of Executives." *Sociometry* 21(1958):140–144.

Downey, H., D. Hellriegal, and J. Slocum, "Environmental Uncertainty: The Construct and its Application." *Administrative Science Quarterly* 20(1975):613–639.

Duncan, R. B., "Multiple Decision-Making Structures on Adapting to Environmental Uncertainty." *Human Relations* 26(1973):273–291.

Emery, F. E., and E. L. Trist, "The Causal Texture of Organizational Environments." *Human Relations* 18(1965):21–32.

Fenn, D. H., Jr., "Finding Where the Power Lies in Government." *Harvard Business Review* 57(Sept.-Oct. 1979):144–153.

Fleming, J. E., "Public Issues Scanning." Presented at the *39th Annual Meeting of the Academy of Management,* Atlanta, August, 1979.

Gricar, B. G., "Responses to Regulation." Presented at the Eastern Academy of Management Meeting, Buffalo, NY, May 1980.

Hannan, M., and J. Freeman, "The Population Ecology of Organizations." *American Journal of Sociology* 82(March 1977):929–964.

Hacker, A., "The Press vs. the Corporation." *The New York Times Book Review* (Feb. 25, 1979):9.

Hargreaves, D. J., and J. Dauman, *Business Survival and Social Change.* New York: John Wiley, 1975.

Holmes, S. L., "Adapting Corporate Structure for Social Responsibility." *California Management Review* XXI (1978):47–54.

Jemison, "Strategic Decision Making Influence in Boundary Spanning Roles." Presented at the *39th Annual Meeting of the Academy of Management,* Atlanta, Georgia, 1979.

Kasper, D. M., "Note on Managing in a Regulated Environment." Boston: Intercollegiate Case Clearinghouse, 1-379-032, Harvard University, 1978.

Lawrence, P. R., and J. W. Lorsch, *Organization and Environment.* Boston: Harvard Graduate School of Business Administration, 1967.

Leone, R. A., "The Real Costs of Regulation." *Harvard Business Review* 55 6(Nov.–Dec. 1977):57–66.

Lodge, G. C., *The New American Ideology.* New York: Knopf, 1975.

Manne, H. G., and H. G. Wallich. *The Modern Corporation and Social Responsibility.* Washington, D.C.: The American Enterprise Institute, 1972.

McGrath, P. S., *Managing Corporate External Relations.* New York: The Conference Board, No. 679, 1976.

Miles, R. H., *Macro Organizational Behavior.* Santa Monica, CA: Goodyear Publishing, 1980.

Miles, R. E., and C. C. Snow, *Organizational Strategy, Structure and Process.* New York: McGraw-Hill, 1978.

Mills, D. Q., "Flawed Victory in Labor Law Reform." *Harvard Business Review* 57 3(May–June 1979): 81–102.

Newgren, K., "Social Forecasting: An Overview of Current Business Practices." In A. B. Carroll (ed.), *Managing Corporation Social Responsibility,* Boston: Little, Brown, 1977.

O'Toole, J., "What's Ahead for the Business Government Relationship." *Harvard Business Review* 57 2(March–April, 1979):94–105.

Parsons, T., *Structure and Process in Modern Societies.* New York: Free Press, 1960.

Patchen, M., "The Locus and Basis of Influence on Organizational Decisions." *Organizational Behavior and Human Performance* 11(1974):195–211.

Perry, J. L., and H. L. Angle, "The Politics of Organization Boundary Roles in Collective Bargaining." *The Academy of Management Review* 4(1979):487–496.

Pettigrew, A. M., *The Politics of Organizational Decision Making.* London: Tavistock, 1973.

Pfeffer, J., and G. R. Salancik, *The External Control of Organizations.* New York: Harper & Row, 1978.

Post, J. E., *Corporate Social Behavior.* Reston, VA: Reston Publishing, 1978.

Preston, L. E., and J. E. Post, *Private Management and Public Responsibility.* Englewood Cliffs, NJ: Prentice-Hall, 1975.

Selznick, P., *Leadership in Adminisstration.* New York: Harper & Row, 1957.

Speckman, R., "Influence and Information" An Exploratory Investigation of the Boundary Role Person's Basis of Power." *Academy of Management Journal* 22(1979):105–117

Sethi, S. P., *Up Against the Corporate Wall.* Englewood Cliffs, NJ: Prentice-Hall, 1977.

Shapiro, I.S., with J. T. Dunlop, A. D. Chandler, and G. P. Schultz, "Business and Public Policy." *Harvard Business Review* (Nov.–Dec., 1979):85–102.

Sonnenfeld, J. A., *Corporate Views of the Public Interest: Perceptions of the Forest Products Industry.* Boston: Auburn House, 1981a.

———, "Executive Apologies for Price Fixing. Role Biased Perceptions of Causality." *Academy of Management Journal* 24(1981b):192–198.

———, "Dealing with an Aging Workforce." *Harvard Business Review*(Nov.-Dec., 1978).

Sonnenfeld, J. A., and P. R. Lawrence, "Why Do Companies Succumb to Price Fixing?" *Harvard Business Review* 56 4(1978):145–157.

Stagner, R., and N. Rosen, *Psychology of Union Management Relations.* Belmont, CA: Wadsworth, 1965.

Starbuck, W. H., "Organizations and Their Environments." In M. Dunnette (ed.), *Handbook of Industrial and Organizational Psychology,* Chicago: Rand-McNally, 1976.

Steiner, G. A., *Business and Society.* New York: Random House, 1974.

Stinchcombe, A. L., "Social Structure and Organizations." In J. G. March, (ed.), *Handbook of Organizations,* Chicago: Rand-McNally, 1965, pp. 142–193.

Thompson, J. D., *Organizations in Action.* New York: McGraw-Hill, 1967.

Tung, R. L., "Dimensions of Organizational Environments: An Exploratory Study of their Impact on Organization Structure." *Academy of Management Journal* 22(1979):672–693.

Votaw, D., and S. P. Sethi, "Do We Need a New Corporate Rsponse." *California Management Review* (Fall 1969). Reprinted in D. Votaw, and S. P. Sethi, *The Corporate Dilemma.* Englewood Cliffs, NJ: Prentice-Hall, 1973, pp. 170–190.

Weick, M., *The Theory of Social and Economic Organization* (1907). New York: Oxford, 1947 (tr.).

Yankelovich, Skelly, and White, *Public Affairs in the Forest Products Industry.* Washington, D.C.: American Forest Institute, 1979.

THE PUBLIC AFFAIRS FUNCTION:
REPORT ON A LARGE SCALE
RESEARCH PROJECT

Edwin A. Murray, Jr.

The increased prominence of social and political forces and their influences on corporations in the past decade have led business firms to focus
more attention on their surrounding environments. One outgrowth of this
greater awareness and interest has been the emergence of a new and
distinct corporate function designed to deal with public issues and social
and political change. This function, generally known as "public affairs,"
involves responsibility for managing a company's external relations, including its interactions with government agencies, the news media, consumers, and the local community.

For the past three years, a research project on the way in which
companies conceptualize and manage the public affairs function has been
conducted at Boston University's School of Management. The research
has included extensive case studies of firms in several sectors of the

Research in Corporate Social Performance and Policy, Vol. 4, pages 129–155
Copyright © 1982 by JAI Press Inc.
All rights of reproduction in any form reserved.
ISBN: 0-89232-259-4

economy, interviews with public affairs executives and general managers, and a survey of 1,000 corporate public affairs offices. More than 400 usable responses were received, allowing us to analyze data in six basic areas: creation and growth of the public affairs functions; federal government relations activities; state and local government relations; interaction with corporate planning; the public affairs mission; and evaluating the public affairs function.[1]

One purpose of this article is to present some of our major findings. Another purpose is to discuss the research process itself because several issues of interest to researchers in the area of corporate social performance and policy are involved. In particular:

1. What *types* of research are there to be done with respect to corporate social performance and policy?
2. How can a stream of research successfully be *initiated* and *sustained?*
3. What are the best *ways* of doing such research?

Although the following discussion pertains chiefly to large scale research, elements of our approach and conclusions drawn from our experience would seem to have relevance for smaller scale research efforts as well.

In the following sections, the development of our research, its design, methodologies used, and results to date will be described. Throughout, important features of research *process* will be highlighted. Finally, the implications of this research for further work in the field will be considered.

INITIATION OF THE PROJECT

The genesis of our research can be traced to three factors: the state of the literature; the people involved; and the availability of financial support. In point of fact, the relative importance of these factors probably should be assigned in reverse order. It was the prospective availability of funding that prompted our initial project team (Post, Dickie, and myself) to consult the literature in preparation of a research proposal.

In 1978, the Shelby Cullom Davis Foundation of New York announced a competition for funds to be administered by its Educational Grants Program to support "programs for improving understanding and communication between the academic and business community." Specifically encouraged were proposals for "research and other inquiries into the relationship between business and the community." (Substantive issues aside, the application procedures were appealing in their own right because they called for proposals not exceeding six typewritten pages in length!)

The opportunity to prepare and submit a grant request appealed to us because the topic represented enough breadth of scope to accommodate our converging intellectual and research interests. Lastly, the fields of literature with which we were conversant seemed to offer only limited empirical insights into relationships between business and the community. We thought research on the corporate public affairs function could contribute significantly to those parts of the management literature which deal with business and society, corporate responsiveness, environmental scanning, strategic planning, and boundary spanning.

We chose to research corporate public affairs departments because we saw them as a new phenomenon—a recent corporate structural response designed to enhance communications between business firms and the larger society. We recognized that despite their proliferation, relatively little was known about these offices, their functions, or their effectiveness. There was a dearth of literature relating to their underlying concepts, operating policies, and specific practices. Therefore, our project was designed to provide an empirical study of such corporate structures in order to:

1. Analyze the various forms and ways in which they actually operated;
2. Identify appropriate criteria by which the general public and corporate managers might assess their performance;
3. Analyze those structures and approaches which had been most successful to date.

Upon receiving a favorable response to our grant proposal, our project team began a five-stage research process. It involved:

1. A search of the literature
2. Four in-depth case studies
3. A large-scale questionnaire survey
4. Analysis and presentation of preliminary findings, and
5. Consolidation and selective continuation of particular research tracks.

These different phases of the research process, as well as highlights from our intermediate findings, are discussed in the following sections.

FIRST STAGE: LITERATURE SEARCH

The initial phase of the project involved an analysis of public affairs practices derived from secondary research materials. We consulted sources in the form of published reports by the Conference Board

(McGrath, 1976, 1977, 1979 and Brown, 1979), files and other information made available to us by the Foundation for Public Affairs, the Public Affairs Council, and the Public Relations Society of America, and interviews with staff members of the Business Roundtable, Conference Board, Public Affairs Council, and several corporate public affairs departments.

The information we gathered facilitated the preparation of a "state of the art" memorandum that outlined areas of existing knowledge as well as areas in need of further research. For example, surveys undertaken by the Conference Board and the Public Affairs Council during the 1970s were at least five years old, and researchers at both organizations urged us to update the information. The principal question we wished to answer was "What constitutes the current state of the art?" In particular, three areas seemed worthy of more focused examination:

1. How are government relations activities managed?
2. What is the relationship between public affairs and corporate planning?
3. What is the impact of public affairs on top management policy making?

Some major areas of the management literature and some of the previous work by others found most pertinent to our study should be briefly noted.

The Corporation in Society. Drawing upon the "interpenetrating systems" model first suggested by Parsons (1960), Preston and Post reasoned not only that the "larger society exists as a macro-system, but that individual (and particularly *large*) micro-organizations also constitute separable systems within themselves, neither controlling nor controlled by the social environment" (Preston and Post, 1975, p. 25). Post further stated that the interpenetrating systems model "provides a general framework within which the analysis of a specific corporation-society relationship can be undertaken. In addition, and perhaps more importantly, the interpenetrating systems perspective provides some sense of where the important issues lie in the relationship of a specific firm to its social environment" (Post, 1978, p. 63).

Corporate Responsiveness. Examining the internal, administrative implications of managers trying to respond to social demands, Ackerman (1975) identified a three-stage "social response process." According to Bauer, this form of "corporate responsiveness" actually reflected important organizational learning processes which could have significant payoffs in both social and economic terms:

> We are witnessing the development of a *responsive* corporation, one that is learning to institutionalize novelty. And if the corporation is in fact learning, it should be increasingly capable of handling new issues whether they be *business* or *social*. It is reasonable to expect the development of a new breed of managers. They will probably have different values, as has been rather widely suggested. But, probably more importantly, they will be accustomed to and skilled at organizational change. (Bauer, 1978, p. 100)

Environmental Analysis. One of the most important functions for a company seeking a good "fit" with its external and changing environment is that of "environmental scanning" (Aguilar 1976). However, Utterback has urged that less attention be paid to the development of more formal analytical or forecasting techniques and that greater attention be paid to the integration of environmental assessments into corporate strategic planning processes. For him, "the most critical issue . . . is understanding the process through which organizations can accommodate themselves to changes in their environment" (Utterback, 1979, p. 143).

Strategic Planning. Arguably, this most holistic of planning approaches—more than any other traditional management activity—should address itself to working out an alignment between an organization and its environment. Ackerman (1975, p. 298), for instance, has suggested that there is a notable similarity between the strategic planning process and the social response process in large, multi-business corporations. Both typically are initiated at the corporate level and thus represent "top-down" phenomena; both seek to allocate scarce resources (either in the form of capital or human resources); and both involve a choice process which yields a portfolio (whether of businesses or social issues) to manage, thereby explicitly acknowledging the need to establish priorities among many competing claims (in terms of business or social opportunities and/or threats).

The parallelism sketched by Ackerman makes particularly relevant the work of Wheelright and Banks (1979). Their research showed that corporate strategic planning systems developed in a five-stage evolutionary process—a descriptive model that, with appropriate modifications, could conceivably characterize the development of public affairs management within a firm as well.

Boundary Spanning. Presumably, rational managers would seek more than just similarities between corporate planning and public affairs management. Actual linkages between the two functions could serve to be mutually enriching in terms of data gathering, analysis, and action planning. However, this type of integration—within the firm among functional specialties as well as outside the firm among various external stakeholder groups—will require the use of skilled "boundary spanning" managers.

According to Child, new "specialist 'link' roles will probably have to be created" (1979, p. 178). In all likelihood, the personalities and interpersonal skills of these integrating specialists, or boundary spanners, will be very important in determining the outcomes of negotiations in which they are involved. However, as organizations undertake an expanded and more systematic, structured role in interacting with their environments, we can expect structural relationships, administrative systems, and organizational processes to play greater parts in determining organizational effectiveness. According to Thompson (1967), the nature of these administrative arrangements would be expected to differ as a function of environmental uncertainty and complexity (see Figure 1).

Illustrative of the types of hypotheses we generated from these areas of the management literature were the following:

1. The more dynamic and heterogeneous the environment, the greater the likelihood that the firm will engage in public affairs activities and have an established department or structure to deal with the environment.
2. Firms with public affairs departments are more likely to institutionalize a sensitivity to public issues throughout the organization than firms without public affairs departments.
3. Firms with public affairs departments are more likely to be effective in dealing with social issues (by minimizing the gap between public expectations and corporate performance) than firms without public affairs departments.
4. The evolution of structure and process in public affairs management, like that of strategic planning, will tend to develop in discernable, evolutionary stages.

However, before we could ask the kind of questions necessary to test these and other hypotheses via a national survey instrument, it was essential that we develop a deeper understanding and greater sophistication with respect to public affairs than we possessed at the time. Clearly helpful would be additional, exploratory research into how firms that appeared to be leaders in public affairs practice actually implemented the activities and programs which they claimed to use. To examine this question, and to further refine our understanding of the state of the art, detailed case studies of public affairs departments and their activities in four firms were undertaken.

SECOND STAGE: CASE STUDIES

Initially, it was our hope to conduct in-depth field studies at 8 to 10 companies, some of which would be considered leaders in the field of

Figure 1. Organizational Characteristics as a Function of Task Environments

TASK ENVIRONMENTS:

	CERTAINTY/UNCERTAINTY DIMENSION	
	Stable	*Shifting*
Homogeneous	• Simple in the structure of boundary spanning units • Organizations with few functional divisions • Coordination by standardization	• Boundary spanning units differentiated only to the extent that their capacity to monitor the environment would be overextended • Organization arranged by geographic space, which is decentralized. • Coordination by planning
Heterogeneous	• Organization consists of a variety of functional divisions • Boundary spanning unit structure more complex • Coordination by standardization and/or plan	• Boundary units would be differentiated functionally to correspond to segments of the environment • Organization operates on a decentralized basis • Coordination by mutual adjustment

COMPLEXITY DIMENSION

* Adapted from Thompson (1967: p.72).

135

external relations and some of which would be notable laggards. We also envisaged a broad representation of corporate America, including at least one firm from each of eight or so major sectors of the economy.

In the end, our rather lengthy shopping list of ideal firms was reduced to four, based largely on personal contacts we had with managers in those companies. Still, we had a fairly broad representation in that our research sites included a bank, a utility, a high-technology manufacturing company, and a petro-chemical manufacturer (see Table 1). Furthermore, the comprehensive and in-depth field studies were supplemented by additional, although less extensive, studies of other firms with complementary characteristics, activities, and/or public affairs structures.

In each of the four case studies, efforts were made to explore the three basic areas we had identified earlier:

1. How are government relations activities managed?
2. What is the relationship between public affairs and corporate planning?
3. What is the impact of public affairs on top management policy making?

To ensure comparability among the four field studies, each researcher sought to gather information that could be organized under the following topical headings:

1. Description of the company and its business(es).
2. Early involvement of the company in public affairs activities.
3. Establishment and development of the public affairs department (and its activities).
4. The management of government relations at the federal, state, and local levels.
5. The company's approach to strategic planning and the relationship of public affairs management to it.
6. Management policy making processes and the relationship of public affairs management to them.
7. The company's response to a representative public affairs issue.

Through extensive interviewing, examination of corporate records, and observation, it was possible to develop a number of insights into each of these aspects of the management of public affairs. Moreover, by *tracking* a particular issue and its handling throughout the organization (number 7 in the previously mentioned list), we sought to determine whether the actual management of the issue conformed to the description of that process provided by public affairs managers and others. In this

Table 1. Comparison of Size and Organizational Structure at Four Research Sites

	Company A (Utility)	Company B (Bank)	Company C (Computers)	Company D (Chemicals)
Size (1979)				
Revenues	$270 million	$1 billion	$3.2 billion	$8 billion +
Assets	$285 million +	$10 billion +	$1.8 billion	$8 billion +
Structure	Functional Centralized	Functional Centralized	Divisionalized Decentralized	Divisionalized Decentralized

way, we improved upon our ability to discern "perceived effectiveness" (as reported by management) from "actual effectiveness" (as observed in the course of events and actual outcomes).

By comparing our similarly structured case studies, we were able to characterize and array several salient features of public affairs management as practiced by the four companies. The way in which external relations were managed seemed to be contingent on a host of firm-specific circumstances. The environments of each of the four firms were changing, although at different rates and in different ways. The sources of change, for example, differed considerably. Table 2 summarizes the nature and source of changes faced by the four companies, and Table 3 compares the stability and complexity of their respective environments as well as the degree of government regulation encountered by these companies.

Given variations in the types and rates of change and the stability and complexity of their environments, the four companies developed different ways of managing external issues. Table 4 compares the four companies

Table 2. Comparison of the Nature and Source of the Major Changes in the Environments of Four Research Sites

	Company A (Utility)	Company B (Bank)	Company C (Computers)	Company D (Chemicals)
Nature of change	Escalating energy costs	Legislative and regulatory changes altering competitive structure; High technology making possible more types of transactions at higher speeds	High technology and international competition	Escalating energy costs altering the costs of raw materials
Source of change	Energy crisis	Government; High technology	U.S. and foreign competition	Energy crisis; International trade

Table 3. Comparison of the Stability and Complexity of the Environments of Four Research Sites

	Company A (Utility)	Company B (Bank)	Company C (Computers)	Company D (Chemicals)
Environmental Stability (certainty and predictability of events)	Relatively stable in terms of • technology • competitive structure • availability of markets • but supplies a problem	Traditionally stable but rate of change accelerating in terms of legal environment, technology, industry structure	Rapid change in terms of • technology • availability of market	Rapid change in terms of • technology • supplies • availability of markets
Environmental Complexity	Relatively simple and clarified by virtue of the role of legislation and regulation	Complex but clarified by virtue of the role of legislation and regulation	Complex	Very complex, especially due to the diversity of the products
Degree of Regulation	Industry and issue specific	Industry and issue specific	Issues only	Issues only

138

Table 4. Comparison of the Strategic Planning Systems, Government Relations, Structure of Public Affairs Offices, Issue Management, and Techniques of Environmental Analysis Used by the Four Research Sites

	Company A (Utility)	Company B (Bank)	Company C (Computers)	Company D (Chemicals)
Strategic Planning System	Handled implicitly by top management and premised primarily on their best judgment	Like Company A but becoming increasingly institutionalized and formalized	Systematic and apparently well integrated and institutionalized in their line management responsibilities	Systematic. Handled expressly and intensively by top management teams and their staff
Government Relations (Federal)	No Washington office. Functions handled by CEO, VP Public Relations and trade associations	No Washington office. Functions handled by a VP for government relations, an executive VP and trade associations as needed	CEO actively managed these relations and integrated them into corporate strategy and operations	Handled through Washington office
Government Relations (State)	Function handled in same was as federal relations aided by part-time lobbyists	Functions handled in same way as federal relations	Proactive. Initiatives taken to support strategic and programmatic priorities	Handled primarily through operating divisions as needed
Structure of Public Affairs Office	Small department with community affairs specialist and public information specialist	Executive VP orchestrates specialists in community relations, media relations, government relations, etc.	Small department with community relations specialist	Larger department with communications specialist. Issues management and special assignment consultants
Issue Management	Managed on an ad hoc basis, chiefly by VP Public Relations	Handled by a committee or by executive VP, who may assign it to a staff specialist	Task force as needed. Strategic programs office creates/develops programs for integration into organization	Handled by issue managers with a blend of line and staff responsibility and authority
Analysis Used	Qualitative consumer surveys	Essentially market oriented. Personal judgment often relied on	Combination market oriented and socio-political	Socio-political • qualitative • public survey

139

in terms of strategic planning, government relations, the structures of their public affairs offices, issue management, and the techniques of environmental analysis which they used.

From these data, certain nascent patterns of behavior could be discerned. For instance, more systematic and sophisticated corporate responses appeared to be forthcoming (and needed) as firms became larger and found themselves in environments characterized by increasing complexity and decreasing stability. Such a spectrum of responses tempted us to infer the existence of a life cycle phenomenon, that is, the evolutionary development of public affairs practices within the firms. We speculated that the phases of such a life cycle might be described as follows:

1. *Ad Hoc:* Management of external affairs through *ad hoc* responses by non-professionals.
2. *Public Relations:* Use of "public relations" professionals, but largely for the purpose of putting the best face on corporate policies or actions after the fact.
3. *Environmental Analysis and Forecasting:* Increased adeptness at reading the firm's external environment and influencing it through functional specialists (in such areas as environmental forecasting, lobbying, and so forth).
4. *Strategic Planning:* Expansion of public affairs to include and integrate several external relations functions, such as a Washington-based office and media relations. The integration of public affairs into strategic planning at the corporate level.
5. *Institutionalization:* The integration of public affairs into plans and actions at the operating level.

The limited data we had, which was chiefly of a cross-sectional nature, was insufficient to support this life cycle model in detail. The differing postures of the four companies may be less a function of the firms' respective developmental stages than the types of businesses they are in and the particular needs arising from their industry and environmental settings. Even though the concept of evolutionary development of public affairs management through organizational learning seems plausible, additional longitudinal studies will be necessary to confirm it.

Nevertheless, the case studies did provide us with some evidence in support of certain of our working hypotheses. They also generated new questions and hypotheses which enriched our research agenda. Most importantly, they notably increased our understanding of how public affairs activities were actually managed in large corporations. This knowledge equipped us to prepare what we believed to be a relatively sophisticated and penetrating questionnaire.

THIRD STAGE: QUESTIONNAIRE SURVEY

The intent of the questionnaire was to gain a representative view of public affairs management in a large number of companies and thereby provide a fuller factual foundation upon which the study could proceed. Guided by earlier surveys by the Conference Board and the Public Affairs Council, hypotheses generated from the literature, and questions arising from our exploratory field research, we drafted a ten-page questionnaire. After pretesting it with a small number of public affairs practitioners, it was revised and sent to a sample of 1,000 firms, of which 401 responded. The companies chosen were large and medium-sized firms from all sectors of American business. Major companies were generally included in the sample on the assumption that they were most likely to have organized public affairs departments or units. Approximately half of the firms were listed as Public Affairs Council (PAC) members; and PAC members constituted about 62 percent of all respondents. Many of the non-PAC companies in the sample indicated that they had not yet established public affairs units. The high response rate (40 percent) was thought to be attributable to several factors: the design and perceived relevance of the questionnaire; careful targetting of specific public officers by name where possible; use of covering letters which related this research to earlier well-known work done by the Conference Board and the Public Affairs Council; use of "pre-alert" telephone calls; aggressive follow up by mail and telephone; and the offer of a final "de-briefing" by way of a written report.

Firms responding to the survey ranged from $21 million to $85 billion in annual sales or revenues. The respondents were evenly distributed at size intervals below $20 billion in sales, but thinned out significantly above that level. Only 2.6 percent of the respondents reported sales or revenues greater than $20 billion. Table 5 characterizes the respondents

Table 5. Organizational Structure and Decision Making
in Responding Companies

Structure and Decision-Making Style	Percentage of Respondents
Operating company, functionally organized, with centralized decision-making	38.8
Operating company, organized by product or service-markets, with decentralized decision-making	36.5
Holding company, with decentralized decision making	12.9
Holding company, with centralized decision making	8.3
Other	3.5

in terms of their self-reported organizational structures and decision-making processes.

MAJOR RESULTS OF THE STUDY

Public Affairs Departments and Functions

As their political and social surroundings have become more complex and "intrusive," companies generally have designed organizational mechanisms and added capabilities to deal with their environments. Table 6 shows data on the establishment of public affairs units within our respondent companies. The decade of the 1970s was the period of most dramatic growth in public affairs offices, with significantly more units created than in the 1950s and 1960s. Indeed, almost 60 percent of all public affairs departments in existence today were created in the 1970s, and nearly one-third in the past five years.

The growth of public affairs is also reflected in the increased sizes of staffs devoted to these activities. Asked to compare current figures with those of 1975, 63 percent of our respondents said professional staff size increased; 29 percent reported no change, and only 8 percent reported decreases in staff size as shown in Table 7.

Corporate budgets provide another measure of organizational commitment to the public affairs function. Table 8 shows that 35 percent of the respondents spend more than $1 million annually. As a percentage of sales or revenues, public affairs expenditures ranged from a low of .0001 percent to 12 percent. Part of this wide range may be attributable to the varying scope of public affairs responsibilities among respondents. For example, some respondents consider corporate adverstising to be part of the public affairs function, thereby raising the level of reported expenditures.

The importance and complexity of the modern external relations function is reflected in the variety of specific activities included within the definition of corporate public affairs by our respondent companies. Table

Table 6.   Creation of Public Affairs Units

Date of Creation	Number	Percentage	Cumulative Percentage
Before 1950	32	8.9	8.9
1950–1959	37	10.3	19.2
1960–1969	80	22.1	41.3
1970–1974	100	27.7	69.0
1975–1980	112	31.0	100.0
Total	361	100.0	

Table 7. Professional Employees
Working in the Public
Affairs Area

*Current Number of Full-Time Professional Staff
Members (1980)*

Staff Members	Percentage of Respondents
1–10	71.0
11–25	18.2
26–100	8.7
101–400	2.1
	100.0

*How does the Professional Staff Employment in
1980 compare to that in 1975?*

More	62.5
About the Same	29.3
Less	8.2
	100.0

9 shows that external affairs management seems to center around two principal areas of responsibility—government relations and community relations. However, other activities often were included, even though they may be handled by specialized departments as might be the case for consumer affairs.

The most senior public affairs officers tended to be fairly high-ranking newcomers in their firms. Data in Table 10 show that they rank at the vice presidential level in over two-thirds of our sample, and in over 60

Table 8. Corporate-Level Public
Affairs Budgets

Corporate Expenditures	Percentage of Respondents*
Less than $100,000	5.8
$100,001 to $500,000	38.3
$500,001 to $1,000,000	20.8
$1,000,001 to $10,000,000	32.9
Greater than $10,000,000	2.2

Note:
* Of the 401 companies in our sample, 274 responded to this question.

Table 9.   Defining The Public Affairs
Function

Activity	Percentage of Respondents Identifying the Activity as Part of Their Public Affairs Function
Community Relations	84.9
Government Relations	84.2
Corporate Contributions	71.5
Media Relations	70.0
Stockholder Relations	48.5
Advertising	40.4
Consumer Affairs	38.5
Graphics	33.5
Institutional Investor Relations	33.5
Customer Relations	23.8

Table 10.   The Senior Public Affairs Officer

A. Title of the most senior full-time public affairs officer

Vice President	68.6%
Director	20.3%
Manager	5.4%
Other	5.7%
	100.0%

B. To whom does this person report?

Vice President	31.3%
Chairman	25.6%
Chief Executive Officer	19.4%
President	16.5%
Other	7.2%
	100.0%

C. How long has this person held the senior public affairs position?

Range:	1 to 30 years
5 years or less:	61.7%
10 years or less:	88.7%

D. How long has this person been with the company?

Range:	1 to 40 years
5 years or less:	26.7%
10 years or less:	46.8%

percent of the companies, the senior public affairs officer reports directly to the chairman of the board of directors, the chief executive officer, or the president of the company. Among respondents to the survey, 62 percent of senior public affairs officers have been in such positions less than five years, and 89 percent have held such positions less than 10 years. Moreover, one-fourth of our respondents indicate that they have been with the company for less than five years, while nearly one-half indicate a tenure of less than 10 years with their current employer. In short, the growth of the public affairs field is mirrored not only in the mobility of its practitioners but also in the significant opportunities this growth provides.

Government Relations

The increase in federal regulations during the 1970s contributed to a dramatic growth in efforts to manage federal government relations more systematically. Of the companies responding, 73 percent said they maintained a significant involvement or presence in Washington. Table 11 indicates the various forms this "presence" has taken among our sample firms. Notably, trade associations remain important despite recent increases in the number of Washington offices. The growth *within* Washington offices, as reflected in staffing and budgets, was also documented by our survey, and paralleled that of public affairs departments as a whole.

The survey asked companies to identify and evaluate the methods actually used to communicate their policies, objectives, and positions at the federal level. Table 12 summarizes the percentages of companies employing different techniques, and Table 13 ranks the importance of these different activities in influencing federal legislation, using a scale of 1 (low impact) to 5 (high impact). In Table 13, we have calculated the mean for each activity and listed the activities in descending order of importance as perceived by the survey respondents. The importance

Table 11. Types of Washington Presence

Types of Presence	Percentage of Respondents Utilizing this Type of Presence
Trade Association	67.8
Frequent Visits to Washington by Senior Executives	58.4
Company Office in Washington	42.7
Washington Law Firm (as needed or on retainer)	38.0
Washington-based government relations counsel	11.9
Washington Public Relations Firm (as needed or on retainer)	8.6

Table 12. Methods Used to
Communicate Company Positions
and Influence Federal Legislation

Method Used	Percentage of Respondents Using the Method
Regular Correspondence	88.8
Lobbying	73.1
Political Action Committees	69.9
Employee Newsletters	63.3
Plant Visits	52.4
Economic Education Programs	33.9
Speaker's Bureaus	29.3
Issue Advertising	23.2

ascribed to lobbying is not surprising, but it is interesting to note how highly respondents regard regular correspondence and political action committees.

To add to this picture of federal government relations, we asked how effective companies thought they were at four kinds of activity in Washington. Respondents ranked their perceived effectiveness on a scale of 1 (low) to 5 (high), and the mean score for each activity was calculated. The following list is in descending order of perceived effectiveness:

Activity	Mean Rank
Serving as eyes and ears	4.0
Representing the company to regulatory agencies	3.4
Influencing proposed legislation	3.3
Influencing compliance with regulation	3.0

Note that the respondents ranked the monitoring function well above their more active influencing functions. This may be a measure of the public affairs professional's knowledge of his or her own limitations, and/or of the circumstances of modern public policy formulation. It is plausible that this also reflects what senior corporate managements are demanding of public affairs, namely, organizational intelligence.

A final question in the federal relations area asked respondents for a judgment on the influence of the "Washington presence" on *corporate* policy. Using the same 1 to 5 scale, the mean figure was only 3.1. Compared to the preceding mean ranks, it shows that respondents have, on the average, placed their influence on their own company's policy *below* their influence on federal policy.

Table 13. Perceived Effectiveness of
Methods Used to Influence
Federal Legislation

Method Used	Mean Rank*
Lobbying	4.4
Regular Correspondence	3.9
Political Action Committees	3.7
Employee Newsletters	3.3
Plant Visits	3.2
Issue Advertising	3.1
Economic Education Programs	2.9
Speakers' Bureaus	2.8

Note:
* 5 = high impact; 1 = low impact

In the survey, we asked a series of analogous questions about the structure and practice of state and local government relations. Space does not allow us to report the results in detail, but the patterns of growth and activity are similar to those at the federal level.

Public Affairs and Corporate Planning

Most companies reported the existence of a systematic strategic planning process, usually under the direction of a fairly small professional corporate planning staff. When asked to characterize their planning efforts, the companies replied as follows:

Nature of Planning Activities	Percentage of Respondents
Informal discussions among top management	10.6%
Formal, 1-year budgeting of financial data	15.7
Formal, 3–5 year budgeting of financial data	15.7
Formal, 3–5 year development of broad comprehensive strategies	58.0
	100.0%

When asked to say *how* public affairs influenced planning, companies responded as shown in Table 14. When asked to assess the actual *influence* these different activities had on the planning process; the firms replied as shown in Table 15 where we have ranked those activities in descending order of their perceived impact. Notably, the preparation of forecasts of social and political trends for either corporate-level planning units or operating units is rated one of the least effective methods to

Table 14.   Activities Used by Public Affairs to
Influence Corporate Planning

Activities Used by Public Affairs to Influence Corporate Planning	Percentage of Respondents Performing These Activities
Identify public issues for corporate attention	92.8
Set or help set priorities for these issues	78.5
Identify public issues for department, division, and/or subsidiary attention	74.2
Set or help set priorities for these issues	64.8
Provide forecasts of social/political trends to the corporate planning office	74.1
Provide forecasts of social/political trends to departments, divisions, and/or subsidiaries	73.0
Review corporate plans for sensitivity to emerging social/political trends	69.1
Prepare a narrative section regarding future social/political trends which is included with directions for preparing corporate plans	57.8
Review department, division, and/or subsidiary plans for sensitivity to emerging social/political trends	55.0

Table 15.   Perceived Influence of Public Affairs Activities
on Corporate Planning

Activity	Public Affairs Influence on Planning Mean Rank*
Identify public issues for corporate attention	3.5
Set or help set priorities for these issues	3.4
Identify public issues for departmental, division, and/or subsidiary attention	3.3
Set or help set priorities for these issues	3.2
Review corporate plans for sensitivity to emerging social/political trends	3.0
Review department, division, and/or subsidiary plans for sensitivity to emerging social/political trends	2.8
Provide forecasts of social/political trends to the corporate planning office	2.8
Provide forecasts of social/political trends to departments, divisions, and/or subsidiaries	2.7
Prepare a narrative section regarding future social/political trends which is included with directions for preparing corporate plans	2.5

Note:
* 5 = high; 1 = low

influence planning, and yet nearly three-fourths of the respondents continue to provide such forecasts.

Presumably, the incorporation of social and political awareness into the corporate planning process forms a critical step in the evolution of an organization that is responsive to its external environment. As firms come to recognize the increasing turbulence and complexity of their environments, this awareness should influence both the near term management of public issues and longer term strategic thinking about the attractiveness of particular industries and lines of business. According to our survey, nearly all respondents reported having *some* influence on the future course of the organization. Nevertheless, when asked what actions would improve the effectiveness of the public affairs function, many pointed to the establishment of a closer working relationship with corporate planning staffs. As our data suggest, enhancing the relationship between public affairs and corporate planning remains an important step in improving the overall responsiveness of the enterprise to a changing environment.

Managing Emerging Issues

We also sought to learn more about how companies go about the near-term management of "emerging issues," i.e., issues deemed to importantly affect the company within the next 3 years or so. Nearly 65 percent of our respondents reported organized efforts to manage such issues, and Table 16 shows the techniques employed in descending order of their frequency of use. However, as we noted previously, frequency of use cannot necessarily be equated with effectiveness.

Our results in this area remain ambiguous. Even though our data indicate that new tools such as issue managers and formal scanning systems are being tried, practitioners and researchers need to look more closely at how current experiments are working and at how they can be improved and brought into wider use. Further study is needed to show which techniques are most useful under varying circumstances and how such techniques can be effectively integrated with public affairs management and overall planning and operations.

Public Affairs and Management Policy

Most public affairs departments appeared to have some involvement in their company's response to shareholder resolutions, and the forms of that involvement are shown in Table 17. Notably, however, fewer were involved in substantive negotiations with resolution sponsors (19.1 percent), monitoring internal operations (26.5 percent), or designing and coordinating responsive internal programs (36.4 percent) than simply

Table 16.   Techniques Used to Manage Emerging Issues
in Descending Order of Frequency of Use

Techniques	Mean Rank*
Monitoring emerging issues	4.1
Lobbying within trade associations	4.0
Scanning to detect emerging issues	3.9
Communicate company positions to managers	3.9
Lobbying at the federal level	3.9
Lobbying at the state/local levels	3.9
Communicate company positions to government agencies	3.8
Communicate company positions to employees	3.4
Use of issue manager	3.1
Change company information systems	3.0
Change company policies	2.9
Interdepartmental Public Affairs issue research committees	2.9
Communicate company positions to the general public	2.9
Change company or subunit objectives	2.9
Communicate company positions to stockholders	2.9
Change company reward and penalty systems	2.3

Note:
* 5 = most frequent; 1 = least frequent

preparing externally oriented presentations for annual meetings (70.3 percent), shareholders (66.5 percent), and institutional investors (42.9 percent). Although not definitive, these data suggest that either public affairs units are not expected to aid in the development and implementation of internally oriented programs which respond to shareholders or that they have not been effective in such roles. Further research on how

Table 17.   Public Affairs Responsibilities in Responding
to Shareholder Resolutions

Activity	Percentage of Respondents Indicating Public Affairs Responsibility
Preparation of presentations for the annual meeting	70.3
Preparation of written responses for shareholders	66.5
Preparation of analysis for management	54.4
Preparation of presentations for institutional investors	42.9
Designing and/or coordinating any internal programs designed to respond to the resolution(s)	36.4
Preparation of analysis for the board of directors	34.7
Monitoring internal corporate operations as a response to the resolution(s)	26.5
Negotiating with sponsors of the resolution(s)	19.1

and to what extent public affairs can and should contribute to such internally oriented implementation efforts seems appropriate.

Insofar as "other" participants in public affairs and management policy were concerned, we found that a public affairs committee, whether at the Board or senior management level, had been established by fewer than one-fourth of our respondents. Where committees did exist, however, it was interesting to note the breadth of their membership—primarily outside directors at the Board level and key staff and operating managers at the corporate level.

The Effectiveness of Public Affairs

The survey also included a number of questions, some open-ended, that were designed to probe for comments on how the effectiveness of the public affairs function was measured. Of the many criteria offered by the respondents, the three categories most often cited (in descending order of frequency) were:

1. *Measures of Audience Response to Communications Efforts.* This criterion included all survey measures of opinion, but it also included less formal judgments about audience response. A key phrase used to describe this was "Acceptance of our views by the public."
2. *Results of Lobbying Efforts.* This criterion included all those respondents who described any outcome of lobbying effort (whether passage, defeat, or modification of legislation or regulations) as their standard of achievement.
3. *Financial or Competitive Impact of Effort.* This criterion included all indications that public affairs was concerned with whether or not it reduced the firm's costs, increased its profits, protected a line of business, or otherwise favorably influenced the "bottom line."

When asked to note changes they would make to improve the effectiveness of public affairs within their organizations, those surveyed most commonly replied as follows:

1. Integration of public affairs into one department.
2. Additional staff and/or budget.
3. Direct reporting to the chief executive officer.
4. Education and involvement of operating managers in public affairs.
5. A more significant role for public affairs in company decision-making process.

It should be noted, however, that a significant number of respondents were frankly skeptical about the measurability of public affairs effectiveness. This and the fact that there exists a broad spectrum of effectiveness criteria (we were able to reduce the categories to no less than thirteen) suggests a continuing need to more closely evaluate measurements of effectiveness for public affairs (and perhaps similar staff organizations).

FOURTH STAGE: PRESENTATION OF FINDINGS

In order to get early reactions to our survey data, we scheduled a one-day "de-briefing" to which we invited a representative from each of the respondent companies. At the seminar, copies of our printed report were distributed and preliminary findings based on the data were presented.

Discussion of our observations and interpretations by the survey participants was then encouraged. From the dialogue, we developed additional insights into the meaning and limitations of our data. We also had suggested to us many new avenues of inquiry to pursue, and were even offered additional research sites to visit as well as expressions of interest in providing continued financial support. In sum, the process of checking the validity of our findings with those people surveyed appeared to be an enormously enriching step in the research process.

From that point on, we proceeded in conventional fashion to prepare several publications and presentations describing our work and results. In addition, new materials for Boston University's Management Policy courses are being developed and plans have been made for an executive development program in the area of public affairs management. In time, this may lead to the establishment of a Masters level elective course and ultimately the preparation of a book-length monograph.

FIFTH STAGE: CONSOLIDATION AND SELECTIVE CONTINUATION

Although our research has already produced these "end products," the survey results have yet to be fully analyzed and a series of specific analyses is being undertaken to more closely examine other aspects of the data. Our research plans include the following:

- *Industry Studies.* Analyses of public affairs patterns by industry and industry sector should provide useful profiles of public affairs practice in industries of varying characteristics.
- *Washington Offices.* Seventy-five percent of the firms surveyed responded to questions about the operation and management of

Washington offices. These data will be separately analyzed and reported.

- *Public Affairs and Corporate Planning.* A more detailed examination of how companies gather and utilize information about government's actions and decisions as an input to the companies' strategic planning processes will be undertaken.
- *Key Characteristics.* The data base is sufficiently large to permit some of the first studies of variations in public affairs practice by size of firm, type of technology, concentration of industry, regulatory characteristics, and geographic location.

Moreover, the survey results will be complemented in the future by more interviews with public affairs practitioners and additional, detailed studies of public affairs practice in a number of case research sites. This should facilitate further interpretation of the survey data and lead to even more refined studies of the public affairs function.

CONCLUSIONS AND IMPLICATIONS

Looking back on our experience to date, several features stand out as relevant to either large- or small-scale efforts to research issues pertaining to corporate social performance and policy.

1. It is of paramount importance that researchers pick problems of interest and relevance to practicing managers. These managers and their enthusiasm for the research can lead to critical forms of support, such as responding to questionnaires, making organizations available for clinical field research, reviewing and reacting to proposals, providing contacts, and even underwriting expenses.
2. There are numerous sources of information available to researchers, simply for the asking. Companies, trade and professional associations, and government agencies—to name but a few—have a great deal to offer by way of both raw data and informed opinions. As a consequence, many good research topics can come directly from the field. They do not necessarily have to emerge, fully formed, from the management literature alone.
3. Increasingly, researchers should think of private funding sources. Not only is there typically less paperwork involved, but with expected cutbacks in government funding, there simply are fewer alternatives. To offset the risk of having research inappropriately influenced by single sources of funding, multiple contributors or

foundations could be sought out. A blend of public and private financing would be ideal.

4.   Finally, in this field, as in many others of a policy nature, there is as yet a great deal of "messiness" which must be both tolerated and managed. Elegant research designs and methodologies are likely to be less appropriate than rather simple, crude approaches. Nevertheless, if researchers are interested in working at this frontier of corporate social performance and policy research, they will be helped by a willingness to embrace multiple research methodologies and alternate between inductive and deductive analyses. Our literature review helped us deductively establish some propositions about what we should be looking for and what we might find in the field. It thereby helped us see the value of clinical field research. Our inductive analysis of the case studies gave us a framework with which to more precisely organize our thinking about public affairs. It thus enabled us to develop a relatively comprehensive and sophisticated questionnaire. And the questionnaire responses, in turn, represented a large data base from which we could deductively (and with more statistical precision) analyze hypothosized relationships. In general, this alternation between deductive and inductive reasoning allowed us to refine and test theoretical models in light of empirical evidence.

Much remains to be done. The growth and significance of corporate public affairs activities which our survey has documented, as well as the variety of management approaches and the complexity of challenges for management in the public affairs area, underscore the importance of this field for continuing research.

ACKNOWLEDGMENTS

The Public Affairs Research Group was formed in 1978 to conduct research on the corporation-society relationship and the management of corporate external affairs. Faculty involved in the research described in this article include James E. Post, Edwin A. Murray, Jr., Robert B. Dickie, John F. Mahon, and Michael Jones, Research Associate.

NOTE

1.   These data are summarized more fully in *Public Affairs Offices and Their Functions: Summary of Survey Responses* (Public Affairs Research Program, Boston University School of Management, Boston, MA 02215).

REFERENCES

Ackerman, Robert W., *The Social Challenge to Business*. Cambridge, Massachusetts: Harvard University Press, 1975.

Aguilar, F. J., *Scanning the Business Environment*. New York: MacMillan, 1976.

Bauer, Raymond A., "The Corporate Response Process." In Preston, Lee E. (ed.), *Research in Corporate Social Performance and Policy*, vol. 1. JAI Press, Inc., Greenwich, Connecticut: 1978, pp. 99–122.

Brown, James K., *This Business of Issues; Coping with the Company's Environments*. New York: The Conference Board, 1979.

Child, John, "Commentary on Strategy Formulation: A Social and Political Process." In Schendel, Dan E. and Charles W. Hofer (eds.), *Strategic Management: A New View of Business Policy and Planning*, Little, Brown and Company, Boston: 1979, pp. 172–179.

McGrath, Phyllis, *Action Plans for Public Affairs*. New York: The Conference Board, 1977.

———, *Managing Corporate External Relations: Changing Perspectives and Responses*. New York: The Conference Board, 1976.

———, *Redefining Federal Corporate Relations*. New York: The Conference Board, 1979.

Parsons, Talcott, *Structure and Process in Modern Societies*. New York: The Free Press, 1960.

Post, James E., "Research on Patterns of Corporate Response to Social Change." In Preston, Lee E. (ed.), *Research in Corporate Social Performance and Policy*, vol. 1. JAI Press, Inc. Greenwich, Connecticut: 1978, pp. 55–77.

Preston, Lee E., and James E. Post, *Private Management and Public Policy*. Englewood Cliffs, New Jersey: Prentice-Hall, 1975.

Thompson, James D., *Organization in Action*. New York: McGraw-Hill, 1976.

Utterback, James M., "Environmental Analysis and Forecasting." In Schendel, Dan E., and Charles W. Hofer (eds.), *Strategic Management: A New View of Business Policy and Planning*, Little Brown and Company, Boston, 1979, pp. 134–143.

Wheelwright, Steven C., and Robert L. Banks, "Involving Operating Managers in Planning Process Evolution." *Sloan Management Review* (Summer, 1979): 45–59.

ETHICAL INVESTMENT POLICIES AND ACTIVITIES OF CATHOLIC RELIGIOUS ORDERS

Richard E. Wokutch

In recent years, universities, foundations, church groups, mutual funds, and labor unions with pension funds have attempted to determine how these funds can be best used to promote their social or ethical concerns, as well as to achieve their economic objectives (*Newsweek*, 1978; Lublin, 1980; Kennedy, 1975; and *Business and Society Review,* 1976). While some of these institutional investors have decided that the pursuit of a maximum rate of return to support programmatic activities is the appropriate goal, others have embarked on a much more activist role, communicating with management, filing shareholder resolutions, divesting stock from certain companies and investing in other companies to influence company policy. The Interfaith Center on Corporate Responsibility (ICCR) reports a steady growth in the submission of socially oriented resolutions to corporations over the last five years. In 1975

Research in Corporate Social Performance and Policy, Vol. 4, pages 157–188
Copyright © 1982 by JAI Press Inc.
All rights of reproduction in any form reserved.
ISBN: 0-89232-259-4

church groups submitted such resolutions to 23 companies, in 1976 to 40 companies, and in 1977 to 56 companies. In 1978, 61 resolutions were submitted to 47 companies; in 1979, 82 resolutions were submitted to 62 companies; and in 1980, 104 resolutions were submitted to 81 companies (ICCR, 1980). Meanwhile, the objectives, activities, and impacts of this movement have been both acclaimed and condemned (Nickel, 1979; Purcell, 1979, 1980).

This paper reports the results of a survey of the "ethical investment" policies and activities[1] of one group of institutional investors with overt moral and ethical concerns—Catholic religious orders. The purpose of the survey was to determine: (1) whether or not these orders were guided by any explicit ethical investment policy, and if so, its nature and means of implementation; (2) the extent and nature of the orders' ethical investment activities; and (3) the relative importance of various sources of corporate social performance information for the orders in making their investment decisions. Before considering the data collected on these points, a brief review of the historical and theoretical context of various institutional investor participation in ethical investment activities is presented.

ETHICAL INVESTMENT: THE BACKGROUND

Eastman Kodak and General Motors were two early targets of organized stockholder movements. Kodak was asked in 1966 to hire minority workers screened by "FIGHT," a local civil rights group. (Sethi, 1971). When management refused, a national campaign was initiated to urge Kodak stockholders to withhold proxy votes from management at the annual stockholders meeting. In 1970 Campaign G.M. succeeded in placing shareholder resolutions regarding product safety, pollution control, operations in South Africa, and corporate governance on the company's annual proxy statement. In both of these cases the percentages of stockholder votes withheld or voted against management were small (generally less than 3 percent). However, supporters claimed credit for subsequent changes which the companies made pertaining to these issues.

These and several other confrontations around the same time marked a turning point in many institutions' investment policies. Previously institutional investors (and especially religious institutions) generally adopted a considerably more passive role with respect to corporate social issues. As far back as the late 1800s some churches simply avoided investments in certain industries, notably tobacco and liquor, on moral grounds (Powers, 1971). Questions about the ethics of investments were raised in the 1930s by the churches, but at that time it was decided by many that ethical concerns could best be advanced by seeking a maximum return on investment and using income for funding appropriate programs. This is still a popular argument against more direct ethical investment activities.

When this issue was once again taken up or thrust upon institutional investors in the late sixties and early seventies, several institutions undertook extensive studies of this issue which bear reviewing. Comprehensive studies were conducted at Princeton (Malkiel and Quandt, 1971), Yale (Simon, Powers, and Gunneman, 1972), MIT and Harvard (Longstreth and Rosenbloom, 1973), as well as by several churches and church-related groups (Powers, 1971).

In these studies, there is quite a bit of disagreement concerning the most effective way for an institutional investor to impress its ethical concerns upon management. The available options can be grouped into eight general categories:

1. Declining to invest in certain corporations or industries.
2. Divesting any existing holdings in certain corporations.
3. Purposely investing in certain corporations, industries, or projects because of their likely desirable social effects.
4. Directly communicating with management, urging it to change certain policies.
5. Proposing shareholder resolutions pertaining to ethical issues or supporting those proposed by others.
6. Initiating or joining in litigation against management.
7. Voting to unseat management.
8. Publicizing opposition to management.

Simon, et al. (1972) presents a detailed discussion of these strategies. Only the points most pertinent to this discussion are considered here.

Strategies 4–8 are frequently viewed as alternatives to the invest/divest/don't invest range of options. There are also indications that some investors combine these strategies in various ways, such as buying stock in a corporation to establish legal grounds for engaging in other activities (e.g., Campaign GM), or publicizing opposition to management in conjunction with any of the other strategies. The existence of these various alternatives and combinations of options has many implications for this study. In particular it precludes the possibility of simply comparing an institutional investor's expressed ethical concerns to its portfolio to determine the degree to which investments are made on the basis of these concerns. The ethical investment policy of the institution must first be identified (if any exists) before its specific investment practices can be analyzed.

Strategy 1 has been traditionally used by certain churches which have declined to invest in firms in the tobacco and liquor industries. Simon, et al. (1972) however, contend that declining to invest in a particular corporation will not influence management's actions. It simply enables the potential investor to remain disassociated from a corporation perceived to be morally objectionable. This may be correct in general; but, it does seem possible to envision certain circumstances in which a significant amount of potential investment funds could be used to induce certain managerial actions. To be effective though, it would seem necessary to communicate to management the conditions for investing or the reasons for not investing.

While many of those concerned with ethical issues in investments advocate divestment of stock in companies with whose policies one disagrees, Powers (1971) contends that stock prices are essentially unaffected by non-economic decisions to sell stock. Furthermore, even if stock prices were driven down, he continues, this would affect management in only two ways: in its ability to secure funds and in shareholder confidence in management as this relates to retaining/replacing them. Powers argues that these factors would not take on great importance if it were known they were due to non-economic factors.

Related to this is the question of whether or not investing on the basis of ethical criteria will result in lower rates of financial return to the institutions. Conflicting evidence has been presented on this point. Malkiel and Quandt (1971), for example, reported that Princeton's investments in firms with operations in Southern Africa had a nearly 3 percent higher rate of return than did their other investments. In the same vein, Vance (1975) provided evidence that "socially irresponsible" firms exhibit better stock market performance than "socially responsible" firms. On the other hand, Moscowitz (1972) (and some respondents to this survey) argued that "socially responsible" firms are better financial investments. Finally, Alexander and Buchholz (1978) argue that there is no relationship between social responsibility and stock market performance. In any event it is clear that brokerage expenses could be substantial to investors selling off their stock in "irresponsible" firms. For example, Newsweek (1978) estimated that the brokerage fees for Harvard, Princeton or Yale to divest themselves of all their stock in companies with investments in South Africa would exceed $500,000 for each institution.

If it is the case that ethical investments represent a financial sacrifice, some interesting questions arise concerning whether the investing institutions can legally make these investments. Most institutional investors are subject to a restriction known as the "prudent man rule." By this, the trustee is required to act as if he/she were managing his/her own funds for the purpose of ensuring the capital and the regularity and size of the flow of dividends of the investment. It is not clear from the rule what activities are outlawed, but it is possible that deliberate choice of a lower-than-necessary rate of return would be illegal.

An issue on which these studies all seem to agree is that there are great difficulties in determining which are the ethical (or "socially responsible") and which are the unethical (or "socially irresponsible") firms. Firms exhibit varied performance along a number of dimensions, such as pollution control, minority hiring, consumer and employee safety, defense contracting, and investments in countries with repressive governments. Thus, the development of an overall assessment of the "ethical" or "socially responsible" status of a corporation is a formidable task. Even in considering only one specific dimension, many difficulties arise in separating the heroes from the villians. For example, there are differing views on whether Blacks in South Africa would be better off if corporations withdrew their investments from that country; recent court cases have questioned the legality and social desirability of preferential hiring and promoting of women and Blacks; and even Dow Chemical, villified during the Viet Nam War, justified its production of napalm as part of its social responsibility to support the government. Despite these problems, researchers and investors continue their attempts to differentiate "socially responsible" from "socially irresponsible" firms.

An approach to corporate social performance assessment which has received much attention in recent years is that of the corporate social audit. One type of social audit is the social impact audit which attempts to evaluate the overall effect of the corporation on society by measuring the social contributions (benefits) and social detriments (costs) arising from the firm's operations. But a problem arises in determining which aspects of corporate operations should be considered:

> Pollution and the hiring and promotion of minorities (including women) receive a roughly consistent priority but after that, things are fairly wide open. Some auditors virtually ignore corporate giving and community programs; others include them. Quite a few stress consumerist issues of various kinds, others go heavy on munitions manufacturing, or investments in South Africa or Portugal. Still others focus on employee well-being—fringe benefits, promotion opportunities and so forth. (Bauer and Fenn, 1973, p. 40)

In response to this problem some researchers have suggested the use of a social process audit approach which would investigate how well a particular socially oriented program is being carried out with respect to its own goals (Blake, Frederick, and Myers, 1976). While this would be useful for the internal management of these programs, it would have limited utility to outside observers (such as ethical investors) who may not share the same goals for the program. In addition, for the purpose of guiding ethical investment activities, the process audit would need to be conducted in a particular corporation on all the programs in which the investor is concerned. Moreover, these audits would have to be carried out on a large enough sample of companies to permit interfirm comparisons by the investor. Clearly this will not be carried out overnight, and the ethical investor is left with few critera. An ultimate objective of this research effort is the development of a value-based social audit methodology which would allow corporate social performance evaluations based on the evaluator's (e.g. investor's) own criteria of social responsibility (Wokutch and Fahey, 1981).

SAMPLE AND METHODOLOGY

The population for this study was Catholic religious orders of priests, nuns, and brothers in the United States. This group was chosen because of the relative lack of constraints on their activities in this area from legal sources (i.e., the prudent man rule) or from more diversely motivated constituencies such as those of universities, banks, pension funds, insurance companies and mutual funds.[2] In addition, their perceived interest in this subject and the fact that the survey was funded by a religious order led to an expectation of a high rate of participation in the survey.

Copies of the questionnaire (see Appendix I) were mailed to 780 "major superiors" of most of the leading Catholic religious orders in the U.S., who were asked to give these to their treasurers. With two mailings, responses were received from 141 treasurers. Of these, 11 indicated a willingness to participate further in this study and were interviewed by phone. The effective coverage is actually higher than the apparent 18 percent response rate, because of the variety of organizational structures of the orders. A major superior may head an entire order or a province of that order, or an abbey, monastery, or other legal/canonical grouping. The provinces, abbeys, and so forth, have varying degrees of autonomy (especially financial) from the order. Thus, in a number of cases, nonresponses indicated that there was no investment portfolio at that organizational level. On the other hand, a response from the treasurer of an order might provide the information on the investment activities of all the provinces, abbeys, etc. comprising the order. For the sake of brevity, all the respondents to our survey will be referred to as "orders" in the remainder of this paper.

It is worth speculating on the representativeness of those orders which responded. There are two potential sources of bias among the respondents; but these may cancel each other out. Orders interested and involved in ethical investing would seem to be more likely than others to respond to the questionnaire. However, due to the open-ended nature of some of the questions, answering the questionnaire took considerably more time and effort for these more involved orders. In fact, feedback from some non-responding orders indicated that this was the reason for their non-response. It is possible that the former factor was stronger than the latter and that this sample is more involved in ethical investment activities than the population as a whole. But at the very least, this survey would shed some light on the activities of the more involved orders.

SURVEY RESULTS

The responses to the survey clearly reveal that there is a wide variance among the orders as to:

1. The extent of ownership of corporate stock and their views on the appropriateness of such ownership;
2. The content of their policies (or lack of them) with respect to ethical investment activities and how these policies are implemented; and
3. The degree of sophistication the orders have reached in their consideration of ethical investment issues.

Major findings with respect to each of these points are discussed in turn.

Extent of Stock Ownership

Although this survey did not seek information on the *extent* of orders' stockholdings,[3] it was nevertheless apparent from the responses and other sources that there is a wide variance among them in this respect. Responding orders ranged in size from those with hundreds of members to one with only eight. The financial resources and, more specifically, the stock ownership of these orders varied with their size, as well as their philosophies regarding how to live out their "spirit of poverty." Of the 141 responding orders, 25 volunteered the information that they had no holdings of corporate stock. The most widely cited reason was that the order was too small or too poor to afford it. The remainder cited the avoidance of risk (on economic as well as ethical grounds) as the reason. These 25 orders are included in the tabulated results of this survey since six of these non-investing orders engaged in broadly defined "ethical investment activities" (such as, declining to invest for ethical reasons, communicating with management, or assisting others in their ethical investment activities), In accordance with their desires for risk minimization, a number of orders—both those with and those without stockholdings—indicated that they placed all or a portion of their funds not needed for current expenses in government bonds or highly rated corporate bonds. Many also mentioned that a sizeable portion of their funds were lent to charitable institutions, for example through the purchase of bonds issued by Catholic hospitals, old age homes, and so forth.

Despite the poverty of some orders and the avoidance of stock ownership by others, the extent of stock ownership by some groups is substantial. The ICCRs 1980 edition of *Corporate Proxy Resolutions* lists the number of shares owned by religious orders in the companies with which the orders were sponsoring or supporting shareholder resolutions during 1980. Twenty-eight orders[4] with 1000 or more shares in one or more of these 84 corporations are so listed. Nine of these 28 orders had more than 10,000 shares of all 84 companies combined, and two orders each had close to 90,000 shares in these 84 companies combined. Undoubtedly these orders also owned substantial numbers of shares in companies for which no resolutions were filed. The total value of securities in American corporations owned by "Christian Churches" (such as, Catholic religious orders and dioceses along with Prostestant congregations) was placed at over $15 billion in 1977 (Catholic Church Investments for Corporate Social Responsibility, 1978). Another estimate placed the value of private holdings of cash and securities of American Catholic orders at $150 million in 1971 (Gollin, 1971). These "private holdings" are separate from holdings of order-affiliated institutions such as universities and hospitals.

While the above is by no means a precise measure of the orders' financial resources, it is suggestive. It indicates that religious groups' sponsorship of shareholder resolutions cannot be dismissed as the work of a few troublemakers with a couple of shares of stock. Evidence from the survey responses also suggests that these stockholdings are by no means speculative ventures to be used capriciously. The orders do rely on these investments both to support current activities and to provide for the long term security of their members.

Ethical Investment Policy

Participants in the survey were first asked whether or not their order had developed *any* policy towards the use of its investments and/or financial resources to achieve social goals. Affirmative answers were given by 62 of 135 orders responding to this question (46 percent). Several other orders said they were developing such a policy, with some indicating that this survey had prompted them to do so. A much higher number (104, or 74 percent) indicated that their investment activities are influenced in one way or another by ethical or corporate social responsibility considerations.[5]

The reported ethical investment policies varied greatly in terms of complexity and the apparent sophistication in the analysis of the issues involved. Many were relatively vague statements concerning the orders' intentions to use their financial resources in a "responsible" or "just" way, or to tell their investment counselors to invest only in "socially responsible" firms. Along these lines, one order stated that they had instructed their broker "not to even propose investments for our consideration unless the company is trying to be just."

On the other hand, 31 orders attached formal policy statements on the use of their financial resources; and most of these showed careful consideration of the issues involved in ethical investing. One such policy statement is reproduced in Appendix II. As is common for these statements, this one ties investment policy to the mission of the order. It is more specific than many in spelling out the criteria of "ethical" corporate conduct; and it notes that these criteria are given to the fiduciary institutions managing the order's investments. Also typical of the orders surveyed, this order relies on various church-related groups, the media, and the corporations themselves to provide the information needed to make decisions on these matters. This order also expects their fiduciary institutions to be aware of public criticism of corporations and to consult them before investing in or divesting from such firms.

This policy statement and all others received avoid the question of how one measures such ethical performance dimensions as protecting human rights or correcting exploitive practices in the Third World. However, the National Council of Churches has developed guidelines for investments which explicitly deal with these and other policy implementation questions (Corporate Examiner, 1973). Five orders specifically cited the National Council of Churches' guidelines as references for their own ethical investment policy formulation/implementation. Given the availability of this document, it is likely that the other orders which have developed policies in this area have been influenced by it as well. These National Council of Churches' guidelines themselves are largely based on the studies by Simon, et al., (1972) and Powers, (1972).

Those 31 orders which attached policy statements on the use of their investments and/or financial resources to achieve social goals comprise an interesting subset of the survey sample, since they have obviously given these matters serious thought before receiving the questionnaire. All of these statements either explicitly call for (24) or implicitly allow (7) ethical investment activities; and all 31 orders had engaged in one or more such activities. This indicates that no order in the sample (at least no order willing to admit to it) had developed a formal policy statement directing them to seek a maximum rate of return on investment to support their own programs, without regard to the nature of the investment. These 31 orders can be assumed to represent relatively sophisticated ethical investors, and their activities are given special attention in this analysis.

Most of the orders which indicated that they had not undertaken any ethical investing activity gave no reasons or explanations. However, the few that did give reasons are worth considering since the same three reasons were commonly cited and may be representative of the other orders as well:

1. They did not have the time or expertise to distinguish "socially responsible" from "socially irresponsible" corporations.
2. They did not have enough money or stock for them to be concerned with the issue.
3. They were in such a tight financial situation that they were unable to consider issues other than financial return.

The issue of lack of information or expertise regarding corporate social performance is one that was repeatedly raised by orders that engaged in ethical investment activities as well. As one order put it, they were frustrated by their "inability to know" regarding these issues. The procedures some orders have instituted to help alleviate this problem are discussed later in this paper.

With respect to the second reason, it is worth noting that other orders with few or no shares of stock nevertheless participate in ethical investment activities. Even a large order with a sizeable portfolio is likely to have only a tiny fraction of the outstanding shares of a particular corporation. Apparently these orders feel there is some value in attempting to sway other stockholders and ultimately to influence management. Moreover, even if they have no ultimate effect on the corporation, some orders feel it is nevertheless important to take a stand on an issue or to disassociate themselves from certain situations.

The reason of financial need preventing orders from engaging in ethical investment activities is clearly a relevant concern for all orders. In times of inflation and high unemployment, orders are likely to have more difficulty meeting expenses with income from donations and members' own paid employment. The same conditions compound the orders' problems with recruitment of new members and the resulting increase in the percentages of retired/non-working members. As indicated previously, orders may rely on income from investments to cover operating deficits and to provide for their retired members. Thus, some orders feel that they can't afford to allow any considerations other than financial to influence their investment decisions. Other orders in similar circumstances have of course made different choices. Several, however, indicated their beliefs that "socially responsible" firms made better financial investments, essentially making the "enlightened self-interest" argument for corporate social responsibility.

Another point of interest is the great variance and intensity of unsolicited comments regarding the value of this research. Most were very supportive, with many stating that they would pray for its success. Most orders (101) also requested results of the study (including several which declined to answer the questionnaire) to help in their own formulation of policy in this area. Other orders, however, indicated that they felt that this research was a waste of time and money. One order questioned whether the funds for the printing and mailing of the questionnaire could not have been better spent "to feed the starving people of Cambodia or to support the inspiring work of Mother Theresa rather than adding to the proliferation of paper-work and bureaucracy with which we have all been inundated." These comments illustrate the orders' belief that their "moral authority" is significant even if their financial clout is not. The external credibility of their stands on ethical matters explains why these investors have been a force to be reckoned with by corporate managers.

Implementation

Religious orders have sometimes been accused of oversimplifying corporate social responsibility issues. In the recent *Fortune* article entitled, "The Corporation Haters," Herman Nickel claimed that:

> In order to attract broad support, the church activists have chosen to present business-related issues as morally clear-cut and simple—when in fact they are usually complex, morally ambiguous and involve difficult policy trade-offs. (1980, p. 128).

In this study, there was evidence of naivete or oversimplification in the responses of a few orders. For example, one order stated that their policy was to avoid corporations that they know are "violating practices of justice;" but noted that, "It is difficult however in some instances where big corporations are involved, for in essence it seems that the multinationals are contrary to justice." Another order stated that *since* it had not as yet developed an ethical investment policy; it simply supported any ethically-oriented proxy resolution that was proposed by another order. Purcell (1981) has indicated that this approach of "tagging along" with whatever proposals were initiated by other orders or by the ICCR may be even more common than the orders were willing to admit in this survey. The majority of the orders' responses, however, reflected a recognition of the complexity of the issues involved and avoided sweeping generalizations such as the above. This was especially true for those orders which were the most active in ethical investment matters and those with formal policy statements on these activities.

In most cases the responsibility for implementing the orders' investment policy (and ethical investment policy in particular) is delegated to the treasurer or a similarly-titled individual. The orders usually also utilize external investment managers who have varying degrees of discretion in making investment decisions. In many cases the treasurer provides the investment manager with a general set of financial, and in some cases, ethical objectives.

There was concern expressed by some orders however that the investment managers were either incapable of or had little interest in carrying out policies like "invest only in socially responsible/just corporations." This problem has led some orders to develop more specific "ethical" investment policy statements such as the one in Appendix II, and to share them with their external investment managers. Even with such policy statements, a considerable amount of responsibility is placed on the investment counselor to distinguish "ethical" from "unethical" firms. When a new issue arises (e.g., the infant formula controversy) some orders will take up the specific matter with their investment counselors. Orders desiring to have more input on a day to day basis have delegated members or committees the responsibility to work with investment managers in selecting stocks and in exercising their rights of stock ownership. In one case a lay person was hired on a full-time basis to explore ethical investment issues.

To determine how widespread the decision-making process was within the orders concerning ethical investment activities, treasurers were asked how members other than those with primary responsibility for implementing the ethical investment activities could participate in this process. Forty-three of 141 responding orders had some type of routine procedure (that is, occurring more than once a year) for providing feedback to the members and/or encouraging input from them regarding their ethical investment activities. These came in the form of regular reports in the orders' newsletters or the activities of standing committees/study groups concerned with this issue. The other 98 reported their activities in this area to their members yearly, informally, or not at all; and they provided for member participation in decision-making on an ad-hoc or interest-only basis, if at all. In general there seems to be an openness to wider member participation in ethical investment activities, but there do not appear to be an overwhelming number of members (or even a majority) who want to be actively involved in these matters.

Overall, there seems to be considerable evidence that the great majority of the orders with corporate securities have decided that these securities can be an important vehicle for promoting their ethical concerns. Most orders, however, also appear to recognize that the issues involved in acting upon these concerns can be very complex. Those orders which have developed policy statements and instituted procedures for dealing with ethical investment issues appear to have clarified the issues for themselves better than those which have not done this.

CORPORATE SOCIAL PERFORMANCE
INFORMATION SOURCES

Since the lack of information on corporate social performance was so prominently cited as a deterrent to the development and implementation of an ethical investment policy, it is interesting to consider the orders' perceptions of the value of various sources of this information. The treasurers were asked to rate the importance of various sources (see Table 1) of corporate social performance information. Of the 141 responding orders, 121 rated these information sources. The aggregated responses, separated into those of the more "sophisticated" and less "sophisticated" respondents, are shown in Table 1.

Organizations concerned with corporate social performance were clearly the most important source of information for both groups of orders. Interestingly, every information source except investment counselors received a higher importance rating by those orders which supplied policy statements than by those which did not, perhaps indicating the greater awareness by the former concerning these matters. The lower

Table 1. Sources of Corporate Social Performance Information

	Aggregated ratings[a] (rank in parenthesis)	
	Orders Supplying Formal Ethical Investment Policy Statements	Other Orders
Organizations concerned with corporate social performance	1.48 (1)	2.15 (1)
Other (than business) newspapers and magazines	2.61 (2)	3.22 (5)
Business periodicals and newspapers	2.77 (3)	3.08 (3)
Corporate annual reports and other business publications	2.90 (4)	3.14 (4)
Television and radio	3.16 (5)	3.67 (6)
Word-of-mouth	3.35 (6)	3.75 (7)
Investment counselors	3.61 (7)	3.03 (2)
Federal government	3.84 (8)	3.90 (8)

Note:
[a] Ratings based on a 5-point scale where 1 indicates "extremely important," 5 "of very little use." In computing the results, blanks were assigned a rating of 5. Number of responses to this question: 121.

rating of investment counselors may reflect the previously noted distrust on the part of some orders of the interest and competence of such counselors on ethical investment matters.

Respondents were also asked to specify those organizations or other sources from which they received their information. Those which were mentioned by three or more orders are listed on Table 2. Of the 121 useable responses, 68 specified a *particular* group or other source for corporate social performance information; 38 different groups or sources were so specified. The most frequently cited were the National Catholic Coalition for Responsible Investment (NCCRI), or one of its 14 constituent groups, and the Interfaith Center on Corporate Responsibility (ICCR). Those which listed specific organizations or other sources which applied social performance information listed, on the average, 2.2 such sources.

ETHICAL INVESTMENT ACTIVITIES

Respondents were asked to describe their ethical investment activities in the preceding five years in each of the eight previously cited categories. They were asked to name the corporations with respect to which these activities were undertaken and the reason(s) for this. Cases in which corporations were named but no reason was given were classified by the researcher where the reason was obvious, or were placed in an "unspecified" or "other" category. Multiple proposals to a company initiated or supported by a given order are listed separately.

Tables 3 through 6 report the survey responses with respect to various ethical investment activities. Table 7 contrasts the participation in ethical investment activities by the more sophisticated respondents which attached formal policy statements with those which did not.

Table 2. Sources Providing Corporate Social Performance Information (Sources Mentioned by 3 or More Respondents)

Sources	Number of Mentions
National Catholic Coalition for Responsible Investment (NCCRI)	49
Interfaith Center on Corporate Responsibility (ICCR)	40
Network	7
Leadership Council of Women Religious, Conference of Major Superiors of Men, etc.	7
Informal communication with members of own and other orders	5
Investor Responsibility Research Center (IRRC)	3
Peace and Justice/Social Justice Committees	3
National Conference of Religious Treasurers	3
Number of orders citing specific sources	68

Divestment/Declining to Invest

Fifty-seven[6] of the 141 treasurers responding to the questionnaire reported at least one of these ethical investment activities. The slightly higher incidence of these activities among those orders which enclosed formal policy statements (45 percent), as compared to those which did not (39 percent), is probably not significant. These two activity categories are considered together in Table 3 since they represent two different modes of avoiding stock ownership in certain industries or corporations. As can be seen, there was a wide range of industries, corporations, or groups of corporations with common characteristics which were avoided for ethical reasons. The most frequently cited industries/groups were defense/armaments producers, firms dealing with South Africa, corporations with questionable activities in the Third World (especially selling infant formula), pharmaceutical companies selling birth control items, and firms engaged in or supporting unfair labor practices. A total of 26 corporations were individually cited. The most frequently mentioned were Dow Chemical, J. P. Stevens, American Home Products, and Nestlé. Since Nestlé stock is not sold in the United States, its mention on

Table 3. Corporations, Industries, and Corporate Groups Not Invested in or Divested from for Ethical Reasons[a] (Those Cited by 3 or More Respondents)

Corporations, Industries, Corporate Groups	*Number of Mentions*
Defense/Armaments Firms	21
Dow Chemical (6)	
Firms Having Commercial Dealings with South Africa	10
Pharmaceutical Companies (Birth Control)	10
Firms with Questionable Activities in the Third World	9
Firms Selling Infant Formula (7)	
American Home Products (4)	
Nestlé (3)	
Firms Engaged in or Supporting Unfair Labor Practices[b]	5
J. P. Stevens (3)	
Secular Hospitals (Abortions)	4
Utilities or Companies Engaged in Nuclear Power Projects	4
"All Corporate Stock"[c]	4
Gambling Enterprises	3
Number of orders reporting at least one of these activities	57

Notes:

[a] Responses also include corporations from which bonds are not bought, and banks in which deposits were not made or from which they were withdrawn.

[b] Includes discrimination, non-reporting of EEO statistics and anti-union activities in domestic operations, and ties with J.P. Stevens. Firms engaged in "unfair labor practices" in the Third World are listed under "Firms with Questionable Activities in the Third World."

[c] In three of these cases, avoidance of risk was cited as the reason for not investing.

three questionnaires may simply be due to misinformation on the part of these orders.

These results should be considered suggestive rather than definitive of the orders' investments since the questionnaire relies on the respondents' memories to report where they have not invested or where they have divested because of ethical concerns. It is likely that other orders have also not invested in the industries, corporate groups, or firms listed because of such concerns but simply forgot or neglected to list them. Clearly, however, the industries, corporations, and corporate groups listed were the ones foremost on the minds of the treasurers.

The activities in the divest/don't invest categories must be viewed in relation to activities in other categories. For example, one order noted that it would refrain from buying stock in defense firms unless it planned to file a resolution with the firm. Thus activities in these two categories do not necessarily mean a consistent policy of "washing one's hands" of firms perceived to be "unethical."

Purposeful Investments

The converse of the divest/don't invest option is purposely investing in certain corporations, industries, or projects because of their likely desirable social effects. The treasurers were asked to list on the questionnaire any investments made for this reason in the last five years. In addition to doing this, many voluntarily listed corporations in which they invested for the purpose of pursuing changes in corporate policy. While it was not clear in every case which of these was the reason for making the investment listed on the returned questionnaire, these investments are grouped as accurately as possible in Table 4. Considering these two groups together, 48 orders[7] indicated that they purposely invested in certain corporations, projects, or industries for ethical reasons. Of these, 35 orders invested to support such enterprises and 16 invested to press for change. Three orders did both. Participation rates were higher in both of these categories for those orders which attached formal policy statements than those which did not: 48 percent versus 18 percent in the support category and 29 percent versus 6 percent in the change category.

Clearly, the most popular vehicle used by the religious orders surveyed for promoting economic organizations whose policies they support is investing in them, or depositing money in financial institutions. Examples include deposits in neighborhood banks or banks supporting local development, credit unions, and cooperatives (21 mentions, of which 10 were for South Shore Bank in Chicago) and minority banks. Also receiving more than three mentions were Catholic hospitals, and institutions providing housing/nursing homes for the poor, aged, or handi-

Table 4. Corporations, Industries, Corporate Groups
and Projects Invested in for Ethical Reasons
(Those Cited by 3 or More Repsondents)

To Support Current Policies	Number of Mentions
Neighborhood Banks, Credit Unions, Cooperatives	21
South Shore Bank, Chicago (10)	
Catholic Hospitals	5
Minority Banks	4
Housing, Nursing Homes for Poor, Aged and Handicapped	4
Other Organizations Helping Minorities	3
Other Church-Related Institutions	6
Other Charitable Institutions or Causes	11
Number of orders reporting this activity	35
To Change Current Policies	
Firms Engaged in or Supporting Unfair Labor Practices	8
J.P. Stevens (5)	
Defense/Armaments Firms	7
Grumman (3)	
Firms with Questionable Activities in the Third World	5
Number of orders reporting this activity	16

capped. Besides South Shore Bank, only 4 specific companies were mentioned as socially beneficial investments.

Of particular interest are the firms in which the orders invested to influence *changes* in corporate policies, such as, to pursue an activist role. The only firms listed more than once in this category are J.P. Stevens, Grumman, and Rockwell International. The purposeful investment in these latter two firms represents an interesting development in ethical investing, given the popularity of avoiding ownership in defense firms that was previously noted. For the most part, the orders invested to press these firms to undertake "conversion planning" (such as, planning the conversion of defense-related production facilities to nonmilitary production in order to ease the adverse economic effects on workers and the surrounding community) (McGivern, 1980).

One line of criticism of ethical investors is that those who purchase stock for the express purpose of changing corporate policies are simply troublemakers rather than concerned stockholders. Without considering the merits of this criticism, a comparison of these results with those discussed below indicates that it is much more common for these orders to direct their ethical investment activities at companies in which they already own stock than to acquire new holdings for activist purposes.

Direct Communication

Table 5 lists firms with which the treasurers indicated that they had been in communication to urge management to change certain policies. Forty-four[8] orders indicated they had engaged in this activity. One order which had divested itself of all corporate stocks and bonds reportedly continued to contact firms concerning these matters. Communicating with management was a particulary popular activity with those orders which supplied policy statements. Twenty (65 percent) of these orders reported such contacts, compared to 22 percent of the others. These orders also contacted more firms, reporting an average of four contacts per order versus an average of two contacts per order for the others.

Commercial ties with South Africa was the most frequently cited topic of communication, followed by questionable practices in Third World countries and unfair labor practices. It is interesting to note that the defense/armament issue is relatively less prominent here than in the divest/don't invest activity category. This may indicate that the orders feel corporate managers are more open to discussion and negotiation about their operations in South Africa and Third World countries and their labor practices than they would be about changing their line of business. Only a few orders have been urging the management of defense firms to undertake "conversion planning."

Table 5.   Corporate Managements Contacted to Change Certain Policies
(Those Cited by 3 or More Respondents)

Corporations, Industries, Corporate Groups	Number of Mentions
Firms Having Commercial Dealings with South Africa	33
Mellon Bank (3)	
Pittsburgh National Bank (3)	
Continental Bank (3)	
Firms Engaged in or Supporting Unfair Labor Practices	27
J.P. Stevens (3)	
Campbells (3)	
Sears (J.P. Stevens ties) (3)	
Firms with Questionable Activities in the Third World	26
Marketing Infant Formula in the Third World (13)	
Nestlé (5)	
American Home Products (4)	
Bristol Myers (3)	
Firms Having Commercial Dealings with Chile (6)	
General Motors (4)	
Defense/Armaments Firms	10
General Electric (3)	
Firms with Adverse Environmental Impacts	6
Nuclear Power Firms	5
Number of orders reporting this activity	44

Banks were the most frequently contacted corporations. Of the 108 reported contacts, 21 were with banks, and almost all of these contacts concerned dealings with South Africa. Oil companies were the next most frequently cited, with 12 contacts. In all, a total of 75 different corporations were specified by the orders as ones which they contacted. Given the number of orders which just cited "many" contacts, it is likely that the total number of corporations contacted by the orders is significantly larger than this. Thus, this particular ethical investment activity appears to be very popular. Questionnaire and interview responses also indicated that communicating with management is often the first step in attempting to influence corporate activities. Usually only after this approach has proved unsatisfactory are the other more extreme, time-consuming and costly ethical investment strategies undertaken.

Shareholder Resolutions

Table 6 lists firms in which orders have initiated or supported shareholder resolutions, grouped by resolution category. A total of sixty-nine orders[9] reported some activity of this type. Again, this activity was more popular with those orders which supplied policy statements. Twenty-four (77 percent) of these orders had initiated or supported shareholder resolutions versus only 41 percent of the remaining respondents.

Resolutions dealing with various firms' activities in/or with South Africa (mentioned 43 times) and with various Third World countries (mentioned 40 times) were the most frequently cited. The orders' support for South Africa resolutions was rather diffuse; resolutions dealing with South African activities were directed at 25 different corporations, with General Motors, the most frequently cited, mentioned only six times. On the other hand, mentions of resolutions dealing with Third World activities were highly concentrated in two companies marketing infant formula, American Home Products and Bristol Myers.

Next in order of frequency were resolutions dealing with a variety of domestic corporate labor practices: discrimination, non-reporting of EEO statistics, anti-union activities, and plant closings (in the steel industry). The most frequently cited firm in this category was J. P. Stevens, and the next most frequently cited firm, Sears Roebuck, was the target of a resolution seeking to end its commercial ties with the company as well. Defense and environment-oriented resolutions were also popular with orders. Defense-related shareholder resolutions directed at 9 corporations were cited 18 times. These resolutions dealt with "conversion planning," as well as foreign military sales. Environmental resolutions directed at 8 different corporations, mostly coal and other natural resource companies, were cited 11 times.

Given the large number of orders that indicated that they supported too many proposals to name them individually, Table 6 should be viewed

Table 6.   Ethically Oriented Shareholder Resolutions
Initiated or Supported
(Those Cited by 3 or More Respondents)

Corporations, Industries, Corporate Groups	*Number of Mentions*
Firms Having Commercial Dealings with South Africa	43
General Motors (6)	
Exxon (4)	
IBM (3)	
Kodak (3)	
Bankamerica (3)	
Firms with Questionable Activities in the Third World	40
Marketing Infant Formula (20)	
American Home Products (9)	
Bristol Myers (8)	
Firms Having Commercial Dealings with Chile (10)	
General Motors (5)	
Other Firms	
Exxon (Foreign Payments) (4)	
Firms Engaged in or Supporting Unfair Labor Practices	26
J.P. Stevens (5)	
Sears Roebuck (J.P. Stevens ties) (4)	
Coca Coal (3)	
U.S. Steel (3)	
Defense/Armaments Firms	18
General Electric (Foreign military sales and nuclear weapons) (6)	
McDonnell Douglas (3)	
Firms with Adverse Environmental Impacts	11
Kennecott Copper (3)	
Number of orders engaged in this activity	67

as suggestive of the direction of the orders' participation in these proposals rather than precisely descriptive of the extent of their participation. These results correspond to the findings of David Fritzsche (1980)
who categorized by subject area/purpose the socially oriented proposals
sponsored by the ICCR in the years 1977–79. While the categories he
used are somewhat different than those in this study, both studies point
to the same trends regarding the focal issues of stockholder activities
for religious groups.

Litigation

Only one order reported undertaking litigation against corporate management—the well-publicized suit against Bristol Myers by the Sisters
of the Precious Blood, concerning marketing of infant formula in the
Third World. Two other orders reported providing financial backing for
this litigation. One other order reported it was actively considering filing
suit against U.S. Steel pertaining to its plans to close old plants while

opening a new one. This order, as well as one of those supporting the Bristol-Myers suit, were among the orders which supplied formal policy statements.

Obviously, litigation can be a very expensive and time-consuming undertaking which most orders are reluctant to undertake. In the Bristol-Myers case, the order had engaged in dialogue with the company and had filed a shareholder resolution on the infant formula issue prior to bringing the suit, which was settled out of court in 1978.

Voting to Unseat Management

A total of 9 orders indicated that they had voted to unseat management or withheld votes for management-selected board candidates in the preceding five years. Only three corporations were mentioned by name— Sperry Rand, J. P. Stevens, and American Home Products—with the first two mentioned by the same order. Three other orders said they withheld proxies when there were no women board members or candidates (two cases) or when there were no women or minority board members or candidates (one case). Four orders indicated that they voted against management on occasion, but did not specify the circumstances. These are clearly protest votes with no real expectation of unseating management, although there is probably some hope that this might lead to some future change in corporate policies or composition of boards. Still, it is clear that direct communications with management and shareholder resolutions are much more popular protest vehicles than board elections.

Table 7. Orders' Participation Rates in Ethical Investment Activities

Ethical Investment Activity	Orders Supplying Formal Policy Statements		Other Orders	
	Number	Percentage	Number	Percentage
Avoidance of Investments/ Divestment	14	45	43	39
Purposeful Investments				
a) To Support Current Policy	15	48	20	18
b) To Change Current Policy	9	29	7	6
Direct Communications with Management	20	65	24	22
Shareholder Resolutions	24	77	45	41
Litigation	2	6	2	2
Voting to Unseat Management	5	16	4	4
Publicizing Activities	5	16	13	12
Number of orders responding	31	100	110	100

Publicizing Activities

Eighteen orders indicated that they sought to publicize externally their various ethical investment activities. Thirteen corporations were cited as targets of this publicity, with only one, Nestlé, mentioned three or more times. Others mentioned included Standard Brands, Gulf, IBM, General Motors, and Bristol Myers. Comparing these responses with those previously presented, it is clear that a great many ethical investment activities are not deliberately publicized. Nevertheless, given the controversial nature of the activities and the highly visible forums in which they take place (for example, stockholders meetings), it is unlikely that these activities go unnoticed. One respondent objected to the wording of this question. She said that her order engaged in "consciousness raising activities" but did not seek publicity for its own sake.

CONCLUSIONS

These summary results reveal that a substantial number of Catholic orders have used a variety of ethical investment strategies to draw attention to and deal with a wide range of issues. The most frequently cited issues, regardless of the ethical investment strategy employed, are commercial dealings with South Africa, various questionable activities in the Third World (especially marketing infant formula), defense issues, and various labor practices. Conspicuously of somewhat lesser concern are environmental issues, including nuclear power.

The fact that there are so many issues and corporations targeted through different ethical investment strategies tends to diffuse the impact of these activities on any one corporation or issue. This helps explain, for example, the inability of most shareholder resolutions to gain even the 3 percent of the vote needed to be included on the next year's agenda (Purcell, 1979). However, it is clear that in most cases *forcing* firms to undertake or end certain activities through winning approval of resolutions or imposing financial hardship on the firm is not the goal of the orders. Even if all the orders focused on one issue in one corporation, they would still need massive support from other investors to force management to do something to which it was otherwise opposed. Many orders thus first seek a dialogue with management to encourage voluntary changes. Other strategies (such as divestiture, shareholder resolutions, litigation) are usually undertaken if and when this fails. Communications with management, and in some cases other stockholders, facilitates the "consciousness raising" that many orders apparently seek. In this context then, the diffusion of ethical investment activities by the orders is not necessarily detrimental to their aims. It may actually achieve the maximum "consciousness raising" effect.

Except in cases where an order finds an activity of a firm so offensive that it feels it must disassociate itself from that firm, there appears to be a preference to work for change from within the company as stock-holders. Many would agree with the respondent who stated that "no stock is untainted" in explaining this preference. The preference for changing "unethical" corporate practices rather than simply avoiding association with them was most notable among the more sophisticated orders with ethical investment policy statements.[10] While this group engaged in all ethical investment activities more frequently then the sample as a whole, differences were much more pronounced in the action-oriented strategies of purposeful investing, communicating with management, and supporting or proposing shareholder resolutions than in the avoidance strategies of divest/don't invest.

Several problems with respect to the pursuit of ethical investment strategies were repeatedly mentioned by the respondents: (1) lack of funds to risk in investments made on other than financial criteria, (2) scarcity of information on corporate social performance, (3) uncertainty about the best way to influence corporate behavior, and (4) internal and external difficulties in coordinating ethical investment activities. With respect to this first problem, it is clear that the range of ethical investment activities considered includes actions other than investing or divesting that are not likely to be *financially* burdensome. In fact, orders without any corporate securities have engaged in some of these activities (for example, communicating with management). Even with respect to actual investing/divesting, there is some support in the literature and in the respondents' own views that the most "socially responsible" firms will in the long run make the best *financial* investments. In any event, there do appear to be a substantial number of viable alternative investment opportunities available to all but the most scrupulous investors.

With respect to the last three problems, it is clear that at least partial solutions are possible through certain organizational actions. Those orders which have made the best progress in resolving these problems are the ones which: (1) have developed a formal and explicit policy concerning ethical investment activities; (2) have appointed an individual or committee responsible for implementing that policy and receiving input from and providing feedback to other members of the order; and (3) have utilized the resources of groups such as the NCCRI and ICCR which can achieve economies of scale in the investigation of these issues. It is clear also that coordination of activities with other concerned investors is necessary if the orders want their ethical investment activities to have an impact beyond "consciousness raising."

There are several implications of this study that management should be aware of in deciding on an approach for dealing with ethical investors. First, it seems advantageous for management to be open for the dialogue which such groups seek and perhaps even to initiate it. This could forestall punitive strategies such as shareholder litigation or extremist proposals, and the publicity and problems associated with being labeled "unethical" by groups whose stands on moral issues have considerable credibility. Given the importance to the orders of information from organizations such as ICCR and NCCRI, these groups represent logical points of contact for dialogue. The respondents apparently pay attention to management's views on controversial issues as expressed in official publications such as annual reports; and management has more control over these than other sources of corporate social performance information.

Second, it would seem that management would be well-advised to pay attention to its social reporting/social auditing activities.

Third, since divestiture of stock, initiation of extreme shareholder proposals and lawsuits appear in many cases to result from breakdowns in communications between these shareholders and management, it might be useful to develop specialists who could help bridge the communication gap between ethical investors and management. Corporate experience in the last decade in negotiations with consumer groups, blacks, women, and their even lengthier experience in negotiations with workers suggest the value of specialized skills and experience in such contacts.

ACKNOWLEDGMENTS

This survey was supported by a grant from Project Extend of the Society of Mary Province of Cincinnati. Further support in this research was received from the Center for the Study of Values, University of Delaware. The author is indebted to Theodore V. Purcell and Barry R. Armandi for comments on a previous draft of this paper.

A previous and much shorter version of this paper appears in the *Proceedings of the Academy of Management Meetings,* San Diego, CA, 1981. There are minor discrepancies in the data reported in these two papers resulting from subsequent analysis done in the preparation of this paper.

NOTES

1. In the survey the term "social investment" was used to discuss those policies and activities. Since "ethical investment" has now become the more widely recognized terminology, this latter phrase is used throughout this paper.

2. One exception is mutual funds, such as the Dreyfuss Third Century Fund, which were set up expressly to invest in "socially responsible" firms.

3. No questions on this were asked because of expected order sensitivities to divulging this information. It was feared that this might deter the orders from answering any of the questions.

4. Nine of these 28 orders responded to this survey.

5. It was clear from the responses that the orders interpreted the term "investments"

very broadly. Included in this figure, for example, are orders which own bonds and a few orders which cited such activities as lending money at lower than market rates for socially desirable projects, depositing money in minority or neighborhood financial institutions, or conversely withdrawing money from or not depositing it in "socially irresponsible" banks.

6.   Thirteen of these 57 did not however cite which corporations, corporate groups, or issues they directed these actions towards, so these responses are not included in Table 3. Those responses which cited a corporate group or issue but not the particular corporation are included in the appropriate category totals.

7.   Seven of the 48 did not indicate specific corporations, industries or projects in which they invested.

8.   Eight orders did not specify which firms they contacted, either indicating that there were too many to list or just citing the subject matter of the contacts.

9.   Of these 69 orders, 28 did not specify which resolutions they proposed or supported, in some cases saying there were too many to list.

10.   Hollenbach (1973) however notes that the preference for avoidance strategies may be appropriate for orders with fundamental missions advocating disassociation from worldly affairs rather than social change. Viewed in this light, lack of sophistication may be a consciously chosen position.

APPENDIX I

COLLEGE OF BUSINESS

VIRGINIA POLYTECHNIC INSTITUTE AND STATE UNIVERSITY

Blacksburg, Virginia 24061

DEPARTMENT OF BUSINESS ADMINISTRATION   (703) 961-6596

November 20, 1979

Dear Treasurer:

In recent years religious institutions have been confronted with difficult choices regarding the proper role of their investments. Many have been concerned with how their investments contribute to achievement of organizational goals through both economic return and the furtherance of social values they support.

This questionnaire is part of a study funded by Project Extend of the Society of Mary to investigate how, and to what degree, religious institutions have used their positions as investors to achieve various social goals. It will attempt to determine the institutions' positions on various corporate social issues, their policies concerning the use of investments and other financial resources for social purposes, and the degree to which these policies have been implemented. With the questionnaire responses, we will also be able to assess whether the corporate social performance information available to the institutional investors is adequate for them to make decisions consistent with their own values and social investment policies.

On the following pages you will find the Institutional Investments Questionnaire. Please ask whoever is repsonsible for making your investment decisions to fill out the questionnaire as completely as possible and return it in the envelope provided. Part A requests information about the formulation and implementation of your investment policy, while Part B asks for an indication of the relative importance of each of a number of business/social issues in making your investment decisions. If you desire to offer additional information on these subjects (e.g. policy statements, lists of investments or investment activities), please return it with the questionnaire; and/or you may indicate in the space provided that you are willing to participate in a telephone interview.

You can be assured that all individual responses will be held in the strictest confidence by the researcher. Research results will be reported on an aggregate basis only, with no participating institutions identified by name.

For the participating institutions who desire to receive the results of this study (check-off box provided at the end of the questionnaire), there will be an opportunity to see how other religious institutions have dealt with these same issues. In addition those who elect to participate in the phone interview will have made available to them a method for evaluating corporations' social performance based on the investor's own values—a value-based social audit. This will be developed with the information generated in the phone interviews.

We appreciate your cooperation in providing information which we feel will assist religious institutions in making difficult investment decisions.

Sincerely,

Richard E. Wokutch, Ph.D.
Assistant Professor of Management

REW:mkt

Name: _____

Religious Order: _____

Position: _____

PART A

1a) Has your organization developed any policy towards the use of its investments and/or financial resources to achieve social goals:

Yes _____ No _____

If "yes" to 1a, please answer 1b through 1d. If "no," proceed to question #2.

1b) What is that policy? (Please attach a policy statement to the questionnaire if you so desire.)

1c) Please describe the process by which this policy was developed.

1d) How is this policy implemented?

—Who or what group is responsible for carrying out this policy?

—How do they make their decisions?

—In what ways are other members of the order involved in the implementation of this policy?

2. How important to you are each of the following sources of information on corporate social performance? (Check as many as apply).

1. Extremely important   4. Moderately unimportant
2. Moderately important   5. Of very little use
3. Average importance

_____ Business Periodicals   _____ Corporate annual
      and Newspapers   reports and other
_____ Other Newspapers and   business publications
      Magazines   _____ Organizations
_____ Television and Radio   concerned with
_____ Investment Counselors   corporate social
_____ Word-of-mouth   performance
_____ Federal Government   (specify) _____
                                _____ Other (Specify) _____
                                _____ Other (Specify) _____
                                _____ Other (Specify) _____

3.   Following are 8 commonly cited actions taken by institutional
      investors *to promote their views of social issues*. Please describe
      any actions your organization has taken in these categories in the
      last 5 years. (Specify the corporation at which the action was
      directed and the reason for this.)

      a.   Declining to invest in certain corporations or industries.

      b.   Divestment from certain corporations.

      c.   Purposely investing in certain corporations, industries, or proj-
           ects because of their likely desirable social effects.

      d.   Direct communications with management urging it to change
           certain policies.

      e.   Proposing socially oriented shareholder resolution or sup-
           porting those proposed by others.

      f.   Undertaking or joining in litigation against management.

g. Voting to unseat management.

h. Publicizing opposition to management on the undertaking of any of the above actions.

PART B

Following is a list of economic/social issues relating to the operation of businesses. Please indicate the *relative* importance of each of these issues in your investment decisions by assigning weights to them. These weights should total to 100 points. Thus, if each of the 10 issues listed (excluding "other") were of equal importance, you would assign a weight of 10 to each. If only economic return were a factor in making investment de cisions, you would assign a weight of 100 to economic factors and a 0 to each other category.

1. Economic factors (dividends, capital appreciation, risk minimization, etc.). _____
2. Pollution control (air, water, noise, solid waste, etc. pollution control.). _____
3. Equal employment opportunity practices in the hiring and promoting of minorities and women. _____
4. Non-involvement in munitions manufacturing. _____
5. Employee safety. _____
6. Consumer Issues (product safety, truth in advertising, etc.). _____
7. Philanthropic activities. _____
8. Fair labor relations and bargaining. _____
9. Absence of significant operations (sales, manufacturing, or purchasing) in countries with repressive governments. _____
10. The value of the product or service to society. _____
11. Other (specify). _____ _____

(□ We would like to offer additional information through a telephone interview, please call us at _____ .)

(□ Yes, we would like a copy of the results of this study. Please mail to

_____

_____

_____ .)

APPENDIX II

[Order Name Deleted]

INVESTMENT POLICY

We have been called by the Chapter of 1976 "to listen to the questions of the world and the challenge of what goes on about us." (1) We have shared our awareness of the Church's vocation to be present in the heart of the world by proclaiming the Good News to the poor, freedom to the oppressed, and joy to the afflicted; by listening to the cry of those who suffer violence and are oppressed by unjust systems and structures, and by hearing the appeal of a world that by its heedlessness contradicts the plan of the Creator.

The   [order]   moved by the love of the poor Christ, wishes to walk in the way of the freely given by putting at the service of mission our work and whatever goods we have, for we are only stewards of these goods. "We wish to become aware of the unjust situations in which we are involved and to join others in the search for justice." (2)

Realizing that it is not always easy to administer our finances in the light of the Gospel, for they are affected by the economic systems under which we live, we wish to promote the goals of production which will support the progress of peoples: "to lessen inequalities, to remove discrimination, to free people from bonds of servitude and to enable them to improve their condition in the temporal order, achieve moral development and perfect their spiritual endowment." (3)

We hope that our funds will be invested in corporations which respect certain principles in their pursuit of profits. Meanwhile, we expect to use our modest shareholder power to support or initiate proposals which direct corporations to adopt policies which promote these principles. In cases where there is public criticism of a corporation for violating these principles, we expect fiduciary institutions to consult the Treasurer before divesting or investing in the stock of such a corporation. The principles are:

1. Provide that at every level the largest possible number of people have an active share in directing company development (i.e., safety of employees and the possibility of their sharing in forms of ownership, decision making and company profits).
2. Protect human rights.
3. Provide equal employment and policy formulation opportunities for minorities and women.
4. Advertise honestly and affirm the dignity of the individual in their promotional and advertising policies.

5. Protect the natural resources of water, land and air.
6. Utilize their profits in a just and responsible manner.
7. Make extensive efforts to convert from a military to a peaceful operation.
8. Include in their planning the correction of exploitive practices in the Third World.
9. *Do not* contribute to the economic support of institutions and governments where a minority in power, legally or through the use of force, inhibits the political, cultural, and economic rights of the majority.

In light of the above and aware that the purpose of investments in financial planning and administration is *not* to accumulate wealth, but to provide a regular and reliable source of income to meet obligations which cannot be sustained by other dependable sources of income, our investment portfolio should be so managed that:

1. There is adequate current income (%). This will be revised annually.
2. The growth of capital should be proportionate to the need for adequate current income.
3. There is diversification.
4. Some portion (amount to be determined) is invested in minority and/or social action oriented businesses.

NOTES

1. Chapter 1976, p. 11.
2. Chapter 1976, p. 13.
3. Populorum Progressio: USCC, p. 15.

Adopted by the Interprovincial Board April 27, 1978.
Given to the Fiduciary Institutions which manage the portfolios for the Provinces of the United States.

REFERENCES

Ackerman, R. W., and R. Bauer, *Corporate Social Responsiveness*. Reston, VA: Prentice-Hall, 1976.
Alexander, C. J., and R. A. Buchholz, "Corporate Social Responsibility, and Stock Market Performance." *Academy of Management Journal* 21 (September, 1978): 479–486.
Blake, D. H., W. C. Frederick, and M. S. Myers, *Social Auditing: Evaluating the Impact of Corporate Programs*. New York: Praeger, 1976.
Bauer, R., and D. Fenn, "What Is a Corporate Social Audit?" *Harvard Business Review* 51 (January, 1973): 37–48.

188 RICHARD E. WOKUTCH

Dreyfuss Public Interest Investing, "The Dreyfuss Fund: Experience With Investing in the Public Interest." *Business and Society Review* (Spring, 1976): 57–61.
Fritzsche, D. J., Department of Management and Marketing, Illinois State University, "A Longitudinal Analysis of Corporate Proxy Resolutions: How Churches Attempt to Influence Corporate Social Behavior." Presented at Academy of Management Meetings, Detroit, MI, August, 1980.
"God and Mammon: Stocks and Bondage." Transcript of an ABC Network conversation with Michael Clark and Michael Crosby, with Bob Clark, ABC, *Catholic Church Investments For Corporate Social Responsibility* 5 5(1978): 1–8.
Gollin, J., *Worldly Goods: The Wealth, and Power of the American Catholic Church, the Vatican, and the Men Who Control the Money*. New York: Random House, 1971.
Hollenbach, D., S.J., "Corporate Investments, Ethics, and Evangelical Poverty: A Challenge to American Religious Orders." *Theological Studies* 34(June 1973): 265–274.
Interfaith Center on Corporate Responsibility, *Church Proxy Resolutions*. New York, 1978.
——, *Church Proxy Resolutions*. New York, 1979.
——, *Church Proxy Resolutions*. New York, 1980.
Kennedy, R., "How the Ford Foundation Deals With Social Issues." *Trusts, and Estates* (April, 1975): 114, 214–217.
Longstreth, B., and H. D. Rosenbloom, *Corporate Responsibility, and the Institutional Investor*. New York: Praeger, 1973.
Lublin, L. S., "Unions Step Up Use of Pension Cash to Push 'Socially Desirable' Projects." *Wall Street Journal* (July 23, 1980): 23–32.
McGivern, M. A., S.L., "Economic Conversion: Planning for Peace." *Catholic Church Investments For Corporate Social Responsibility* 8 6(1980): 1–8.
Malkiel, B. G., and R. E. Quandt, "Moral Issues in Investment Policy." *Harvard Business Review* 49(March, 1971): 37.
"Marching Again." *Newsweek*. May 8, 1978, p. 56.
Moscowitz, M. R., "Choosing Socially Responsible Stocks." *Business and Society Review/ Innovation* (Spring, 1972).
"NCC Guidelines for Mission Investments." *Corporate Examiner*. 3(April, 1973): 3a–3d.
Nickel, H., "The Corporate Haters." *Fortune* (June 16, 1980): 126–128+.
Powers, C. W., *Social Responsibility and Investments*. Nashville: Abington, 1971.
Powers, C. W. (ed.), *People/Profits: The Ethics of Investment*. New York: Council on Religion and International Affairs, 1972.
Purcell, T. V., "Management and the 'Ethical' Investors." *Harvard Business Review* 57(September-October, 1979): 24–26+.
——, "Reprise of the 'Ethical Investors.'" *Harvard Business Review* 58(March-April, 1980): 158–182.
——, "Correspondence to R. E. Wokutch," March 9, 1981.
Sethi, S. P., *Business Corporations and the Black Man*. Scranton, PA: Chandler, 1970.
Simon, J. G., C. W. Powers, and J. P. Hunneman, *The Ethical Investor: Universities, Corporate Responsibility*. New Haven: Yale University, 1972.
Taylor, B., "Planning for the 1980's." Unpublished paper presented at the meeting of the Academy of Management, Atlanta, August, 1979.
Vance, S. C., "Are Socially Responsible Corporations Good Investment Risks?" *Management Review* 64(August, 1975): 18–25.
Wokutch, R. E., and L. Fahey, "Towards a Value-Based Social Audit Approach." Unpublished paper presented at the meeting of the Academy of Management, San Diego, August, 1981.

STRATEGIC ACTION IN THE REGULATORY ENVIRONMENT:
THE CASE OF THE FIRESTONE "500"

Elliot Zashin

The great expansion of government regulation in the areas of safety, health and environmental protection since the late 1960s has drawn vigorous and frequent criticism from the private sector. Corporate managers and their spokesmen complain about financial and organizational burdens of regulatory requirements, and economists and policy analysts charge that the benefits involved have been inadequate to justify the costs (MacAvoy, 1979).

It is difficult to evaluate these general critiques because the estimation of costs and benefits associated with regulatory activity presents formidable problems. Although there is merit in some of the criticisms, the original regulatory objective—reducing public exposure to harm from unacceptable business behavior—remains valid. Moreover, little attention has been paid to the role of business itself in raising the cost and

Research in Corporate Social Performance and Policy, Vol. 4, pages 189–214
Copyright © 1982 by JAI Press Inc.
All rights of reproduction in any form reserved.
ISBN: 0-89232-259-4

reducing the benefits of regulation, particularly through the use of strategic action to cause repeated delays in the regulatory process. A detailed examination of the recall of the Firestone "500" steel-belted radial tire by the National Highway Traffic Safety Administration (NHTSA) provides an unusually clear record of such behavior and permits an analysis of its critical aspects and implications.

STRATEGIC ACTION

Regulatory agencies have considerable discretion in formulating regulation, determining when the criteria of violation have been met, and assessing authorized sanctions. Because the regulatory process has adversarial aspects, regulatory agencies follow a set of procedures similar to those required in courts of law, to ensure that regulatees receive fair treatment. Economists (Owen and Braeutigam, 1978, pp. 3–5) have recognized that the administrative process of regulation—the due process requirements, in particular—creates incentives for regulatees to resort to litigation. By initiating litigation or continuing it by appeals, any party to the regulatory process can impose delays and expenses on the other parties. In effect, the due process requirements give regulatees some leverage in determining the pace of a regulatory investigation, thereby allowing them to delay a final determination. Regulatees can challenge the regulations (and the determinations made according to them) in federal court without appearing to challenge the legislative mandate of the agency.

Because "litigation costs are usually small compared to the stakes in a regulatory decision for an established firm or industry," the strategic use of administrative process may appear desirable to a major corporation. It can maintain the status quo, using the delay "to undertake other measures to reduce or eliminate the costs of an eventual adverse decision" (Owen and Braeutigam, pp. 4–5).

Despite their investigatory powers, regulatory agencies tend to be dependent upon regulated industries for the information necessary to determine regulatory violations. Frequently the best or only source of data is the alleged violator of regulatory standards. Routine mandatory reporting does not provide sufficient information to make official determinations. A regulatee's ability to control the flow of information to the regulatory agency thus becomes a critical element in the regulatory process. Information can be released slowly or selectively, affecting the pace and substance of regulatory investigations. When information is withheld and agencies must use the federal courts to compel production, further delay results. Such delay or difficulty in reaching a judgment on the facts because of insufficient information thus can increase regulatory costs. Since agencies have limited legal and investigative resources relative to the number of regulatees, the latter's control of vital information and due process options can impose a serious strain on an agency's efficiency.

Although regulated corporations have some incentives to cooperate with regulatory agencies—obtaining the agency's good will, maintaining a socially responsible public image, and minimizing potential legal liability—the incentives to use strategic action may easily outweigh them. Strategic action offers the possibility (in the short run, at least) of avoiding the imposition of costly remedial actions and penalties, preventing confidential information from reaching competitors and public (thereby avoiding any competitive disadvantage), avoiding concessions that may be interpreted as admissions of guilt, and keeping regulatory agencies on the defensive by requiring them to defend their regulations and determinations in court.

The subject of corporate strategic action has not been systematically studied. One can glean examples of corporations taking strategic action from newspaper reports, but these are too fragmentary to estimate the actual incidence or effects. Behind the news reports (generally short) of consent decrees and other forms of regulatory decision-making are the unreported day-to-day activities of regulators and regulatees: exchanges of questions and information, protracted negotiations, bargaining, litigation, concessions, and compromises. Neither side is likely to reveal these details because they might well indicate that the regulatory process frequently deviates from the public's conception of what transpires.

In general terms, *strategic action* may be defined as game-like moves that involve manipulating rules and other constraints on the parties to gain advantage in an adversarial setting. In the field of government regulation, strategic action represents an attempt to use the *process* to influence the *substance* of regulation. When substance and process are closely interrelated (as in the case of business regulation), strategic action becomes attractive. Agencies have discretion to set the criteria for determining violations of regulatory standards, but regulatees can affect the utility of whatever criteria are set. For the criteria to be manageable, certain kinds of evidence must be available. In a sense, regulatory agencies are in a bind: the more objectively precise (and therefore more persuasive to the judiciary and policy-makers) the criteria are, the more dependent the agencies are on the regulatees as sources of information. Conversely, reducing the rigor of criteria eases the burden of determining violations, but at the same time increases the possibilities of rebuttal.

Thus, the process-substance interaction creates opportunities for regulatees to influence the impact of regulation. It is not clear that this was an unintended or unanticipated consequence of regulatory legislation. Pro-regulation interest groups may well have recognized the possibilities of strategic use of the administrative process, but also realized that viable legislative proposals required the inclusion of due process elements. Potential delay and deflection may have been expected costs of extending due process, but due process may well have been necessary to achieve regulation.

While the use of strategic action by regulated corporations warrants more empirical study, it seems clear that relevant reform—either of agencies or corporations—is not promising at this time. So we have to fall back on consensual norms to restrain undesirable behavior. At this point, the legitimacy of strategic action must be considered. Many definitions of corporate social responsibility suggest that the legality of corporate decisions and actions does not exhaust the moral obligation of business in our society. Yet advocates of social responsibility have not applied the concept to compliance within the regulatory process. The Firestone "500" case analyzed in this paper reveals many of the complexities. As a first step toward applying normative standards to the regulatory behavior illustrated by the case, the author will examine two other adversarial relations that occur within a legal framework in order to see whether strategic tactics have been recognized as illegitimate. Analogies from plea-bargaining in the criminal courts and collective bargaining in labor-management relations form the basis for a concept of fair dealing which can be applied to regulators and regulatees. Of course, merely espousing an ethic of responsible action will not eliminate problems of strategic action. There have to be incentives for corporations to act responsibly in the regulatory process. This essay concludes with an examination of the prospects for restraint.

THE CASE OF THE FIRESTONE "500" RECALL

The case of the National Highway Traffic Safety Administration's recall of the Firestone "500" steel-belted radial tire in 1978 illustrates the variety of strategic actions open to a corporation: delaying responses to agency inquiries; providing less information than requested; initiating litigation to impede agency investigations and to question the legitimacy of agency action; not complying with agency administrative orders, thereby requiring the agency to seek court process; proceeding slowly in negotiations; and not raising significant issues during negotiations. The case also indicates that a regulatory agency may not, by itself, be able to counter all these strategic moves—even though it, too, may maneuver tactically. In the short run, so this case suggests, strategic action offers a corporation significant benefits, but in the long run, too obvious a use of these tactics may undermine their advantages.

The Firestone "500" case is a complex one and judgments, empirical and normative, are difficult to make. Inference about intentions cannot be avoided altogether and these are always open to question. An attempt has been made to distinguish the practice of strategic action from the motivation by indicating the advantages to regulatees regardless of intent. Yet judgments about the legitimacy of such a practice inevitably will be influenced by perceptions of motivations. Adequate information about such matters is intrinsically elusive and even on the key factual issues, information is not likely to be sufficient. Moreover, no single case study can demonstrate how significant strategic action is as an obstacle to effective regulation. Yet despite these deficiencies, the case is instructive about the incentives, the tactics, and the consequences of strategic action.

First, the options open to the NHTSA and to Firestone as the agency began its investigation of the tire will be outlined, along with suggestions of probable motivations for the choices made by each side. This will be followed by a discussion of Firestone's strategic moves and the NHTSA's responses, including explanations offered by corporate and agency spokespersons, and an evaluation of the entire experience.

Agency Background and Options

A 1973 report by the U.S. General Accounting Office on the NHTSA's efforts to ensure compliance with federal safety standards foreshadows the agency's problems in the Firestone case. Although more than half of the agency's limited compliance testing funds were being devoted to tires, the investigative cycle on tire recalls averaged 14.6 months from test failure to recall notification. The agency told the GAO that it could not control the timetable of the investigation cycle, particularly because the manufacturer had to be accorded due process. Moreover, according to the NHTS Administrator at the time, "manufacturers were always ready to exploit" the fact that the initially adopted safety standards (taken from the industry) and their associated test procedures "were never intended by their authors to be used for compliance type testing and thus, very rarely, if ever, provided a clear-cut 'go' or 'no go' compliance evaluation." He also claimed that manufacturers scattered "red herrings" across the investigative path, "in many cases greatly delaying the final decision."

> It would be naive of us to expect a manufacturer to submit certification data that showed him to be in noncompliance, therefore, it is safe to assume that any data submitted to us has been thoroughly screened . . .

> It would be fair to say that most cases of noncompliance discovered by the Administration have been due to a breakdown in the manufacturer's internal processing and quality controls which are used to assure continuing compliance rather than design error. (U.S. Comptroller-General, 1973)

The specific experience to be investigated here begins in 1977, when the number of private complaints about Firestone tires, particularly the "500" radial, received by the NHTSA increased conspicuously. The agency had conducted a massive public survey during this year and the responses, while only a small fraction of the total, seemed to support the view that the "500" was more prone to problems than other steel-belted radials. Based on this data and perhaps lingering doubts from an earlier limited recall of "500" tires, the agency thought it had good reason to push its investigation as rapidly as possible: If the "500" was indeed defective, then delay meant continued risk of serious accident for "500" users, who still numbered in the millions. Moreover, the agency mandate permitted it to recall tires only if less than three years had elapsed from the time of purchase. Assuming a recall proved warranted, it was in the agency's interest to institute it promptly to maximize recall coverage and thereby minimize the risk to users.

Yet the investigation and final determination of findings could not be too rapid. Administrative due process permitted Firestone to appeal the NHTSA's decisions to the federal courts. Presumably it could win if administrative requirements were not met, thereby delaying the NHTSA investigation significantly. At the same time, the agency apparently recognized that Firestone had a legitimate interest in restricting the recall only to those tires still at risk. Recalling even these would be costly. The NHTSA had to make a convincing case for the existence of a defect; otherwise, Firestone would probably appeal the final determination, delaying the actual initiation of a recall.

Even if the NHTSA could develop adequate evidence of a defect, it wanted expeditious action, so a voluntary recall was preferable and this required some compromise. If the NHTSA pushed too hard, precluding a compromise, Firestone might fight a mandatory recall in court. Even if the company agreed to a voluntary recall, the agency needed continued cooperation because the company could control the pace and thus the effectiveness of recall. So the agency had to be sufficiently flexible and fair to keep open the possibilities of compromise and cooperation, while convincing Firestone that it was a formidable adversary. Achieving credibility as an adversary is no mean task when the regulatees may question the very legitimacy of regulation. In this case, it seems that Firestone had been one of the most aggressively anti-regulation firms in the industry.

The Company's Position

When the NHTSA made its informal request for information to Firestone in December, 1977, company officials apparently were not surprised. The agency had given prior indications that it suspected the

"500" of being problem-prone. Moreover, Firestone and the NHTSA had clashed twice before concerning the compliance of Firestone tires with federal quality standards. In addition, in November, 1977, the head of the Center of Auto Safety, a Ralph Nader spin-off organization, had addressed a public letter to the president of Firestone, calling on him to recall the "500" radial. Company officials saw this as putting pressure on the NHTSA to take some action.

It may be that, at this time, Firestone officials actually believed, as they consistently claimed during 1978, that (1) the "500" was as good as other U.S. manufacturers' steel-belted radials (SBR's); (2) the relatively high adjustment rates dealers were encountering were due primarily to user inexperience with radials, disproportionately adverse publicity, and a liberal adjustment policy for a top-of-the-line tire; and (3) the NHTSA was unfairly singling out the "500" from other SBR's. It is also possible that company officials knew by this time that they had produced a tire that was inadequate even in terms of their own concept of acceptable quality and safety but they hoped they could weather the storm of criticism as the "500" was gradually replaced by the successor SBR.

Possibly, the views of Firestone officials lay between these extremes. They knew the "500" had been troublesome—there had been complaints from dealers concerning the high adjustment rates, and a variety of changes had been experimented with to eliminate the problem of belt separations—but they believed that SBR's in general were prone to this problem and they were not willing to concede that the "500" was unique. The industry was a competitive one and Firestone had been an early entrant into the SBR market. Introducing a new product usually involves a "learning curve" as the idiosyncracies of a product are revealed. Thus, some evolutionary risks and costs are obviously involved. Apparently, Firestone did not think it should have to bear the brunt of dissatisfaction with the early performance of the SBR.

The Company's Options: Cooperation vs. Noncooperation

Whatever Firestone officials' actual views, cooperation with the NHTSA probably would have meant an extensive recall. Firestone officials thought the NHTSA had only a methodologically rather questionable survey and private complaints as a basis for its investigation.[1] Providing the agency with extensive company records might well give it the evidence it would regard as adequate to determine the presence of a safety-related defect in the tire. Such a verdict would generate considerable pressure on Firestone to agree to a recall. Firestone's cooperation might help the NHTSA to make a case it really did not have, at the very time when company officials suspected that the agency was under pressure to prove it could take effective action. In addition, agreeing to a voluntary recall might be regarded as a *de facto* admission by Firestone that the tire had a safety-related defect even if no physical defect in the tire materials or construction was definitively confirmed. This "concession" might help those suing Firestone for damages resulting from accidents alleged to be caused by the tire. Finally, even a voluntary recall, if publicized, might result in unfavorable publicity, and the tire had already received considerable adverse notice.

On the positive side, cooperation probably would cause the NHTSA to be more conciliatory about the terms of an acceptable recall, would avoid fines, and enable the company to present itself in its public relations as responsible and concerned about the safety of its products.

In contrast, noncooperation would harden the adversarial relationship with the agency by challenging its political credibility, but it would also make it harder for the agency to prove its case against the tire. Moreover, if Firestone could get a favorable federal district court to assume jurisdiction, the company might be able to defend itself successfully against a mandatory recall. Delay would reduce the impact of a recall even if, at some point, it became inevitable.

On the other hand, during the skirmishing with the NHTSA, adverse publicity probably would continue, leading perhaps to a continued loss in sales, as well as more litigation. Firestone could be presented in the media as irresponsible; the agency would be antagonized and thus less conciliatory about the terms of a recall. Finally, in the worst possible outcome, an unsuccessful litigation against a mandatory recall, there would be fines and more negative coverage.

Good/Bad Faith and the Options

Assuming that Firestone officials were in "good faith," neither active cooperation nor noncooperation would seem to be optimal. Some middle course, avoiding a hardened adversarial stance but also not being too forthcoming, probably would be better. Even if a recall ultimately proved unavoidable, it could be delayed and its terms negotiated as a compromise (both factors reducing its financial impact). Firestone could point to its willingness to see the controversy resolved, while stressing its liberal adjustment policy, so it would not appear callous about the consumers' safety. If, in the end, a mutually satisfactory compromise could not be worked out, Firestone could fight a mandatory recall in court.

Assuming that Firestone officials were in "bad faith," the likely consequences of the two basic options were somewhat different. To cooperate fully meant either admitting at the outset that the "500" SBR had safety defects, or, while not admitting to previous knowledge of the deficiencies, providing information to the NHTSA that probably would lead the agency to conclude that company officials had concealed this.

Firestone would, in effect, be assisting in undermining its own credibility. Thus, cooperation would result in an early and extensive recall; the agency would get the data it needed promptly and it could reach its findings quickly. Cooperation might win some concessions from the NHTSA when the terms of a recall were being negotiated, but the agency might be chagrined that Firestone did not come forward sooner. Thus, it might be disposed to impose sanctions. Any efforts by Firestone to save its reputation would be undercut by its previous concealment.

As above, noncooperation probably meant a more adversarial and even acrimonious relationship. The same negative consequences as above would occur, but in this case, the strategy promised, in the short run at least, to conceal the evidence of bad faith. To the extent the company could limit the information it had to provide the NHTSA, it could continue to resist a recall without appearing to be hypocritical. The less information the agency obtained, the less optimistic it might be about winning any litigation over a mandatory recall. Thus, it might ultimately be willing to compromise to settle the controversy. Perhaps it would agree to another limited recall and Firestone's bad faith might escape revelation.

So under the assumption of bad faith, cooperation had little to recommend it, unless the company was prepared to make a major change in its position, offer a *mea culpa,* and promise to act more responsibly in the future. Noncooperation had great risks, but it offered the only way out of a very serious bind—if it succeeded in limiting the agency's access to information.

The Company's Choice: Noncooperation

Whatever the motives of Firestone officials, active cooperation did not appear desirable; they chose a course much closer to active *noncooperation.* When the NHTSA first made its informal inquiries, Firestone did not flatly refuse to answer them, but the company claimed that it would take months to compile all the information the NHTSA sought. Apparently, the company was slow in providing information, and even when it was supplied, it did not fully meet the agency's expectations. Firestone asked for more time, and there were repeated requests for information before the agency issued (in early April, 1978) an administrative order to compel Firestone to respond.

According to Firestone attorneys, the agency requests were so extensive that compliance was virtually impossible; the company lacked an automated information retrieval system capable of producing an adequate response promptly. However, had Firestone really wanted to cooperate, it probably could have expedited the data retrieval. In December, 1977, and the first months of 1978, Firestone officials probably saw no reason to let the agency build a case by delving into confidential company records, because they were skeptical of the agency's basis for singling out the "500" SBR and because these records would have revealed how aware they were of the belt separation and dealer adjustment problems.

When the NHTSA announced its formal investigation of the tire at the end of February, 1978, Firestone officials apparently decided to go on the offensive. Filing suit in early March in the Cleveland federal district court against the Department of Transportation and the NHTSA to prevent use of the disputed survey in the investigation and public release of the results may have been a tactical move to put the agency on the defensive. Firestone attorneys claimed they thought the NHTSA was about to release the results, thereby generating more adverse publicity about the tire. However, the agency asserted at the court hearings that it had no intention of releasing the survey at that time. The Firestone suit was brought before a judge whom the company must have known would be favorably disposed. He issued *ex parte* both a temporary restraining order, until arguments for and against a permanent injunction could be heard, and a broad discovery order which permitted Firestone to inquire into agency activity relating to the survey.[2]

As it turned out, the suit against the survey must have seemed a mixed blessing to Firestone officials. Before Judge Manos could rule on the company request for a permanent injunction, the Center for Auto Safety released the survey results.[3] Assuming the information had been leaked, Firestone officials asked Judge Manos to institute contempt proceedings against the Department of Transportation (DOT) and NHTSA officials. He ordered all documents related to the investigation sequestered until he could determine how the CFAS had obtained the information. NHTSA attorneys denied that DOT officials had any knowledge of the release, and Joan Claybrook, head of the NHTSA, testified that she had no idea how the survey results had reached the CFAS. Firestone was given permission to take depositions in Washington to find the source of the leak.

According to Claybrook, the sequester order and the staff time that had to be diverted to the court proceedings significantly delayed the investigation into the "500" tire. (Judge Manos eventually limited the sequester order.) A permanent injunction would have barred the agency from using the survey as a basis for a finding of defect, but it is not clear that this in itself would have handicapped the agency very much. At the same time, the suit may have conveyed the impression to the media that Firestone wanted to conceal information of vital significance. A *Fortune* article (Louis, 1978) asserted that this episode brought Congressman John Moss, chairman of the Subcommittee on Oversight and Investigations of the House Committee on Interstate and Foreign Commerce, into the case. Moss was pro-consumer and had played a role in the formation of the agency. Company attorneys, in retrospect at least, suspected the agency of appealing to Moss to help them find a convincing basis for determining that the tire had a safety-related defect.

In April, the agency decided to go into federal court to obtain compulsory process for its administrative order. Firestone attorneys claimed they were willing to reach an accommodation with the agency and that the refusal to comply was really *pro forma;* but at the same time, they tried (unsuccessfully) to get the case transferred to Judge Manos' court. By this time, the patience of agency officials probably was exhausted. Yet they had to wait nearly four months to get a favorable decision. On August 15, 1978, Judge Flannery ordered the company to release the information that NHTSA had sought.[4] As the court-appointed deadline approached, Firestone finally put all the documents at the agency's disposal in a warehouse in the District of Columbia. Initially, the documents were not organized to be responsive to the agency's interrogatories, but upon request Firestone labelled them to assist the agency's examination. The company claimed that the documents remained under its control, but the agency rejected this contention. Firestone attorneys said that company staff went to great lengths to supply the documents in response to the court order because they did not want to jeopardize contemporaneous mid-August efforts to negotiate the controversy with the assistance of Clark Clifford, a well-known Washington lawyer with Democratic Party connections.

The attempt to stymie the NHTSA investigation apparently failed because the company decided that the effects of the unfavorable publicity were becoming too costly. The company had received another round of adverse publicity at the Moss subcommittee hearings in July and again at the NHTSA hearing in early August, and a number of significant revelations had appeared in the press.[5]

Publicly, Firestone had not budged in its defense of the tire's safety. Before the Moss subcommittee, Vice President John Floberg put the blame for the blowouts and other "500" failures primarily on mishandling by owners (for example, underinflating tires) and on the "adverse and erroneous publicity" the tire had received. Similarly, at the NHTSA hearing on its preliminary finding of a safety-related defect, Firestone representatives claimed that the tire was comparable in all respects to all other first generation steel-belted radials produced by U.S. manufacturers; they contended that no specific defect in the design or manufacture had been conclusively identified. Neither the agency nor Moss was persuaded.

The Recall

The NHTSA recommended a recall, basing its finding of a defect on inferences from the evidence *in toto*. It claimed that the consumer reports of failures and the unusually high adjustment rate demonstrated a pattern of excessive failures and that it had legal precedent for this way of proceeding. On September 1, Congressman Moss joined the agency in recommending a recall. He was convinced by the evidence his staff collected and presented at the hearings that the tire was defective and dangerous to users. The subcommittee report cited the relatively high adjustment rate of the tire, the number of claims settled by Firestone for tire failure damage, and the high average number of failures per customer. The subcommittee report also criticized the company for issuing only "belated and minimal warnings" to owners that the tires needed unusually careful maintenance to avoid serious deterioration problems (U.S. Congress, 1978). Firestone attorneys felt the subcommittee had bailed out the agency by helping to develop a basis for justifying an adverse determination on the safety issue.

Firestone now had a strong incentive to negotiate a voluntary recall and try to put the controversy behind it. What the NHTSA might learn from the supplied documents probably would hurt Firestone's position even more. Yet the company still had a substantial interest in limiting the *extent* of the recall, and apparently did not attempt to expedite the negotiations. An agreement in principle was not reached until late October and then only under the threat of a final determination by the agency of a safety-related defect and court proceedings for a recall. The initial agreement began to disintegrate immediately as different interpretations of its details surfaced; negotiations resumed, and a formal agreement was signed in late November.

According to a news report in the *Washington Post* (Dec. 27, 1978), Joan Claybrook, head of the NHTSA, asserted that Firestone took three to five days to resolve every issue. In one instance, it took a week to get an answer to a simple question posed to Clark Clifford. Claybrook attributed some of this delay to the highly bureaucratic nature of the Firestone organization. She inferred that there was considerable internal conflict among officials, so that those who had been responsible for the former policy (i.e., continuing to market the "500" when they knew it was defective) stalled when it came to supplying information necessary for the recall. In addition, Clifford had asked the agency to be patient because he was new to the tire industry and was learning about it as he worked on the case. Claybrook's remarks in this interview suggest that the agency thought Firestone had legitimate concerns in the negotiations (e.g., fear of being defrauded by junk dealers seeking compensation for used tires), and appropriately wanted time to design protections against such developments. On the other hand she thought the stalling was, in part, a result of wanting to save money. Firestone's president denied the stalling charge; he said that many details in the final agreement had not been discussed when the original agreement in principle was reached. He claimed that neither side had wanted to sign an incomplete agreement. This may well have been the case, but Firestone's actions suggest that a better and more fully articulated argument might have been negotiated much earlier if the company had chosen to be more cooperative.

THE EFFECTS OF STRATEGIC ACTION

It might now appear that the strategic use of litigation, control of information, and negotiating tactics gained Firestone at most several months' delay in the imposition of a recall that was quite sizable. But it must be recognized that had it not been for the Moss hearings, the adverse publicity, dropping sales, and dealer discontent, Firestone might have delayed the recall much longer. It might have chosen to force the agency to issue a mandatory order and try to enforce it through court processes. Although the agency's newly obtained knowledge would have strengthened it in such a court fight, the ultimate consequences of losing for Firestone (if it did lose) would have been pushed far into the future. Moreover, the costs of a recall at that point, plus fines and legal costs, might have been no worse than the costs of a voluntary recall in the fall of 1978. So one can argue that what limited the effectiveness of strategic action was not the agency's actions, but certain factors over which it had modest influence. The NHTSA did create some negative publicity for Firestone, but the CFAS and the Moss hearings probably had a much greater impact.

Furthermore, the agency's vulnerability to strategic action appears to have been greater than these events suggest. Based on the NHTSA's interpretation of the Firestone documents, one can say that the company's strategic action began much earlier and that the "500" recall represented at best a partial success for the regulatory process. After the limited, voluntary recall of "500" SBR's in late 1976 (through early 1977), the NHTSA had received failure reports on tires not included in the recalled batch that Firestone had said was "contaminated." According to newspaper reports of Claybrook's remarks, the documents led the agency to conclude that Firestone's offer to recall the "contaminated" batch probably represented a substantial containment of the extent of the actual problem. Moreover, other documents suggested that Firestone knew, at the time it challenged the NHTSA in an earlier "500" bias-ply tire case, that the problem of failing adhesion of steel belts to tire walls was a time-dependent problem and that testing one batch of new tires (which Firestone agreed to) probably would not reveal any violation of federal standards. Compliance with standards only at the time of manufacture does not fulfill the manufacturer's obligation under the law. The tires that had failed the test had been sitting in a warehouse for some time.

The Firestone documents indicated that by 1975, the company knew a great deal about these kinds of problems with its tires, including but not limited to the "500" SBR. It had used litigation and control over information strategically for several years, succeeding in keeping knowledge of the extent of its problems from the agency and avoiding extensive recalls prior to the fall of 1978.[6] Had the "500" tire failures not appeared so disproportionate compared to other SBR's, the NHTSA with its limited resources might not have pushed its investigations so far. It is impossible now to determine what percentage of Firestone tires really failed to meet quality control standards or had safety-related defects, but if more information had been available earlier, the impact of regulation on Firestone probably would have been much greater.

The ironic aspect of the case is that Firestone's responses to the NHTSA may have played a crucial role in its becoming the "culprit." Although the company's public actions sometimes made it appear as a corporate bad guy—an insensitive, irresponsible firm that might be giving its whole industry a bad name—the strategic actions and even much of what it concealed from the NHTSA provide only circumstantial evidence concerning the safety of the tire. One cannot say on the basis of the Moss subcommittee hearings and other information available to the outside observer that any definitive finding that the tire was defective was ever made. To a large extent, it appears that the substantially higher adjustment rates of the "500" compared to other Firestone SBR's and to the largest selling lines of seven other companies served as a surrogate measure of comparative safety quality, while specific accidents in which blowouts of "500" 's were the proximate causes served as indicators of the serious consequences of the defects. To this day, Firestone spokesmen claim that evidence on relative failure rates of comparable SBR's does not show the "500" to be inferior.

Yet at the time, the adjustment rate data were the best available evidence of comparative tire quality, whatever the differences in adjustment policies. Firestone may well have been right in December, 1977, that the evidence to support its being singled out for more intensive investigation was not very substantial. And it is not altogether clear that the "500" was the only SBR creating potential safety problems for drivers. But Firestone's actions, particularly its refusal to comply with the NHTSA's administrative order, clearly distinguished it from the other major tire companies. Had Firestone maneuvered somewhat more diplomatically, it might have avoided a recall the justification for which is still somewhat controversial.

Firestone spokesmen give some plausible reasons for the company's taking the actions here labelled "strategic," but it is not possible to determine the extent to which these are essentially *post hoc* rationalizations. In any event, a definitive judgment on the good or bad faith of Firestone executives is not essential to the conclusion that strategic action can frustrate the purposes of regulation and that the consumer may be the victim. To the extent that all observers might agree that there was some safety problem with the "500" SBR, and thus that some drivers were at risk (although the specific risk was very difficult to determine and varied depending on the tire and the circumstances), then strategic action and the resulting delays worked against the public interest. Whether the reasons were good or bad, the actions Firestone management took were strategic, intended to delay and impede a finding by the agency that the "500" had a safety-related defect and should be recalled. It seems clear that Firestone chose to take an adversarial stance toward the agency and that a mutually acceptable resolution of the controversy was not its primary concern until the costs to the company of refusing to compromise became substantial. Yet even if one assumes good faith motivations, Firestone may have overplayed its hand, and the strategic action approach may not have been optimal.[7]

REFORM PROPOSALS

If strategic action in response to regulation may not be in the interest of either the corporation and industry involved or the general public, then some reforms intended to reduce the likelihood of this behavior may be suggested. The most significant of these are: (1) giving the NHTSA (or other agencies) more resources to collect, analyze, and disseminate information on product quality; and (2) restructuring corporate decision-making to increase the chances that problems such as the "500" posed would not be concealed.

Strengthening the NHTSA

In the present political climate, the powers of regulatory agencies are not likely to be significantly strengthened, but a case can be made for giving the NHTSA more resources for independent compliance testing and for collecting adjustment data from the major companies. At the time of the GAO report (1973), the NHTSA was requesting this information only as part of its inquiries, but the agency mandate permits collection of adjustment data on a regular basis. Public surveys, if properly constructed, might also play a role in providing early warning information. Self-initiated consumer complaints will provide only limited, unsystematic, and highly subjective evidence.

Improved information collection might enable the agency to initiate investigations before corporations have been distributing a product for several years. Yet the costs sunk in development and production preparation alone are very substantial, and the losses caused by an immediate recall (especially if the product has to be scrapped) could go totally uncompensated. At present, the regulatory process permits a corporation to delay (if not avoid) some of the costs of an imperfectly engineered product, thereby putting the consumer at some risk. One might say, with the advantage of hindsight, that Firestone should have delayed its entry into the SBR market until it was more satisfied with its adhesion results. However, in the early 1970s, the uncertainties of evaluating which course—holding back or plunging ahead—promised greater net benefits were considerable. The lure of gaining a significant share of a new market, plus the ability to manipulate the regulatory process (should it be necessary), probably will lead a competitive company to move ahead. To protect the consumer from bearing these risks, government would have to slow the pace of innovation. This would mean much greater intervention into the realm of corporate decision-making, and that seems even less likely than a general strengthening of regulatory agencies at this time.

Another alternative would be to increase the regulatory agency's efforts to educate the public and disseminate product quality information so consumers could make better choices. For example, extensive performance testing of major competing lines might permit the NHTSA to inform consumers about product strengths and weaknesses, particularly when it cannot make a good case for a recall. However, this would require greatly expanded resources for testing, and publication of such comparisons probably would put the agency in a more adversarial posture vis-à-vis the industry as a whole.[8]

Restructuring the Corporation

What changes in the organization of the corporation might alleviate the problem of strategic action? Christopher Stone (1975) proposes a restructuring of corporate decision making in order to achieve more responsible decisions. He effectively criticizes the deficiencies of using legal sanctions (and by implication, the regulatory process) to constrain undesirable corporate behavior. Instead, he favors legislation to require certain major corporations to appoint outside directors with specified powers, responsibilities, and resources, as well as the establishment of information nets designed to bring important facts and considerations relating to questionable corporate behavior before the highest level decision-makers.

Presumably, these reforms could inhibit corporate strategic action because outside directors would be made aware of the problems inducing managers to resort to such tactics and would raise objections. In the

"500" case, it seems that top executives knew about the tire problems at a relatively early stage (concealment by middle managers or engineers was not an issue), so independent-minded outside directors armed with this information might have been persuasive in urging Firestone to withdraw the "500" or at least to enter into a negotiating posture sooner. The option of such a director to go public, if his colleagues would not change their stance, might also have some real influence, although this would require atypical behavior. The critical problem with Stone's proposals is not their putative effects; these probably would be salutary. However, the necessary legislation would be at least as difficult to draft and pass in Congress as legislation strengthening regulatory agencies.

Other Reforms

Industry self-policing (e.g., establishment of an organization to monitor comparative data on product quality) might be worth exploring, but arrangements that could win industry support and still have credibility with the public and the regulatory agencies probably would be difficult to develop. In the "500" case, reliable industry-wide data on SBR adjustments and known tire failures might have resolved the controversy sooner and certainly to the advantage of the consumer. An independently conducted survey supported by the agency and the industry might also have helped. However, other major firms may have been content to let Firestone bear the brunt of the SBR controversy.

Whistle-blowing offers some possibilities, but legal protections are controversial, and in any case, creating an ethic of whistle-blowing, as Ralph Nader has been trying to do, is a long-term effort. Active consumer organizations can play a role in informing the public about safety issues and at least alert consumers to certain dangers. However, the resources of such organizations do not permit them to undertake much independent testing, and their immediate audiences are limited, so much depends on whether the national media give their releases coverage. In this case, the CFAS apparently helped catalyze efforts to investigate the "500" tire.

SOCIAL RESPONSIBILITY AND THE ETHIC OF FAIR DEALING

One cannot feel confident that any of the reform alternatives are likely to have much impact on the regulatory relationship in the near future. Therefore, an appeal to corporate social responsibility has a place in efforts to address the problem. Although the continuing debate about the implications of social responsibility has created some doubts that the concept will ever have a major impact, it still may have some promise as a constraint on corporate behavior. But social responsibility cannot be left so ambiguous that it has no behavioral implications; the failure to address the regulatory relationship is a particularly glaring omission in the literature.

An ethic of fair dealing must have some appeal to corporate executives if they are to constrain their behavior in the regulatory relationship. This suggests that there be some reciprocal elements, i.e., that the constraints apply as well to the behavior of the agency, and that fair dealing can be shown to bear on the long-term (what is often called the "enlightened") interest of the corporation, even though in any particular situation, a short-term narrow assessment of benefits and costs may support strategic action vis-à-vis the regulatory agency.

What, if anything, do the parties to the regulatory relationship owe each other? At present, corporation executives may choose to regard the existence of regulatory agencies and regulations as reducing their responsibility to purchasers of their products, while not creating any new obligations on their part vis-à-vis agencies. The passage of regulatory legislation may be interpreted as evidence that political office-holders reject both corporate morality and the market as sufficient to prevent the production and sale of harmful or defective products or the harmful consequences of the production process itself. In other words, once regulations come into existence, corporate officials may decide their only obligation is to obey the law, for example, conform to the regulations and not violate government standards. Obviously, what constitutes compliance with regulations is often a complex matter. An ethic of fair dealing might spell out the nature of reciprocal obligations between regulator and regulatee.

How have notions of fair dealing been developed in other institutionally adversarial relationships? Are there any analogous relationships involving parties with conflicting interests who interact to reach a mutually acceptable resolution of differences within judicially-enforced boundaries? And if so, might these by analogy offer support for the practicality of mutual restraint and provide some content for the ethic? An analysis of plea bargaining in the judicial process and collective bargaining in labor relations provides some useful ideas.

Plea-Bargaining

The practice of plea-bargaining between public prosecutors and defense attorneys offers a starting point, even though the analogy is not too close. The opposing attorneys have some clearly conflicting interests. Defense counsel is expected to provide an effective legal defense for the accused regardless of personal opinions as to the client's actual conduct and guilt, while the prosecuting attorney seeks to obtain some kind of conviction of the formally accused individual. The plea-bargaining situation is an ambiguous one because there are few definite, publicly prescribed rules to govern it, and courts do not officially acknowledge its existence; judges deal only with the plea itself. However, prosecutors engaged in plea-bargaining are under some legal constraints. They cannot legally suppress discoverable or exculpatory evidence; an indictment where no probable cause is thought to exist would be fraudulent.

Yet there is a realm in which bluffing (as it is called) can occur without violating these legal norms. Legal scholars have raised the questions: Are there any ethical norms governing this realm, or are all forms of bluffing within the law generally considered acceptable? In other words, how truthful are the parties expected to be to each other in seeking to work out a mutually acceptable plea? One recent study (McDonald, Cramer, and Rossman, 1980) indicates that some norms are widely subscribed to by prosecutors and defense attorneys, although their purview seems rather modest.

Most prosecutors do not believe that they have to reveal to defense attorneys information about *all* the weaknesses in their cases (e.g., logistical or administrative problems) that may reduce the probability of obtaining a conviction in a case. They also apparently do not feel obliged to tell defense counsel about constitutional weaknesses. Moreover, they do not consider it illegitimate to accept cases into the system when they know that the evidence does not yet meet the standards of proof required at later stages of adjudication, nor do they see themselves as trying to bluff legally innocent defendants into convictions. At the same time, the prosecutors draw the line at outright lying. For example, they would not say in court that they were ready for trial if that was not true, and many indicated they would tell defense counsel that they were not ready, if directly asked. They also feel obliged to deal with certain legal aspects of conviction, such as making sure that the statute of limitations has not run out.

Thus, although the norms apparently give prosecutors considerable leeway in conveying the impression that a case is actually stronger than they think it to be, some limits are observed. The authors attribute this in large part to the importance of credibility to lawyers, both prosecutors and defense attorneys. Successful plea-bargaining depends on there being a definite sense of trust between the adversarial parties. Defense attorneys must believe in the prosecutors' essential truthfulness and willingness to honor commitments or the negotiations will not achieve their goal. That would be inconvenient for prosecutors if it occurred frequently. It appears that credibility is important for defense attorneys, too, because public prosecutors can make their job much harder if they choose to. They can force defense counsel to go through the time-consuming process of filing motions for discovery to obtain any information to which they are entitled.

So, these authors suggest, self-interest provides a strong incentive for rejecting some defensive/offensive tactics that are *not* illegal. Nonetheless, some of the differences between plea-bargaining and corporate-agency relations reveal the problems of working out mutually acceptable restraints in the latter situation. In plea-bargaining, there appear to be congruent interests in reaching an agreement and the parties realize the necessity of some degree of trust to achieve the plea-bargain. Deceit and reneging on commitments would undermine trust, but the notion of fair dealing is rather limited. In the regulatory context, the mutual interest in restraint may be less, and at the same time, the rules of fair dealing must be more extensive because the standards of legal conduct in the regulatory context are less explicit. Bad-faith action in the plea-bargaining situation may jeopardize a prosecutor's case or even result in an attorney's losing the right to practice, but regulators and regulatees may be more uncertain about the negative consequences of bad-faith actions. Moreover, in the regulatory context, there may be fewer instances of negotiation where the previous outcomes have a significant influence, although the Firestone case illustrates that regulator-regulatee interaction may occur intermittently over many years.

Collective Bargaining

The duty to bargain in good faith in the law of labor relations offers another analogy, one that confirms the possibility of giving a good-faith ethic substantial content. Although labor law experts indicate that the phrase has defied precise definition, the federal courts and the National Labor Relations Board (NLRB) have grappled with the concept and their efforts have yielded some indicia. The behaviors that have been selected as indicators (positive and negative) are instructive:

1. Willingness to compromise, for example, by granting numerous concessions;
2. Advancement of proposals, assuming they are not patently unreasonable or harsh;
3. Rejection of previously accepted proposals;
4. Injection of new proposals after months of bargaining;
5. Introduction of new issues after an agreement has been reached;
6. Willful avoidance of meeting or delaying tactics;
7. Failure to supply requested information promptly;
8. Attempts to place conditions on bargaining or executing a contract;

9. Attempts to bypass a union with majority status in order to deal directly with employees; and
10. Commission of unfair labor practices during negotiations.

If the employer claims that compiling the data will be unduly burdensome, it must assert that claim at the time of the request for information so that an arrangement may be made to lessen the burden. . . . Where it does allow the union free access to its records and fully cooperates with the union in answering questions, an employer need not furnish information in a more organized form than that in which it keeps its own records (Morris, 1971, pp. 315–16).

The courts have explicitly recognized that the bargaining situation is one of opposed interests. Exerting economic pressure against the other party to influence its willingness to agree is not in itself inconsistent with the duty to bargain in good faith. Moreover, the law recognizes the legitimacy of an impasse after extended, intense bargaining has taken place. In other words, good-faith bargaining may not produce an agreement.

The definition of good-faith bargaining in labor relations law suggests that the problems of determining the parties' state of mind and motivations can be circumvented by focusing on their observable conduct vis-à-vis the other party in its totality. Moreover, the parallels between what constitutes good faith in the regulatory relationship and what has been defined in labor relations are considerable. Of course, there are differences in the two relationships. The union and the employer are peers whose bargaining is regulated by the NLRB and the federal courts. The regulatory relationship is asymmetrical, because the agency is endowed with public authority. However, this may be reason for the regulatee's having a greater responsibility to deal fairly. Bad faith in collective bargaining defies public authority only because of the statutory requirement; otherwise, it would be only a challenge to a private organization. Bad faith by a regulatee challenges public authority.

Mutual interest may be somewhat clearer in the labor-management bargaining relationship; without a contract, the two parties may not be able to cooperate in the economic functioning of an enterprise. However, the absence of a contract will not necessarily bring operations to a halt, and the bargaining parties may not feel equal pressure to reach an agreement. Indeed, it is open to the parties to use economic pressure to create increased incentives to agree. On the other hand, the regulated corporation is not necessarily trying to reach an agreement with the agency. "No agreement" may be a desirable situation, and the corporation may choose to test the agency's ability to impose any outcome whatsoever. Similar situations can prevail in the union-management relationship, but in a sense this is why the obligation to bargain in good faith was made a legal requirement. The ethic of fair dealing is intended to provide analogous restraints in the regulatory relationship.

Fair Dealing in the Regulatory Relationship

What might "fair dealing" in the regulatory relationship imply? A definition might include the following:

1. That both sides be truthful concerning matters of critical fact;
2. That corporations be responsive to specific inquiries that are within the agency's authority;
3. That the agency not abuse the information supplied;
4. That both sides negotiate in "good faith";
5. That neither side avoid crucial considerations in order to obtain greater discretion under the conditions of an agreement;
6. That nominal compliance with the law is not sufficient;
7. That the legal process not be used obstructively or primarily as a bargaining ploy.

In the context of the Firestone "500" case, these principles do not imply that the corporation could legitimately expect the NHTSA to reveal to it the deficiencies in the investigatory findings or that the NHTSA could expect the corporation to come forth and make the case for recall on its own. But they do suggest that Firestone should have been more responsive to the NHTSA's requests for information. The difficulties of supplying what the agency requested were real, but Firestone was capable of a "crash" effort when it decided that was warranted. Fair dealing might suggest that the agency should have discussed candidly with Firestone the grounds for its selection of their tire for unique treatment. Firestone would have been within the limits of fair dealing in seeking to bar public release of the survey (but not its use by the agency). Firestone could legitimately expect the NHTSA not to "try" the case in the media.

When Firestone first agreed to the general terms of the voluntary recall, it apparently chose to interpret the language of the agreement in the way most conducive to reducing recall costs. Assuming that Firestone had reservations about the terms or realized the ambiguities and their implications, these should have been raised beforehand, rather than held in reserve for further negotiations.

When Firestone finally supplied the information the NHTSA requested in response to the court order, it apparently unloaded a huge amount of documents on the agency near the court's deadline and not in a form that made them easy to use. This may have been unavoidable at that stage, but more compliance earlier would have averted this kind of situation.

With respect to item 7, obstructive use of the legal process, it is hard to draw the line. For example, a corporation may threaten to fight a mandatory recall in court, knowing that its case is weak and that litigation can only serve to delay an adverse verdict. Under our legal system, an appeal to the law is generally considered legitimate as long as a plaintiff's lawyer can make some kind of case. This is why drawing lines is difficult. If a corporation has knowledge of its own culpability when it embarks on defensive litigation, and if it chooses the latter primarily as a means of delay or to gain a concession in return for dropping the litigation, this would seem to be bad-faith obstruction. A similar constraint applies to regulatory agencies; initiating litigation as a bargaining ploy indicates bad faith. However, it would seem that the limited legal resources of government agencies would discourage such tactics, whereas for large corporations, such legal expenses might well be a minor item.

It is hard to reach a judgment on this aspect of fair dealing in the "500" case. Firestone's attempt to bar the NHTSA from using its survey may have been an obstructive use of litigation. Firestone claimed that the agency lacked OMB authorization to conduct it, but the real substance of the controversy was the validity of the survey and the conclusions the agency wanted to draw from it. A court would not be the best forum for deciding those issues. Firestone had other opportunities to impugn the methodology and inferences drawn from the survey. Firestone's refusal to respond to the agency's administrative order may also have been an obstructive use of the legal process. The federal district court in which the NHTSA brought suit dismissed all of the company's contentions, but several months elapsed before the agency got its verdict. If Firestone's main concern was the burden of providing the documents, it would appear that compromise was possible. However, it seems that Firestone did not want the agency to have access to certain kinds of information. This probably was less negotiable, but perhaps also less justifiable.

On the other side, there were suggestions that the NHTSA may have been making bad-faith threats to institute a mandatory recall. The Justice Department allegedly was not optimistic about the prospects of the case were it to be argued in the Cleveland federal district court. However, it seems plausible that once the NHTSA had the Firestone documents, agency officials considered their case much strengthened and they were quite prepared to pursue the case. The Justice Department would not have controlled the agency's decision to proceed.

Obligation and Incentives for Fair Dealing

Because regulatory agencies can legally require regulated corporations to take certain actions, as well as impose sanctions, fairness to the corporation requires due process procedures. However, it is the due process procedures that create the possibilities for strategic action by the corporation. Therefore, fairness to the agency would seem to require that the corporations abide by an ethic of fair dealing. Of course, in the labor relations arena, the courts stand ready to induce bargaining in good faith by legal compulsion. In the regulatory relationship, a strong sense of social responsibility and perhaps industry peer pressure may induce the same result.

Fair dealing may, in fact, be only a morality of prudent reciprocity. The parties to the relationship may choose to exercise some restraint on their conduct because they want to facilitate negotiation and compromise. Corporations under health and safety regulations have some interest in cooperating with regulatory agencies. Cooperation may reassure consumers and employees at a time when there is considerable skepticism about manufacturers' claims, and it may well help to avert demands for more stringent regulatory rules or legislation.

Compromise may be viewed as preferable to remaining long in a zero-sum competition; and fair dealing can prevent the degeneration into a negative-sum situation. When one party engages in bad-faith behavior, the other party can retaliate in kind, and the bad-faith exchanges may escalate. On the other hand, fair dealing and self-restraint may create the possibility of cooperative resolutions that would not have seemed likely in an adversarial setting.

The most troublesome aspect of strategic action may well be that it is most attractive to the bad-faith regulatee, the firm that wants to conceal its knowledge of potentially damaging information. In such cases, the risks and costs to employees or consumers may be the most serious, but the bad-faith firm probably will not be constrained by such a fair-dealing ethic, even if it recognizes some elements of reciprocity. Thus, proposing an ethic of fair dealing for corporations under regulation may amount to little more than telling bad-faith firms to act in good faith, and that is hardly likely to be effective unless the ethic is widely adhered to by other firms. A skeptical observer might conclude that subscribing to an ethic of fair dealing seems to define social responsibility in terms of rather limited obligations for what are very powerful corporations.

Conclusion

It is important to recognize that an ethic of fair dealing is a necessary but not sufficient definition of social responsibility: Necessary, because rejection would imply denial of the legitimacy of public regulation; not sufficient, because of its minimal content. The problem of strategic action in its broadest dimensions raises the fundamental issue of the accommodation between corporate capitalism and our representative and plebiscitary democratic institutions. Frequently, we hear talk that most of the corporate world has accepted the legitimacy of the welfare state in the relatively limited form it has taken in this country. In a sense, the attack on regulation raises that same issue in another form, even though the argument is often disguised in terms of cost-benefit analysis. To maintain its own legitimacy in our society, corporate capitalism obviously has had to make concessions to the authority of the public sector. Corporations cannot portray themselves as "good citizens" while maintaining serious reservations about a feature of the modern liberal state as fundamental as the regulatory structure designed to protect the public from unacceptable business behavior.

NOTES

1. See *The Safety of Firestone 500 Steel Belted Radial Tires,* Hearings of the Subcommittee on Oversight and Investigations of the Committee on Interstate and Foreign Commerce, House of Representatives, 95th Congress, May 19, 22, 23, July 10, 1978, pp. 160–62, for the exchange between Congressman David Stockman and Clarence Ditlow, Director of the Center for Auto Safety, concerning the validity of the survey.

2. NHTSA appealed the original ruling to the Circuit Court of Appeals, alleging that Judge Manos lacked jurisdiction; Firestone asked the same court to dismiss the NHTSA's motion to dismiss Firestone's case. The Circuit Court denied both motions.

3. CFAS Director Ditlow claimed that he was not aware of the court order. The survey apparently was inadvertently included in materials released by NHTSA to CFAS in response to a Freedom of Information Act request. In light of the company's sensitivity about the survey, it would appear that greater caution should have been exercised by NHTSA. However, agency officials denied that there had been a deliberate leak.

4. *U.S. v. The Firestone Tire and Rubber Company,* 455 F. Supp. 1072 (1978).

5. For example, the *Akron Beacon-Journal* reported in July that Firestone had discovered serious problems in some of its SBR's during its own tests but had not informed the Government. The NHTSA released to the press correspondence between Firestone and Montgomery Ward revealing compensation the tire company paid for excessive tire adjustments.

6. The Firestone documents apparently convinced the NHTSA that its case against the "500" tire was valid and that the company had concealed important information from it that would have changed the outcomes of these earlier cases. After the final agreement was signed, Claybrook released selected documents to the press to show that Firestone had known about the deficiencies of the tire. She said that, technically, the company had been guilty of putting tires on the road that it knew did not meet federal standards. She also said that she would seek the maximum fine ($800,000) because of what the agency had learned about the circumstances of the earlier "500" recall. See *Washington Post,* December 23, 1978. Firestone protested the release of these documents, and never offered a *mea culpa.* The issues raised by this incident cannot be explored here; but the relation between sanctions and the purposes of regulation needs to be examined.

7.   A recent statement by John Nevin, President of Firestone, is strongly critical of Firestone's strategic action and endorses an early voluntary recall. Nevin was not associated with Firestone during the period involved in this incident. See John Nevin, "Product Quality, Corporate Competitivity and Consumerism" (paper presented at "The Future of Consumerism" Conference, Washington, D.C., October, 1981).

8.   Claybrook was moving in this direction shortly before her tenure ended; for example, the NHTSA's 35 mph crash tests of American and foreign cars. See Allan Parachin, "Crusade for Safety: The Next Consumer Drive," *Los Angeles Times,* November 23, 1980.

REFERENCES

Louis, Arthur M., "Lessons from the Firestone Fracas." *Fortune* (August 28, 1978):45–48.

MacAvoy, Paul, *The Regulated Industries and the Economy.* New York: Norton, 1979.

McDonald, William F., James A. Cramer, and Henry H. Rossman, "Prosecutorial Bluffing and the Case Against Plea-Bargaining." In McDonald and Cramer, *Plea-Bargaining.* Lexington, Mass.: Lexington Books, 1980.

Morris, Charles J. (ed.), *The Developing Labor Law: The Board, the Courts, and the National Labor Relations Act.* District of Columbia: The Bureau of National Affairs, Inc., 1971.

Owen, Bruce, and Ronald Braeutigam, *The Regulation Game: Strategic Use of the Administrative Process.* Cambridge, Mass.: Ballinger, 1978.

Stone, Christopher, *Where the Law Ends: The Social Control of Corporate Behavior.* New York: Harper & Row, 1975.

U.S. Comptroller-General, *For Safer Motor Vehicles; More Effective Efforts Needed to Insure Compliance with Federal Safety Standards: National Highway Traffic Safety Administration, Department of Transportation.* Washington, D.C.: 3(April 24, 1973):B-164407.

U.S. Congress, House, Subcommittee on Oversight, and Investigations of the Committee on Interstate, and Foreign Commerce, *The Safety of Firestone Steel Belted Radial Tires.* Hearing, 95th Cong., Washington: Government Printing Office, August 16, 1978.

THE TWO-PART PROBLEM OF REGULATORY COMPLIANCE:

COMPLIANCE REFORM AND STRIP MINING

Barry M. Mitnick

The impacts of regulation have received greatly increased attention in recent years. Included among this work have been a number of attempts to measure the costs of regulation (for example, Arthur Andersen and Co. 1979; DeFina 1977; Weidenbaum 1981; U.S. Senate, Committee on Governmental Affairs 1978) and a few attempts to assess its benefits (for example, Ashford and Hill 1980). The work on costs has tended to dramatize the magnitude of the impacts on the firm of regulatory compliance; the extent of *net* societal costs and particular cost or benefit distributions remains, however, a matter for scholarly analysis and debate. The basic rationales for government regulation have been the subject of renewed attention; considerable uncertainty has existed among

Research in Corporate Social Performance and Policy, Vol. 4, pages 215–242
Copyright © 1982 by JAI Press Inc.
All rights of reproduction in any form reserved.
ISBN: 0-89232-259-4

recent analysts regarding the appropriate forms and loci for such intervention in economic and social behavior (see, for example, Mitnick 1980a).

In this climate, public policy (and its analysis) has increasingly reflected a sensitivity to nongovernmental means of achieving social goals and a willingness to examine a wide range of regulatory alternatives—and substitutes. "Privatization," which often involves the use of market-centered means to substitute for government-administered controls, has even been the subject of popular discussion in the press (Lee 1981; Ubell, 1981). Thus the work on regulatory reform both responds to problems experienced by private sector managers under regulation and holds promise for creation of new, possibly problematic—or facilitative—environments for the exercise of managerial initiative.

An important component of the recent renaissance in regulatory studies has been the increased attention paid by both scholars and practitioners to innovative forms of regulation. While the ultimate extent of implementation of these new methods (as well as of any improvements in regulatory efficiency) is as yet unclear, a large number of cases of consideration and/or use of such "innovative techniques" has been documented (U.S. Regulatory Council 1980a, b). This paper deals with one class of these new forms, that referred to by the former U.S. Regulatory Council (now part of the Office of Management and Budget) as "compliance reform." The discussion proceeds in the context of strip mining regulation for purposes of illustration.

Compliance reform is concerned with the development of efficient and nonintrusive means of insuring compliance to regulatory goals by regulated parties. Thus compliance reform aims to use "federal resources more effectively," reduce the "burden" of compliance carried by regulated parties, and stimulate "a deeper commitment in the regulated public to the goals of regulation" through "the use of closer-to-home expertise" (U.S. Regulatory Council 1980a, p. 25). Compliance reform includes such techniques as self-certification of compliance, third-party auditing or certification of compliance, penalties that match the benefits that regulated parties gain from noncompliance, advisory (information rather than violation-citation-oriented) inspections, and negotiated settlement (encouragement or mediation of dispute settlement without imposition of regulatory solutions). While compliance reform can feature attenuation or reduction in scale of actual regulating activity, it does not include deregulation; some degree and form of regulation is assumed to remain.

The analysis that follows focuses on self- and third-party auditing/certification. (For other, recent views on self-regulation, see Garvin 1981a, b; papers by Grumbly and by Bardach in Bardach and Kagan

1982; Tobin 1979, 1982.) It should be noted that in discussing these "compliance reform" techniques we shall not be treating all of the issues surrounding the question of compliance. In essence, we shall consider the advantages and disadvantages of particular monitoring/policing techniques, holding other factors (for example, penalty levels, regulation content and adjudicatory procedures, and so on) constant.

THE COMPLIANCE PROBLEM AND INCENTIVE RELATIONS

Any form of regulation gives rise to a *dual or two-part compliance problem:* both regulators and regulatees must be controlled in order to achieve the regulatory objective. "Control," of course, can include voluntary adherence to the role performance expected of each party. Regulatory design must therefore pay attention *both* to the compliance of regulators with the regulatory goals and tasks set for them, and the compliance achieved on the part of the regulatees.

The two-part compliance problem may be analyzed through consideration of the incentive systems that may structure compliance in each area. Backoff and Mitnick (Mitnick, Backoff, and Rainey 1977; Mitnick 1980a) have proposed a model of what is termed an *incentive relation* that permits the systematic mapping and analysis of such systems. In brief, it is argued that the concept of "incentive" is to be understood as a relation, rather that as an object, as something transferred, or as a thing of particular value. Incentives always presume the existence of an incentive sender, an incentive receiver, and a sender-receiver relation. The sender-receiver relation includes the rewards transferred, the "incentive message" by which the sender specifies the behavior on which the reward is contingent, and other relational factors. The relation may be influenced by elements in its proximal and distal environments, such as internal organizational structure, technology and so on; external group characteristics; and influences from the wider society. To understand the two-part compliance problem we therefore map the incentive relations that exist between and among the regulatees, the regulators, and other parties as incentive receivers and senders. The regulated industry, for example, may create a successful incentive relation with the regulators, as in so-called regulatory "capture."

The incentive systems perspective seems a natural and appropriate one to adopt in the context of analyzing control systems. In fact, its present form in the work of Backoff and Mitnick emerged from more general work on the theory of agency (see, for example, Mitnick 1980a, b; Mitnick 1980a references other work on agency). The agency research seeks to develop general models of social (including regulatory) behavior of "acting for," that is, agents "acting for" principals. Principals may manipulate aspects of the incentive system between them and their agents in order to promote agent behavior of the kind desired. The relevance of agency and incentive system models to control systems, including prescriptive design of such systems, follows directly.

While the major focus of this paper is on the two-part compliance problem and the utility of certain compliance reform techniques, the analysis also proceeds on two other levels: an an illustration of the application of incentive relation analysis to regulation, and as an illustrative assessment of the utility of the compliance reform techniques in strip mining regulation. Appropriate references reflecting the basic compliance reform technique analysis, the incentive model application, and the case in strip mining are therefore incorporated in the text.

An Illustration

To illustrate the two-part compliance problem, consider a recent strip mining case in Kentucky. (This account is based on DiSalvo 1980.)

In October 1977, Darrell Yother of Kentucky awoke to discover that an earthen sediment pond to catch strip mine run-off had been built by a coal mine operator in the middle of Madlock Hollow Road, the only road to Mr. Yother's house. Mr. Yother was forced to walk with his 8½-month pregnant wife through a half-mile of rain and deep mud to the main road. Having deposited his wife with relatives, Mr. Yother went to the county courthouse to request action against the operator. County officials, allegedly sensitive to the coal operator's family, which "controlled much of the political action in the county," refused. Mr. Yother went next to the state regulatory authority, the Department for Natural Resources and Environmental Protection (DNREP), which also refused to act immediately. The inspector who considered the case, when asked later why he had taken no action, replied, "I forgot." When asked if any action would be taken, he said, "No, it's too late." Mr. Yother then sued the company and, in addition, filed charges against the company at DNREP's central office in the state capital, Frankfort. The coal company settled quickly in order to avoid delaying a pending application for a strip-mine permit.

While Mr. Yother's experience in third-party auditing is relevant to the central concern of this paper with the evaluation of techniques of compliance reform, it also illustrates the two-part compliance problem and the two-part incentive system which produces or resolves it. In this case there appeared to be both a failure in compliance by the regulated party, the coal operator, and by lower level officials charged with administering the law as it then existed. We may speculate that in the coal operator's incentive relation with the state regulatory body (and with local officials) the perceived probability of enforcement of whatever penalties existed was rather low. Alternatively, of course, the company may have been ignorant of proper (or regulated) procedures in constructing sediment ponds. Given Mr. Yother's experience, the second possibility seems less likely to have been the primary reason. When the probability of enforcement of penalties was significantly increased through the private lawsuit and, in particular, the threat of delay in permit issuance, the company settled quickly.

Ignorance of the "incentive message"—the specifications that are accompanied by the promise of rewards or penalties—is not, however, uncommon. Regulations can be complex and can require considerable technical expertise to interpret and to implement. In addition, even where the regulations themselves may emphasize "performance" over "design" standards (that is, emphasize end goals rather than specific compliance activities), regulatees may lack the expertise to design by themselves compliance activities that can achieve those performance standards (see, for example, Menzel, Hedge et al. 1981, pp. 18-19, on the lack of expertise among coal operators in West Virginia). Design standards involve significant costs of development, and create lengthy and complex regulations that may inhibit use of new technology and may be insensitive to local conditions. Nevertheless, one argument for their use has been in effect that regulatees simply lack the capability to convert an end-goal oriented incentive message into effective compliance (Kirschten 1979, p. 1980).

Furthermore, considering the second compliance problem, regulators (in this case, strip mining inspectors), may be judged either to lack sufficient expertise to relate ongoing mining activities to performance standards or to use the discretion they possess under performance standards to regulate in the spirit of the law. As with Mr. Yother's state inspector, regulators may "forget" because they are overly sensitive to the regulated party's interest, because the regulator does not know how to comply with the regulations or to respond to a complaint under them, because the regulator's job convenience dictates that nothing be done, and so on.

The tension between performance and design standards in regulation—in part, a tension over the degree of discretion permitted lower-level line regulators in their incentive relation with the superior regulatory authority—can reflect the level of trust between regulatory levels. In the history of strip mining and its regulation at the state and local level, there is no shortage of Mr. Yothers. We turn now to some related compliance issues in the federal-state system of strip mining regulation.

COMPLIANCE ISSUES IN STRIP MINING REGULATION

Federal-state relationships during the implementation of the Surface Mining Control and Reclamation Act of 1977, which appears to have been passed in response to a history of abuses like that described above, have hardly been congenial. State laws and enforcement practices have varied greatly from state to state, and, within states, varied over time. Under the 1977 Act, state regulatory bodies have the opportunity to assume "primacy" in enforcement over the federal body, subject to federal approval. The state bodies have felt that federal regulators have not been sensitive to these variations and to the changes that have occurred. In addition, there has been a perception of basic enforcement philosophy differences between federal and state regulators. The federal regulators are perceived, stereotypically, as going by-the-rules and creating adversary relationships with regulated firms, while the state people are seen as more compromising and cooperative (Menzel 1981; Menzel and Hedge 1981; Comptroller General of the U.S. 1979; Haurwitz 1981b). The early OSM has been described by William Harger, president of the Western Pennsylvania Surface Coal Operators Association: "It was a new broom and it swept pretty damn hard and pretty clean" (Haurwitz 1981b). One OSM regional director reported an instruction from his superiors specifying that "Regional Offices should not fraternize with operators; that we (OSM) were environmentalists and you can't talk with the industry" (Menzel and Hedge 1981, p. 20).

State regulators have in some cases appeared resentful of the rigidity of federal controls on state enforcement activity. For example, J. Anthony Ercole, head of Pennsylvania's Bureau of Surface Mine Reclamation, commented, "we are going to dance to a federal tune. So far we have been working for the (federal) Office of Surface Mining, not with it" (Watson 1979; see also Watson 1978b; Edgmon and Menzel 1981; Menzel and Hedge 1981).

On the other hand, state regulatory bodies have enjoyed enormous growth due to federal grants to support implementation of the 1977 Act (on OSM grants to the states, see Edgmon and Menzel 1981). In Ohio, for example, the total program budget (including both state and federal contributions) in the state's Division of Reclamation has gone from $762,000 in 1977 to about $2.26 million in fiscal year 1981 (personal communication, Jeffrey L. Wilson, Division of Reclamation, Ohio Department of Natural Resources, July 27, 1981). Of the latter amount, only about $920,000 is from state funding. Such growth is usually welcomed in any organization, and should certainly be welcomed by the traditionally small and understaffed state reclamation bodies.

Critics in industry and in state government have argued that the federal regulations, both interim and, particularly, those proposed by the federal body as permanent, are the product of "deskbound" bureaucrats with only theoretical technical, not field experience (Omang 1980, p. A12). The regulations are said to be insensitive to local, state, and regional differences (Edgmon and Menzel 1981). The size of requisite sedimentation basins may differ, for example, depending on expected rainfall; dry Western climates may require different run-off precautions than wetter Eastern ones.

Supporters of federal regulation reply that reliance on diverse state programs alone, or the permitting of widely varying standards by locale, would give an edge to coal from states with more lenient regulation (*Pittsburgh Post Gazette* 1980; Edgmon and Menzel 1981). State officials across the country have from time to time expressed fears of growth of competition among state regulatory regimes (personal communication, official of Division of Reclamation, Ohio Department of Natural Resources, May 1, 1981). Since companies may thus move to such more lenient states, or expand operations relatively more in such states, there will be a market-like downward push on the severity of regulations; states may attenuate regulations in order to keep or attract mining firms. Strategic exploitation of regulatory regimes is common to a number of regulated areas, such as corporate chartering, chartering of financial institutions, toxic substance regulation, and truck registration (see Mitnick 1981; Rowland and Marz 1979).

Coal companies have in general been hostile to regulation; this is obviously a key consideration in evaluating the effectiveness of such compliance reforms as self-certification. There are other complications as well. Larger firms can more easily respond to complex regulation than can smaller firms; they have the capital and cash flow, and can support inhouse expertise to design and manage the firms' responses. J. Allen Overton, Jr., president of the American Mining Congress, has remarked with regard to recent social regulation that "All this creates a paradise for lawyers and a banquet for accountants, but it is pure hell for the practical businessman. . . . Coal companies have to maintain armies of attorneys, accountants, and engineers just to keep abreast of the regulatory avalanche, not to mention trying to understand them and figure out how to comply with them without going broke" (Fine 1978). It is likely that only the larger firms can afford these armies. There is also evidence that larger firms tend to do a better job at reclamation than smaller ones (Omang 1980).

Thus, under regulation, the greater response capabilities of larger firms should give them a competitive advantage over their smaller rivals. In fact, there appears to be a steady trend toward concentration in the industry. According to a mining official in one state, over 60 percent of the small operators left the business as independent operators between February 1978 and September 1979. And, according to Congressional testimony by the president of the Mining and Reclamation Council of America in March 1979, 1,000 of the 1,750 small operators were expected to be gone by the end of that year (Comptroller General of the U.S. 1979, p. 27). James W. Trapp, executive secretary of the Ohio Coal and Energy Association, an association of small operators, has asserted that the effect of the 1977 Act on the members of his organization will be "to have their 'heads put on the chopping block' " (Trapp 1978). And one small operator who has left the business says "I have been beat into the ground so bad from federal regulations that I have no desire whatsoever to return to the open pit mining business" (Haurwitz 1980a).

Federal officials have maintained that factors besides the stringency of federal regulation are most important in explaining this exodus. They note in particular the adverse market conditions and high transportation costs for small operators (Comptroller General of the U.S. 1979, p. 27; Watson 1978b).

At any rate, the large companies, although in general hostile to strip mining regulation, may actually prefer to see its retention as long as it provides them with an advantage over smaller competitors. Of course, what would be preferred is the most lenient form that still provides the advantage. Since it is costly for firms to change their internal response patterns (costly in hiring, firing, training time, equipment acquisition, and so on), many large firms may even be quite happy to keep an existing, moderate degree of regulation (that is, regulation that is more than enough to insure competitive advantage).

Support by large operators for relatively stricter regulation can also reduce public pressure for the strictest regulation; the operators can coopt the issue. Furthermore, it may simply be easier for regulators to catch larger operators (on compliance and firm size, see Marcus 1978). And larger, more easily monitored companies may find it in their interest to report violations by their smaller competitors. Even small operators may support enforcement efforts if their location, capital resources, or staffing makes compliance feasible, and if they feel enforcement of moderate laws will prevent the publicized abuses by less-well-off competitors that could lead to stricter regulation (for one such case, see Watson 1979; see also Haurwitz 1981a). These arguments have obvious consequences for the success of compliance reform techniques like self-certification and third-party auditing.

Perhaps the strongest argument why coal companies may actually defend a relatively small or moderate level of regulation is that the regulation in effect legitimizes and legally defends their operations. As long as the companies can demonstrate compliance, challenges from public, environmental, and local community groups, as well as from adversely affected individuals, can be successfully defended through the administrative process and any court proceedings. Regulation not only controls; in effect, it limits liability. It legitimizes the conduct of an activity that is inherently disturbing or destructive to the environment; one is reminded of the "license to pollute" arguments used against effluent charges (see, for example, Mitnick 1980a, p. 375). And because of the externalities produced through surface mining, there are always likely to be people made unhappy by it. Regulation can reduce, as well as protect the industry from, such externality-originated complaints.

While we have pointed out some reasons why the mining industry (or at least some sectors of it) may give some support to regulation, it is pertinent to recall the illustrative aspects of the Yother case. While comparative advantage and some protection can be generated through regulation, a residuum of basic adversariness is likely to remain. The two-part compliance problem—both the regulatee and the regulator problems—must be resolved through appropriate regulatory design.

We turn now to consider the advantages and disadvantages of two major types of compliance reform in strip mining regulation: self-certification and third-party auditing. In the following section, we focus on the problem of controlling regulatees, the context in which compliance reform is usually discussed. After assessing the two techniques in this context, we analyze the second part of the two-part problem by reporting some results of a questionnaire study of the incentive relations facing regulators in a large Midwestern state.

PART ONE OF THE TWO-PART PROBLEM: CONTROLLING REGULATEES

In discussing the problem of regulatee compliance, we shall focus on two of the compliance reform techniques identified by the U.S. Regulatory Council (1980a, b): self-certification, and third-party monitoring, auditing, or certification.

In self-certification, regulated parties are responsible for attesting to their own compliance with applicable regulations. Perhaps the best known use of this technique is by the Internal Revenue Service (IRS) in the preparation of tax returns. Even here, however, the IRS plans for and conducts a certain level of auditing, and support for the profession of certified public accountants may be viewed as a form of third-party monitoring. Another example is the Department of Transportation's requirement that automobile manufacturers certify compliance with regulations (U.S. Regulatory Council 1980a, pp. 26–27).

Third-party monitoring, auditing, or certification employs a third party—not a member of the regulatory body or of the regulated entity—to examine the compliance status of the regulated party. The powers granted to the third party can vary. The third party may merely collect information on compliance; may assist the regulated party in attaining compliance, perhaps through provision of expert advice (as can be the case in an advisory inspection, which is a related technique); or may legally certify to the regulatory body that the regulatee is in fact in compliance. The third party may or may not be certified or approved by the regulatory body; be a member of an industry-related group such as consumers, public interest activists, members of a trade association; or be paid by the regulatory agency or the regulatee.

Obviously, the trustworthiness of the third party is a major issue. Baseball clubs employ umpires through their league association as third party auditors—and, indeed, as direct regulators—and still manage to retain the image of the umpire's integrity and objectivity. But most regulated industries might find this hard to do. Many if not most applications of both self-certification and third-party auditing probably rely on some degree of second-level auditing by the regulatory body. Thus tax return audits not only regulate taxpayers directly; they also, in effect, audit the work of the professional tax preparers.

The existence of randomized second-level auditing together with stiff penalties and a high probability of their application when infractions are discovered may thus help to policy self- or third-party certification. In addition, of course, self- and third-party certification may be aided through socialization to and/or reinforcement of any relevant societal norms of compliance. It is a commonplace observation that the U.S. tax collection system seems to work so relatively well only because of beliefs in the legitimacy of the government and the civic obligation to pay taxes (on regulatory compliance and enforcement generally, see, for example, Diver 1980; McKean 1980).

We now review some advantages and disadvantages of the two compliance reform techniques, indicating differences where appropriate. The analysis is illustrated with reference to strip mining regulation.

Advantages

- Self- or third-party certification can provide an agency with an expanded field staff, an advantage when the agency is short of staff, when on-the-spot observation is necessary and cannot be maintained by the agency for long periods or at closely-spaced intervals, or where events are changing rapidly and the agency cannot monitor all regulated parties continuously and simultaneously (that is, as above, when it is in effect short of staff). Staffing problems have been endemic to strip mining regulation, of course, reflecting traditional budgetary shortfalls.

- Self- or third-party certification may be useful where the agency lacks inhouse expertise, whether because certification needs are occasional and do not justify a full-time staff member, or because resources are insufficient to support an expert who *is* needed full-time. In both cases, of course, the basic problem is resource scarcity. One of the fears of federal strip mining regulators (and of those who pushed for federal regulation) has been that lack of state expertise in enforcement could nullify even the most restrictive federal performance goals. Hence, as discussed earlier, we see extensive reliance on detailed design standards (that is, detailed specification of the incentive message) for essentially educational/informational as well as performance insurance reasons.
- Self- or third-party certification may be advantageous where professional or societal norms require certification by group specialists. Professional autonomy norms (in addition to profession protectionism) dictate that physicians and lawyers, for example, perform self-certification. Aside from localism or state's rights claims, which are certainly part of the rhetoric of strip mining regulation controversy, we do not see such norms in this area. Such norms would, of course, be a feature of the dispositional state of the incentive receivers.
- Self- or third-party certification "makes the government appear to be less meddlesome" (U.S. Regulatory Council 1980a). While this comment can be taken to refer to localism claims as noted above, it refers primarily to both a libertarian ideology and the psychic costs of perceived repetitive government intervention. Insofar as strip mining companies tend to be heavily regulated both in the safety and in other environmental areas, these attitudes and perceptions can be significant. These are dispositions by incentive receivers to not comply simply because of the nature of the incentive sender and the existence of other incentive relations. Compliance is in principle promoted whenever such oppositional factors are reduced or eliminated.
- Self- or third-party certification may be "useful when many products, firms, or organizations must be monitored" (U.S. Regulatory Council 1980a, p. 26), that is, when there are many incentive receivers. Here again, of course, resource scarcity is at the root. This has typically been the case in strip mining, although, as noted earlier, the number of small operators has been decreasing rapidly.
- Self- or third-party certification may be useful whenever there is a coincidence of goals between regulatee and regulator, that is, between incentive sender and incentive receiver. This may occur due to third-party constraints on the regulatee, for example, the

interest of the consumer in a safe, high quality product. In strip mining, however, coal consumers do not produce such constraints and, except for competitive advantage and legitimacy protections (as discussed earlier), a community of interest is generally lacking. Of course, if there were a true and stable community of interest we might well question the need for any regulation at all.

Coincidence of goals can also occur due to protections afforded by the regulation. Self- and third-party certification could meet the desires of large companies for lenient or moderate levels of regulation that could provide legitimacy and protection from parties adversely-affected by externalities of production and that could provide competitive advantages with respect to smaller companies less able to comply with the regulation. Reasonable levels of willing compliance are at least conceivable in the strip mining case, but the adversary posture of regulators and companies and the history of abuses cast some doubt on their likelihood.

- Self- or third-party certification may be advantageous whenever effective second-level auditing is feasible. This may occur where randomized auditing backed by effective penalties can be implemented, as with the IRS. This technique may feasibly require such conditions as relatively standardized, time-limited cases that may be assessed rapidly and objectively, with noncatastrophic consequences from monitoring failure. Strip mining would not seem to qualify: there is wide variation among cases; monitoring needs can be relatively frequent and problematic cases can extend for months or years; consequences of monitoring failure can be catastrophic (see, for example, DiSalvo 1980; but cf. perceptions of West Virginia inspectors, Menzel, Hedge et al. 1981, pp. 20–21); and assessment can be time-consuming and require the subjective expertise of on-the-spot inspectors.

- Self- and third-party certification, although appearing to lack enforcement capabilities, can be self-policing since better situated companies (that is, agents) may have reason to report violators (that is, noncompliant agents) and/or to institute legal or regulatory proceedings against them. Of course, penalties for noncompliance must exist and be meaningful. Such self-policing has occurred in at least one case, in Pennsylvania (see Watson 1978a, c; Watson 1979).

- Self- (and possibly third-party) certification may require less regulatory paperwork, which is increasingly costly and resisted by regulated parties. In the case of strip mining, even inspectors who share the program's end goals have begun to resent the flood of paperwork required by the interim regulations; the permanent regulations could be worse. Inspectors assert, as noted above, that the regulations exhibit a lack of knowledge of field work requirements. One state official estimates that his agency has purchased over one million sheets of paper since August 1977 (personal communication, July 27, 1981). The incentive receiver's (agent's) costs in merely administering compliance (paperwork) are of course not borne by the incentive sender (principal) and can be impediments to receiver compliance.

- Self-certification is potentially more effective where control requires knowledge of idiosyncratic, local circumstances for which it is difficult to write rules (incentive messages) of general application and for which regulators with generic training lack special, localized expertise to develop specialized interpretation of broad rules. While the we-have-special-conditions complaint is loudly heard in strip mining regulation controversy (see, for example, Omang 1980), it is heard whenever general rules are applied to particular cases. Since at face at least some of the complaints regarding the federal regulations seem justified, and have been in some cases acknowledged and addressed in modifications, we may count this as a possibly minor advantage for these techniques in the strip mining case.
- Third-party certification can provide the educational/expertise substitution that was described earlier for design standards. It can provide an expert interpreter of the rules and designer of local arrangements to achieve performance standards (that is, interpret the content of incentive messages). Since lack of reclamation expertise by companies has been a problem, use of third parties in this area might be an advantage for the strip mining case. But federal regulators have rightly or wrongly distrusted the competence and integrity of state officials. Moreover, third-party auditors are unlikely to be more competent than full-time specialist state officials.

Disadvantages

- Both self- and third-party certification may require a grant of statutory authority to the federal agency to delegate certification powers (U.S. Regulatory Council 1980a, p. 26). This authority rarely exists and may be difficult, given the present political climate, to get through the legislature unless it is clearly identified with a reduction in regulation. This is as true of strip mining as of any other area. In addition, third-party certification may require more regulations— to qualify third-party inspectors. Such a grant of authority deals of course with the formal legal status of the sender-receiver relation.
- If the results of monitoring or auditing are to be usable in a legal proceeding, the certifying party must be "a professional, well-qual-

ified, independent examiner" (U.S. Regulatory Council 1980a, p. 26). Such examiners would, of course, be third party agents (if they were not the industry itself) engaged by the incentive receiver and certified by the sender to report receiver compliance activities to the sender. Obviously, the regulated industry is not likely to qualify unless it can establish itself as a profession like law or medicine. Similarly, the reports of consumer or public interest groups may be suspect. The difficulty of finding such an examiner is a clear disadvantage, particularly in strip mining regulation, where the positions of all interested parties have become highly polarized.

- In third-party certification, use of the outside party may raise liability questions (U.S. Regulatory Council 1980a, p. 26). These may be difficult to resolve and, as above, require additional regulations rather than economize on regulatory activity.

- Both self- and third-party certification may require resources and supporting regulations to perform second-level auditing of the performance of the regulatory agent, resulting in additional costs to the incentive sender, the second-level auditor.

- Self-certification may be biased; where the third party is paid by the regulated party, bias is also likely. Bias can also exist where the third party has a clear conflicting interest, such as those of environmentalist groups in the strip mining case. Even where a community of interest exists between the regulatory body and the third party, a history of adversary relations between regulator and regulatee might produce results judged by some not to be disinterested (cf. the lobbying alliance between the OSM and environmentalist groups, Keller 1980, p. 2184).

- Self-certification cannot provide a substitute for the educational/expertise content of detailed design standards. Incentive receivers (coal operators) may lack the ability to correctly interpret and implement the incentive message (surface mining regulations). According to the OSM (Kirschten 1979, p. 180; Edgmon and Menzel 1981), this has been a problem in strip mining regulation.

- For both self-certification and third-party certification, the nature of the local economy and local attitudes toward the regulated activity may strongly influence the quality of compliance; these are elements of the incentive receiver's proximal and distal environments. It is not clear, for example, that the Department of the Treasury should resort to self-certification of whiskey production in rural West Virginia and Kentucky. For the strip mining case, the local economy is often depressed (at least in the East) and dependent on the mining industry (Prochnau 1980). There is therefore less of a chance for formation of citizen groups who could perform third-party auditing through reports of violations. There is greater pressure from the local community on auditors to bias their reporting, and any third party from the local community may have strongly-held attitudes about the desirability of protecting local enterprise. And the community's views are likely to be shared by workers who are both local and precariously employed.

- If third-party certification depends on citizen groups or activism in a rural area, as it might in strip mining, there may be problems. Rural areas may exhibit lower levels of educational attainment and of political activism; skilled political brokers or activists as well as followers may therefore be scarce.
- Third-party certification schemes involving expectations of local-level activity by, for example, public interest groups comparable to national-level activity may be ill-conceived. Levels of public interest and other group activity vary from region to region and state to state. Ostensibly national organizations with Washington headquarters have varying regional interests and strengths.

Consider, speculatively, the Sierra Club as a third-party monitor in strip mining regulation. The Club is based in San Francisco, with a strong national presence, of course, in Washington, D.C., and activist members throughout the country. While it has played a role in environmental controversies across the country, let us assume the Club has a relatively stronger focus on wilderness and national park areas, most of which are in the West. Could we expect the same quality of third-party monitoring in rural West Virginia as in Yosemite?

In addition, there are clear East-West differences in regulatory compliance (Omang 1980). Newer, larger Western companies tend to be more compliant, while most of the history of abuse and the present reclamation problems are in the East. There is expected to be a transfer of funds from the coal mining tax for reclamation established by the 1977 Act from Western taxpayers (coal companies) to Eastern reclamation projects. Under these conditions can we expect major Western groups to be effective monitors for Eastern interests? Monitoring agents must be recognized to have interests that can conflict with those of the incentive sender.

- Third-party certification must be structured to facilitate access to the regulatee, that is, facilitate reporting of actual incentive receiver behavior to the incentive sender. There is currently a question in some states as to whether citizens, including the press, may accompany inspectors and/or observe mining sites without the permission of property owners. The Division of Reclamation in Ohio, for example, tends to welcome the press, feeling that media exposure can be helpful (personal communication, Jeffrey L. Wilson, Division of Reclamation, Ohio DNR, May 1, 1981). Pennsylvania, however, recently restricted the press to visits with company permission only. The local press then raised questions about the possible dangers from lack of "public scrutiny" and speculated that the state administration may be wishing to boost one of the state's major industries (Haurwitz 1980b). Requirements of notification and permission remove the element of surprise. The difficulty of guaranteeing access of a (possibly private) third party to the private property of the regulatee, while protecting the rights of the firm and its owners, seems a disadvantage of this technique.

- If third parties are to be groups such as environmental organizations, third-party certification can carry the standard problems, well-discussed in the literature on interest group behavior, of creating, coordinating, and maintaining effective group action. Cost, information, and free-rider problems can be difficult to surmount on a continuing basis.

- Third-party certification by public, community, or other citizen groups may prove unworkable if an imbalance in skills and resources, and existing provisions and participatory requirements in the legal system, give advantages to the regulated industry. Recently a coal company sued environmentalist groups for libel; an environmentalist said he feared the suit would have a "chilling effect" on environmental advocacy (Franklin 1980; *New York Times* 1980). The threat of such suits may be effective even if many are unsuccessful, since they are costly to defend.

- If third-party certification is not formalized but, rather, left to the informal processes of interest group observation and violation reporting, significant changes in effectiveness may occur with changes in such distal environmental factors as political officeholders (as in the Pennsylvania situation described above), economic conditions, local ordinances and attitudes, nationwide private contributions to relevant organizations, and so on. Thus, informal third-party certification may be unstable and inconsistent.

- Self- and third-party certification may not, as discussed earlier, be able to copy adequately with the need for rapid or widely coordinated regulatory intervention in the case of crisis or catastrophe, as may occur in strip mining. There is no mechanism for coordinating the responses of regulatees quickly across the affected region. Thus these techniques may be ill-suited to coordinate responses to a single incentive sender across a number of dispersed incentive receivers.

Brief Assessment

The support for use of such compliance reform techniques as self-certification and third-party certification appears weak in the context of strip mining regulation. There appear to be significant problems in use of these techniques in insuring incentive receiver (coal company) responses to the incentive messages (regulations) sent by the incentive sender (OSM). There may yet be, of course, a place (if not a central one) for other compliance reform techniques not considered here in detail, such as advisory inspections. While self- and third-party certification appear inappropriate for strip mining, they may, as the U.S. Regulatory Council began to document (1980a, b), be useful elsewhere. At any rate, the analysis of basic advantages and disadvantages may be applied in other regulatory issue areas to facilitate choice of regulatory solutions to the first component of the basic two-part problem in regulation.

PART TWO OF THE TWO-PART PROBLEM: CONTROLLING THE REGULATORS

Having considered compliance reform and control of regulatees in strip mining, we turn now to the second part of the control problem in regulation: control of the regulators. Compliance reform in this context is concerned with the development of efficient and nonintrusive means of insuring consummate performance by regulators. Remember that, even if compliance reform for *regulatees* is successful in reducing the magnitude of regulating activity required, some regulatory activity is presumed to remain; compliance reform is not equivalent to deregulation.

To illustrate the problem of control of regulators in strip mining regulation, we shall describe some results of an exploratory study of the incentive system facing regulators in a state reclamation agency in a large Midwestern state. In particular, the incentive relations existing between the regulated industry and the state regulators, and those between the federal Office of Surface Mining and the state regulators, will be examined. It is of course expected that compliance of regulators to policy and task directives may be affected importantly by the nature of these incentive relations.

In early 1979, when final federal regulations under the Surface Mining Control and Reclamation Act of 1977 were in the process of being promulgated, a questionnaire was sent to all inspectors and inspector supervisors in the state agency plus three who had very recently left that agency. Responses were voluntary, assurances of confidentiality were made, and the agency head wrote a cover letter sent with the questionnaire that supported the effort. The response rate was about 85 percent (29 responses). Part of the questionnaire was adapted from that employed by Rainey (1977) in order to permit future comparisons. The questionnaire was supplemented by interiews with state officials. (Also on this study, see Mitnick 1980a, b.)

The incentive relation between the mining industry and the state regulators consists of a sender (industry), a receiver (regulators), and a sender-receiver relation operating in a particular environment. The industry potentially controls a set of regulator rewards which are associated with certain preferred courses of regulator conduct. Transfer of these rewards is of course constrained by the sender-receiver relation and by aspects of the environment (for example, ethics regulations and other legal constraints); it is not in general feasible for the industry to offer outright bribes.

There are some rewards, however, whose transfer is less constrained. These include status/prestige, friendship, contributions of the industry to increasing the regulator's convenience on the job (that is, reducing work load) through such activities as supplying needed information, and the possibility of a future job in the industry. Note that the future job reward is one way in which otherwise forbidden financial rewards may be offered (on this reward structure and on the literature in regulation that proposes and discusses it, see Mitnick 1980a).

The regulators are also engaged in incentive relations with their regulatory organization through the employment relation and, potentially, with the federal Office of Surface Mining which, like the industry, also controls some future job possibilities. The agency relations constructed in this manner engage in an *incentive competition* for the regulators. In the following analysis, we shall systematically review the evidence for each major reward in each of the major external incentive relations— that with the industry, and that with the federal agency.

Pay and promotion possibilities are severely restricted in the state agency. Perceptions of the inspectors regarding their possibilities in these areas compared with other jobs bore this out: approximately two-thirds of the inspectors reported that they thought pay was higher in federal government or private industry jobs, and all inspectors reported that they perceived that a "higher paying job" was the major reason for all or most of those who left the agency. Three-quarters of the inspectors said that the opportunity for promotion within the agency was somewhat limited. Although Civil Service provides job security, the position of inspector is usually taken by recent college or associate degree graduates; the median tenure among a dozen recent departures from the agency was about three years.

A number of rewards were considered "important" and "extremely important" by more than half of the regulators; not all of these rewards were perceived by most regulators as "mostly" and "extremely available." The survey results are tabulated below:

Reward	Considered Important (percent)	Perceived Available (percent)
Higher pay	86	7
Promotion	72	14
Job security	75	73
Respect and friendliness from your colleagues or co-workers	79	72
Sense of worthwhile accomplishment in your work	100	58
Development of your abilities through your work	100	62
Good feeling about yourself, as a result of your work	93	66
Doing work that is helpful to other people	69	42
Making important decisions and exerting an important influence on your organization	58	21

Clearly, there are significant gaps between the rewards considered important and those considered available in their work by inspectors covered in this study (but see the high job satisfaction levels reported by West Virginia inspectors; Menzel, Hedge et al. 1981, pp. 20, 24).

Conceivably, some of the rewards available to inspectors may come from the regulated industy. Among them, the possibility of a future job stands out. Eighty percent of the inspectors thought that most or some of their colleagues took their present jobs in anticipation of a future job in the industry (although only 46 percent said that they had themselves considered working for a mining company when they were choosing a career), and all the inspectors thought their training in the agency would be useful for work in the industry. Seventy-two percent thought they would or might work for a mining company someday, and 62 percent reported that they had formally or informally talked with mining companies about a future job.

Inspectors thought their jobs provided more security than private industry jobs (76 percent of those responding); security was of course identified as one of the more important rewards. Work load may be reduced if the inspectors have a need for information that is met by the industry. Such a need might arise because of the on-the-job training that occurs in the regulatory agency, together with the lack of job experience among the largely short-tenured regulators. Sixty-two percent said that they still needed to learn at least "a moderate amount"/"some important things" in order to "really know" their jobs. About one-third of the regulators said that they knew a "moderate" amount or less about the present strip mining regulations. Thus, industry supply of information could function as an inspector reward.

In deciding whether to issue a permit or license, 89 percent of the inspectors said that they relied at least partly on their own investigation, as against information supplied by the mining companies. The inspectors do have some discretion in following the regulations and perceive that they do; 75 percent said they had a "lot" or a "fair amount" of choice and can play a "major" or a "medium role in affecting whether a permit is issued." Only 14 percent said they had to follow the regulations to the letter and had no room for judgment (45 percent disagreed). The existence of inspector discretion could enhance the potential impacts of any industry influence.

Furthermore, the inspectors felt fairly friendly toward the industry. Seventy-eight percent thought the then current regulations, which were being superseded by more stringent federal ones, were adequate to very good; eighty-five percent thought the current regulations were at least "a little tough" (25 percent thought them "very tough"). Eighty-nine percent thought the industry was being hit "about right" to "much too hard"/"deserves a break" by the current regulations. Ninety-four percent thought the mining companies were "a little" to "extremely cooperative." Eighty-three percent felt at least "a little friendly" toward mining company people (over half felt "moderately friendly," a finding consistent with the West Virginia inspector study by Menzel, Hedge et al. 1981, pp. 18–19). Almost a third had off-the-job social contacts with mining company people, with an average of eight contacts per month. Friendships could increase the regulator's convenience, through facilitating information transfer; they could, in addition, of course, be a way for the industry to anticipate and remain better informed about current regulatory developments.

The potential for the industry to have significant influence through their incentive relation with regulators seems clear. In fact, there is *no* data to support undue industry influence on regulatory decision-making in this agency; in actuality the agency's actions in implementing the federal Act have been used as a model by the federal Office of Surface Mining (OSM) (personal communication, official in state agency, 1979). This suggests a look at another of the inspectors' incentive relations— that with the federal regulators.

The data clearly suggest a dual career path, and the pattern of agency departures supports this. Of 20 departures through March 1979, 40 percent went to a regulated coal company and 40 percent went to the Office of Surface Mining. Menzel and Hedge (1981, p. 46) report that 29 of 71 OSM inspectors in their survey came to OSM from a state agency (but see their West Virginia survey; only 9 percent reported a willingness to change jobs; Menzel, Hedge et al. 1981, pp. 20, 24). Inspectors are well aware of this; all in the present survey perceived that most or some inspectors departed for a federal inspector job, all thought their training useful for such a job, and 62 percent had talked, informally or formally, with the federal agency about a future job. Salaries in the state agency studied were at this time 20 to 80 percent lower than private mining companies and the OSM. The federal agency also provides job security through Civil Service, a job security which is not perceived to exist in the private sector.

Federal employment should not be a bar toward supply of friendship rewards, whether from within the agency or from within the industry. The federal agency has greater promotion possibilities than the state agency, can provide more status/prestige/recognition than the state, and affords the regulator the opportunity to make more important decisions than those at the state level. It may also provide more of a "sense of worthwhile accomplishment" (since the regulator may perceive more power), may give more opportunity to "develop one's abilities," and, as with other jobs, possibly provide a "good feeling about oneself as a result of work" and allow the "doing of work that helps others."

In the absence of the federal alternative, the dominance of the industry incentive relation would seem apparent; there would certainly be more reason to expect the occurrence of the long-term favorable relationship often referred to as "capture." Even if industry hired only the most competent (not the most competent *and* the most "captured") state inspectors, we might expect a long-term tendency toward favoring the industry. The industry would control the sources of other rewards and inspectors might perform self-selection in choosing to work for the state agency, while anticipating future industry work. Furthermore, some net, overall industry orientation might result from any subset of inspectors that, as a result of the reward system, does acquire a pro-industry bias, even though their colleagues do not.

The very existence of the federal promotion ladder, what has been termed an "incentive safety valve" (Mitnick 1980a, b), may then serve to police lower-level regulators. State regulators desiring promotion to the federal body could conceivably be more likely to adhere to federal standards and norms of behavior in order to be accepted into that body at a later date. Menzel and Hedge (1981, pp. 33, 34) note, however, that several sources of federal-state inspector conflict can occur, including resentment over higher salaries, reaction against federal claims of having hired the "best" state inspectors, and discomfort with the preference for stricter regulation and alleged aloofness of federal inspectors in previous years.

Having described the dual promotion ladder as it existed in 1979 and noted the potential of such a mechanism to resolve the second part of the dual control problem in regulation, we must report that the ladder probably no longer exists in strip mining regulation. Given the depressed state of the coal industry, few state inspectors may be leaving at all. General regulatory retrenchment at the federal level, fewer vacancies to fill in the OSM, and future uncertainties regarding federal Administration plans for regulatory rollbacks have capped the federal ladder; some former state officials now in the OSM have even begun to inquire about the availability of state positions (personal communication, state reclamation official). At this writing, Secretary of the Interior James Watt is implementing a plan to reduce the total OSM staff by 40 percent, and by more in some states; Pennsylvania is to go from 26 to 9 inspectors as the federal force drops from 128 to 69 (Haurwitz 1981b). This has been accompanied by reports of low staff morale (personal communication, Midwestern state reclamation official, July 17, 1981).

If this trend in the federal regulatory system continues, and if a reviving economy and a rollback in other environmental (particularly, air pollution) regulations (or reduced enforcement) permits use of more coal, expansion may occur in the coal industry. This may increase the demand in the industry for personnel trained in reclamation—that is, the demand for state inspectors. At least one state official in a large Midwestern coal mining state has predicted that the exodus of state inspectors will then resume, but in a single, not double stream—to the coal industry (personal communication, May 1, 1981). The consequences for compliance, given the incentive relations that were analyzed earlier, seem obvious.

MANAGEMENT OF COMPLIANCE IN THE TWO-PART INCENTIVE SYSTEM

As the preceding discussion has often implied, management of compliance in regulated firms often involves more than a passive response to regulatory requirements. This is true with respect to both parts of the two-part incentive system we have described.

Strategic Use of the Two-Part Incentive System

The two-part incentive system is a control system ostensibly designed to insure regulator activities consistent with efficient and effective regulatory administration, and regulatee activities compliant with the aims and/or terms of the regulation. In practice, such incentive systems can be manipulated; actual behaviors can depend, for example, on who controls reward transfers and the effective content of incentive messages. Regulatees may succeed in strongly influencing these systems, as the literature on "capture" suggests (see, for example, Mitnick 1980a).

Strategies for manipulating the regulatee and regulator systems have recently begun to be studied (Leone 1977; Owen and Braeutigam 1978; Mitnick 1981). These include manipulation of a number of aspects of the sender-receiver relation, including rewards, incentive messages, information feedback from receivers to senders, formal structure of the sender-receiver relation, and so on. Regulated parties can manipulate future job and work load/convenience rewards, supply of selected/distorted/excessive information, supply of expert testimony, choice and timing of litigation, availability of innovative compliance technologies, choice of alternative regulatory incentive relations (for example, movement from federal to state regulatory regimes), compliance activity mix (for example, cross-subsidy choice), and other factors.

General Managerial Benefits/Opportunities from Compliance

Apart from strategic manipulation of the incentive systems, firms can realize real benefits from compliance activities (see, for example, Leone 1977, Mitnick 1981, for a fuller discussion). These include the creation of new markets (for example, in the manufacture of compliance equipment such as seatbelts or air pollution control equipment) made possible by the regulatee incentive system; the realization of comparative advantages under that incentive system due to differing firm endowments of size/capital, resources, location, technological capability, personnel expertise/skills; and the provision, in exchange for compliance, of legitimacy and real legal protections against challenge to the firm's production of negative externalities.

Managerial Benefits/Opportunities under Compliance Reform Techniques

The use of the compliance reform techniques discussed in this paper, self- and third-party certification, can provide particular managerial benefits or opportunities. The autonomy of management to make basic business decisions is often a strong-held value; perhaps one reason for the frequent opposition of management to unionization is the transfer of control of work conditions, reward structures, and other factors to the collective bargaining agreement. Similarly, regulation can take the form of intervention in decision-making areas that managers may prefer to retain for themselves, whether or not the substance of compliance would be affected one way or the other. Self-certification can restore at least the semblance of managerial autonomy, since it places responsibility for monitoring and administering compliance on managers rather than on government inspectors.

Self-certification may leave managers more autonomy in setting compliance schedules, both for inspection and for detailed compliance activities. It may provide managers with the opportunity to better integrate compliance activities with production/service activities; managers, rather than more distant regulators, have better knowledge of the idiosyncratic aspects of their firm's situation and can thus implement more efficient and effective monitoring and compliance methods. Since managers may be able to select (and, conceivably, keep on retainer) third-party inspectors, some of the above benefits may be attainable under third-party certification as well.

Self- and third-party certification may have the potential for realizing a cooperative rather than adversarial style for compliance; the implied threat of the random visit of the suspicious government inspector is replaced with ongoing internal (or, with third-parties, negotiated) reviews. There may be contributions to the level of compliance from the development of inhouse or retained or local (third-party) expertise. And firms may come to understand more of the aims and methods of compliance when regulation is integrated into regular internal firm operations rather than standing outside as a source of sometimes apparently arbitrary intervention. The regulator becomes a local adviser and facilitator rather than a distant dispenser of fiat. Given the long-term interest of society— including many of the firm's constituencies—in realizing many regulatory aims, and the basic coerciveness of any scheme of government regulation, it may be in the long-term interest, profit and otherwise, for firms to embrace such cooperative compliance.

Against these potentially significant benefits and the other advantages analyzed earlier are the manipulatory possibilities mentioned and the other disadvantages listed above. Self- and third-party certification may prove to be valuable and workable regulatory alternatives, achieving both corporate and public policy aims. But this may occur only if they are not seem as opportunities for escape from—rather than adaptation to—the compliance requirements set in regulation ultimately through the representative process. Whether or not they are so seen can depend, of course, on the managerial incentive system—and on basic managerial values.

CONCLUSION: THE PORTFOLIO OF REGULATORY SOLUTIONS

While this paper has not been optimistic regarding the utility of two compliance reform techniques in strip mining regulation, there is a point inherent in the foregoing analysis that should be made clear. If regulatory analysis is now willing (as it did not used to be) to consider innovative techniques, it is important to remember that panaceas, even innovative ones, will not be found. Neither privatization, as exemplified by the compliance reform methods, nor emphasis on renewed but reformed public-sector-centered approaches, are likely to provide universal solutions. The best (and it can be a very desirable best) that can be achieved is identification of an "arsenal" or, more neutrally, a portfolio of regulatory techniques, each with careful specification of the contingencies in which it can perform well. We have taken this perspective in beginning to try to delineate carefully the contingent advantages and disadvantages of the two compliance reform methods. In addition, analysts must not lose sight of the fact that they are dealing with a dual or two-part compliance problem; identification of the extant incentive relations is important in understanding, and, perhaps, modifying behavior through modification of the relations. The faults, if there be any, are both in our tools and in ourselves.

ACKNOWLEDGMENTS

I gratefully acknowledge the helpful comments and/or assistance of Robert W. Backoff, Charles Call, Steven Cover, Karen Denning, Lori Hunter, Stephen Linder, Margery M. Mitnick, Lee Preston, Hal G. Rainey, Rebecca Roberts, Bert Rockman, Charles Stubbart, Fred Thompson, and, especially, Jeffrey L. Wilson. I would also like to thank the Research Program in Corporate Social Policy at the Graduate School of Business, University of Pittsburgh, for its partial support of this paper under a grant from the General Electric Foundation. The discussion of the state regulator questionnaire study is based in part on B. M. Mitnick, "Agency, Incentive Relations, and State Regulation of Strip Mining," *Proceedings of the Academy of Management,* 41st Annual Meeting, San Diego, California (August 2-5, 1981). Discussions of this study also appear in Mitnick (1980a, b). Earlier versions of this paper were presented at the 1981 Annual Conference of the Association for Public Policy Analysis and Management, Shoreham Hotel, Washington, D.C., October 23–24, 1981; the 1981 Annual Meeting of the American Political Science Association, New York Hilton Hotel, New York, NY, September 3–6; and the U.S. Regulatory Council Colloquium on Innovative Techniques in Regulation, Washington, D.C., May 21, 1981.

REFERENCES

Arthur Andersen and Co., *Cost of Government Regulation Study for the Business Roundtable.* Report and Appendix. New York: The Business Roundtable, and Chicago: Arthur Andersen and Co., March 1979.

Ashford, Nicholas A., and Christopher T. Hill, Center for Policy Alternatives at M.I.T., *The Benefits of Environmental Health and Safety Regulation.* Report prepared for the Committee on Governmental Affairs, U.S. Senate, 96th Congress, 2nd Session. Washington, D.C.: U.S. Government Printing Office, March 25, 1980.

Bardach, Eugene, and Robert A. Kagan, eds., *Social Regulation: Strategies for Reform.* San Francisco: Institute for Contemporary Studies, 1982.

Comptroller General of the United States, U.S. General Accounting Office. "Issues Surrounding the Surface Mining Control and Reclamation Act." CED-79-83 (September 21, 1979).

DeFina, Robert, "Public and Private Expenditures for Federal Regulation of Business." Working Paper No. 22. St. Louis: Center for the Study of American Business, Washington University, November 1977.

DiSalvo, Charles R., "If Enforcement Is Left to the States . . . Kentucky Coal: Who'll Guard the Henhouse?" *Commonweal* 107, No. 3 (February 15, 1980): 85–87.

Diver, Colin S., "A Theory of Regulatory Enforcement." *Public Policy* 28, No. 3 (Summer 1980): 257–99.

Edgmon, Terry D., and Donald C. Menzel, "The Regulation of Coal Surface Mining in a Federal System." *National Resources Journal* 21 (April 1981): 245–65.

Fine, Ira, "U.S., Industry Debate Regulations on Coal." *Pittsburgh Press* (September 6, 1978): A-2.

Franklin, Ben A., "Coal Mining Company Sues Its Environmentalist Critics." *New York Times* (August 11, 1980): A16.

Garvin, David A., "Self-Regulation: Problems and Prospects." Working Paper HBS 81–78. Graduate School of Business Administration, Harvard University, April 1, 1981a.

———, "Deregulating and Self-Regulating." *The Wharton Magazine* 5, No. 3 (Spring 1981b): 57–63.

Haurwitz, Ralph, "Ex-Miner, Feds Still Wrangling." *Pittsburgh Press* (July 27, 1980a): A-9.

———, "Public Losing Its Look At Strip Mine Inspections." *Pittsburgh Press* (November 30, 1980b): A-1, A-18.

———, "Mine Mess Strips Away Law: Back to the Dark Ages." *Pittsburgh Press* (March 8, 1981): K-1; (March 9, 1981): B-1; (March 10, 1981): B-1; (March 11, 1981): B-1; (March 12, 1981): B-1. (1981a)

———, "U.S. Foisting Strip-Mine Enforcement on State." *Pittsburgh Press* (November 1, 1981b): B-7.

Keller, Bill, "How New Business Lobbyists Put Their Press on Congress . . . But With Mixed Feelings." *Congressional Quarterly* 38, No. 31 (August 2, 1980): 2176–84.

Kirschten, Dick, "The Coal Industry's Rude Awakening To the Realities of Regulation." *National Journal* 11, 5 (February 3, 1979):178–82.

Lee, Susan, "Privatization: Nobody Does It Better." *Wall Street Journal* (November 18, 1981): 30.

Leone, Robert A., "The Real Costs of Regulation." *Harvard Business Review* (November/December 1977): 57–66.

McKean, Roland N., "Enforcement Costs in Environmental and Safety Regulation." *Policy Analysis* 6, No. 3 (Summer 1980): 269–89.

Marcus, Alfred, "'Command and Control': An Assessment of Smokestack Emission Regulation." Working Paper No. WP-308. Graduate School of Business, University of Pittsburgh, 1978.

Menzel, Donald C., "Implementation of the Federal Surface Mining Control and Reclamation Act of 1977." *Public Administration Review* 41, No. 2 (March/April 1981): 212–19.

Menzel, Donald C., and David M. Hedge, "The Interorganizational Milieu as a Focus of Research on Policy Implementation." Paper presented at the 1981 Annual Meeting of the American Political Science Association, New York, September 3–6, 1981.

Menzel, Donald C., David M. Hedge, with G. G. Sayre, K. A. Perry, G. H. Williams, and C. R. Pollard, "Implementation of the Federal Surface Mining Control and Reclamation Act of 1977: Regulatory Problems and Impacts in West Virginia." Preliminary Report. Morgantown, WV: Policy Analysis Group, Department of Political Science, West Virginia University, August 25, 1981.

Mitnick, Barry M., *The Political Economy of Regulation: Creating, Designing, and Removing Regulatory Forms.* New York: Columbia University Press, 1980a.

———, "Incentive Systems in Environmental Regulation." *Policy Studies Journal* 9, No. 3 (Winter-December 1980b): 379–94.

———, "The Strategic Uses of Regulation—and Deregulation." *Business Horizons* 24, No. 4 (March/April 1981): 71–83.

Mitnick, Barry M., Robert W. Backoff, and Hal G. Rainey, "The Incentive Systems Approach to the Study of Public Organizations." Paper presented at the 1977 Annual Meeting of the American Political Science Association, Washington, D.C.

New York Times, "Environmentalist Wins Stay of Mine's Libel Judgment." (September 18, 1980): A20.

Omang, Joanne, "Strip Mining: There Are Pitfalls and Pratfalls Aplenty Where Eastern Standards Meet the West." *Washington Post* (November 24, 1980): A1, A12.

Owen, Bruce M., and Ronald Braeutigam, *The Regulation Game: Strategic Use of the Administrative Process.* Cambridge, MA: Ballinger, 1978.

Pittsburgh Post-Gazette, "U.S. Surface Mining Office Criticized by Pa. Congressman." (March 28, 1980): 5.

Prochnau, Bill, "The Billion Dollar Dream Just a Wisp of Coal Dust." *Washington Post* (September 13, 1980): A-1, A-12.

Rainey, Hal G., "Comparing Public and Private: Conceptual and Empirical Analysis of Incentives and Motivation Among Government and Business Managers." Ph.D. dissertation, School of Public Administration, Ohio State University, 1977.

Rowland, C. K., and Roger M. Marz, "Interstate Inequities in the Implementation of Toxic Substance Regulation: The Case of Pesticides." Paper presented at the Symposium on Regulatory Policy, Loyola University of Chicago, Chicago, Illinois, December 4, 1979.

Tobin, Richard J., "Federal Regulation of Hazardous Consumer Products." Paper presented at the Symposium on Regulatory Policy, University of Houston, Houston, Texas, November 19–20, 1979.

———, "Safety-Related Defects in Motor Vehicles and the Evaluation of Self-Regulation." *Policy Studies Review* 1, No. 3 (February 1982): 532–39.

Trapp, James W., "Surface Mine Regulations: Could They Be Costly?" *Ohio Energy News,* Ohio State University, 1 2 (Summer 1978): 3 4.

Ubell, Earl, "The Privatizing of Regulation." *Newsweek* 98, No. 21 (November 23, 1981): 35.

U.S. Regulatory Council, *Innovative Techniques in Theory and Practice: Proceedings of a Regulatory Council Conference.* Washington, D.C.: U.S. Regulatory Council, July 22, 1980.

———, "Regulating with Common Sense: A Progress Report on Innovative Regulatory Techniques." Washington, D.C.: U.S. Regulatory Council, October 8, 1980.

U.S. Senate, Committee on Governmental Affairs, *Study on Federal Regulation,* vol. 6 and vol. 6 Appendix: *Framework for Regulation.* 95th Congress, 2nd Session. Washington, D.C.: U.S. Government Printing Office, December 1978.

Watson, Wyndle, "Coal Operators Planning Suit Against Law-Breaking Miner." *Pittsburgh Press* (October 22, 1978a): A-8.

———, "Strip Law Will Add Little to Coal Cost, U.S. Official Says." *Pittsburgh Press* (October 22, 1978b): A-19.

———, "DER Official Calls Miner Suit Vendetta." *Pittsburgh Press* (December 17, 1978c): B-11.

———, "Surface Coal Miners Enlist State Aid to Battle U.S. Laws." *Pittsburgh Press* (May 13, 1979): A-16.

Weidenbaum, Murray L., *Business, Government and the Public*. 2nd ed. Englewood Cliffs, NJ: Prentice-Hall, 1981.

CORPORATE SOCIAL REPORTING:
EIGHT DECADES OF DEVELOPMENT
AT U.S. STEEL

Robert H. Hogner

Development and publication of empirical data pertaining to corporate social performance has generally been viewed as a phenomenon of the 1960s and 1970s. Although the idea that such data might be compiled had been suggested earlier, the first major attempt at implementation is commonly thought to be the Eastern Gas and Fuel annual report insert, "Toward Social Accounting" (1972). Interest in corporate social reporting has been dismissed by some as a short-run fad, and the work itself described as "phantasmagorical accounting" by a leading analyst (Jensen, 1976). A recent chance discovery has revealed a history of formal social reporting going back to the turn of the century by one of the nation's largest and most important business enterprises, U.S. Steel. This paper describes and analyzes the social performance data published by U.S. Steel in its annual reports over eight decades, and relates this

Research in Corporate Social Performance and Policy, Vol. 4, pages 243–250
Copyright © 1982 by JAI Press Inc.
All rights of reproduction in any form reserved.
ISBN: 0-89232-259-4

record to more recent concepts of corporate social accounting and reporting.

CONCEPTUAL ORIGINS

Current scholarship traces the conceptual origin of corporate social accounting to a monograph published by Kreps (1940). According to Carroll and Beiler (1975), Kreps utilized the term "social audit" in "a manner similar to that employed today—as a concept for measuring the social performance of business." Other analysts (for example, Steiner, 1972) had credited Bowen (1953) with first proposing that business make a "social audit" of its activities.

It is proposed here that corporate social accounting, in addition to being a tool for the "measurement and appraisal of the social performance of business," is an indicator of corporate "legitimacy needs." Not only does the technique provide "stakeholders" within and without the firm with information on extra-market activities, but evidence of practitioner use indicates a managerial perception that the information presented on extra-market activities is *important*. In some respects, this argument reflects the Preston and Post (1975) "interpenetrating systems" model for corporations. There, "a larger society exists as a macro system," but at the same time "individual (and *particularly* large) micro-organizations (here, corporations) also constitute separable systems within themselves, neither controlling or controlled by the social environment." They note that:

> the interpenetrating systems model can accommodate both the separateness and possible conflict of managerial and societal goals on one hand and the process of managerial/societal goal adjustment on the other. (p. 26)

Corporate social accounting, when seen from the interpenetrating systems model perspective, becomes the indicator referred to above, monitoring the boundary of corporate and society-at-large responsibilities, at least as they are perceived by those preparing the accounts. If corporate social accounting does, indeed, take on such a meaning, then one should see distinct variation over time in "socially responsible *and* reportable" corporate behaviors. Corporate social accounting is not then a technique whose usage necessarily becomes more frequent and technically substantive as the firm evolves over time, but as a technique whose usage waxes and wanes, depending upon political, social, cultural, technological, and economic forces—in short, the full range of social forces operating internally and externally on the firm.

In this study, corporate social accounting is viewed as an indicator of the changing institutional structure of business in response to changing societal demands. A single firm's complete set of annual reports is reviewed for corporate social accounting content with particular attention to what extra-market activities are reported on at any particular time. What is revealed is that corporate social accounting is not a new technique, but was practiced, albeit in sometimes rudimentary fashion, as early as the first decade of this century. This revelation provides partial verification of the thesis developed above that corporate social accounting will increase or decrease depending upon the *interpenetration* of corporate and societal forces and behaviors.

PRACTICAL ORIGINS

For purposes unrelated to this analysis, the author had the opportunity to review a series of annual reports of United States Steel Corporation for the mid-1930s. A number of items were reported on in those reports which, today, would be immediately recognized as evidence of creative corporate social accounting. Examples to be cited are a decrease of $547,625.52 in the amount invested in "assisting employees in the purchase of homes, through loans payable in installments" and "garden plots numbering 80,475 and covering 12,918 acres . . . were planted and worked by employees" (U.S. Steel, 1932:11). This discovery, at the time, seemed interesting although not sufficient to warrant further exploration. However, after it became apparent that, *one,* awareness of this early corporate social reporting was extremely limited, and *two,* corporate social accounting was seen by analysts to have an early theoretical base, but not a practical one, a study to establish the full extent of U.S. Steel social reporting was undertaken. In this study, a full set of United States Steel annual reports were examined, covering the period 1901–1980. Reporting of extra-market activities, i.e., those activities not directly related to the production of the firm's market goods, were recorded as to type of reporting—general comment, statistical record, or statistical year-to-year comparison—and nature of activity—vegetable gardens and seeding, direct employee relief, worker safety, etc. This data was then analyzed for year-to-year variation, and an eight decade history of U.S. Steel corporate social accounting was assembled.

Table 1 lists the types of corporate social behavior reported on in U.S. Steel annual reports. Reporting directly related to goods-for-market production (distribution sales, etc.) was excluded: for example, the construction of a community pool in Pittsburgh was included, but an employees' bath house was not. It should be evident from Table 1 that U.S. Steel, over its eight decade history, has engaged in extensive corporate social reporting.

The summary in Table 1 and the more detailed data in Table 2 reveal that what is perceived by U.S. Steel as reportable corporate social ac-

Table 1.   Activities Covered by U.S. Steel Corporate Social Reporting
(and periods reported)

1. Dwellings built for workers: 1905–1928
2. Community Development (hospitals, streets, schools, stores, etc.): 1907–1927
3. Sanitation of workers: 1912–1939
4. Worker Safety: 1915–1980
5. Vegetable gardens on company land, usually with company seeds, fertilizer, etc.:
    1916, 1932–1938, 1943–1944
6. Mortgage assistance for employees: 1918–1942
7. Direct Relief to Workers in grant form: 1930–1938
8. Sex composition of work force: 1943–1957
9. Philanthropic Contributions (U.S. Steel Foundation): 1953–1970
10. Pollution efforts: 1966–1980

Source: Annual Reports, United States Steel Corporation, Pittsburgh, Pennsylvania. 1901–1980.

tivity has varied over time. Allowing employees to use company land
for vegetable gardening, and supplying them in many cases with seeds
and fertilizer, is first mentioned in 1916 as a passing reference. In 1932,
when U.S. Steel iron production dropped to 3.5 million tons from a 1929
level of 18.5 million tons, and average employment dropped to 164,348
from the 1929 level of 254,495, the company *chose* to report that the
practice had been continued:

> During the past year, owing to business conditions, vegetable garden work has
> considerably accelerated, with most satisfactory results. Garden plots numbering
> 80,475 and covering 12,918 acres . . . were planted and worked by employees. It
> is estimated that the value of the produce from these gardens amounted to $1,213,504.

By 1937 the tone of reporting, but not the data, had changed:

> As in previous years employees cultivated vegetable gardens during the summer of
> 1937, although interest in this work was somewhat curtailed owing to improved
> plant operations. A total of 40,250 garden plots was worked during the year, covering
> 6,247 acres . . . which yielded to the employee so occupied raw produce of an
> estimated value of $540,000. These garden projects, in addition to providing fresh
> vegetables for the table, have afforded wholesome and instructive outdoor occu-
> pation with its physical and other incidental benefits to employees and their families.
> The subsidiary companies, as usual, rendered assistance to the employees in plowing,
> plotting and fertilizing the land and in securing vegetable seeds.

Therefore 1937 was the final year, through 1980, that the company reported on vegetable gardening on company land.

Other social reporting categories go through similar phases of "reporting significance." No reporting on sanitation has occurred since 1939.
Conversely, contemporary references indicate that funds were spent on

Table 2.   U.S. Steel Social Reporting Data, 1915–43[a]

Year	Accident Prevention	Sanitation	Veg. Gardens (Acres)	Mortgages (Net Sum)	Welfare (Credit)[b]
1915	608	953			
1916	848	1,403	2		
1917	999				
1918	1,110				
1919	1,131	3,209			
1920	1,420	4,227			
1921	1,062	3,615		8,479	
1922	1,175	2,253		8,143	
1923	1,763	3,019		7,975	
1924	1,912	3,231		8,908	
1925	1,414	3,642		12,296	
1926	1,867	3,218		14,996	
1927	1,271	3,227		15,803	
1928	1,077	3,053		14,649	
1929	1,006	3,058		13,899	
1930	1,164	3,379		12,388	
1931	863	2,360		10,312	471 (801)
1932	379	1,136	1,214 (12,918)	9,764	577 (2,690)
1933	412	1,275	1,800 (16,506)	8,245	2,345
1934	513	1,807	989 (11,235)	7,223	1,106
1935	607	1,984	955 (10,046)	6,248	695
1936	713	2,786	654 (7,518)	5,529	500
1937	950	3,950	540 (6,247)	5,633	104
1938	664	2,714		5,273	354
1939	888			4,840	
1940	1,046			6,248	
1941	6.4			6,682	
1942			(2,200)		
1943			(1,800)		

Source: Annual Reports, U.S. Steel Corporation, Pittsburgh, Pa. 1915–1945.
Notes:
[a] No data were reported in 1944 and 1945. All data reported as $1000s, except as noted.
[b] In 1933, welfare and credit were combined to one reported figure.

pollution abatement prior to 1966, but no formal reporting took place
until that date. Reporting on the sex composition of the work force began
in 1943 after President Roosevelt's executive order on hiring, and ended
in 1957.

The social expenditures reported were *not* insignificant in light of other
activities, as the data on Table 3 on corporate housing expenditures
illustrate. During the four year period 1918–21 a specific housing assistance plan was in operation, and housing expenditures amounted to
between 4–9 percent of all capital expenditures in those years.

Table 3. Corporate Housing
Expenditures 1918–1921

Year	Housing Expenditures (Percent Total)	Total Capital Expenditures
1918	$4,719,022 (4.1%)	$113,761,874
1919	7,530,125 (8.7%)	86,704,121
1920	5,448,140 (5.3%)	102,111,851
1921	3,262,275 (4.9%)	67,013,347

Source: Annual Report(s) United States Steel Corporation, Pittsburgh, Pennsylvania. 1918, 1919, 1920
and 1921.

Not all reported information was "positive," either by standards in effect at the time or by those today. For example, clear references are made to decreases, on a year-to-year comparison basis, for mortgage assistance. Segregated housing developments in Alabama are reported in 1917–19; and construction for a school for white children is reported in 1918. In 1925, "churches for colored employees at Edgewater and Bayview Works and community bath houses for white and colored employees at Edgewater and Docena Works," are reported under construction.

Carrol and Beiler (1975), in their analysis of the Kreps social audit proposal, presented a paradigm for analyzing contemporary corporate social accounting. This framework analyzed corporate social accounting models along seven key dimensions; definition of the activity, purpose, apparent motives, nature of issues audited, use, methodology, and by whom conducted. Analysis of U.S. Steel's corporate social reporting activity based on this paradigm is presented in Table 4. This analysis shows that the U.S. Steel activity resembles contemporary social accounting very closely. One missing element is that in the U.S. Steel experience very little effort was devoted to *appraising* the reported performance.

In summary, the United States Steel Corporation Annual Reports, prior to 1945 provide a rich history of corporate social performance. All of the pre-1930 reporting includes the development of so-called "company towns," and reflects a paternalistic corporate stance. In our own era, however, such a stance *might* be viewed as a corporation recognizing, and reporting on, broader responsibilities to society.

DISCUSSION

This discovery that corporate social reporting is an old idea with a practical base, suggests that it is an example of institutional behavior

Table 4. Conceptual Framework of U. S. Steel Social Accounting

Carroll and Beiler Criteria	U. S. Steel Annual Reports
Definition	Reporting of company activity deemed significant
Purpose	Varies, depending upon period and category of performance. Initially reflected "normal" corporate behavior.
Apparent motives	Initially to satisfy "contractual" reporting requirements with stakeholders. Evolved into: 1. satisfying the firm's social conscience 2. public relations 3. enhancement of firm's, and capitalism's, legitimacy.
Nature of issues audited	(See Table 1)
Use	Public Document
Methodology	Monitor, measure and report social expenditures, using the forum of the annual report.
By whom conducted	Management

whose frequency of occurrence depends on a matrix of societal forces. Changes in reporting practices reflect a shifting of the matrix of forces affecting corporate behavior, resulting in a concentration on the reporting of activities that society is perceived as valuing most at the time. There may also be significant variation between actual activity and what is reported.

The need for further study should not, however, prevent some speculation about the factors accounting for U.S. Steel's corporate social reporting and changes over time. U.S. Steel apparently defined "private enterprise" differently in 1915, 1940 and 1980. Specific trends involved at various times were: growth of company towns; response to the depression; extremely hostile response to labor organizing; response to wartime personnel and material needs; and response to the environmental movement. The company primarily reported on activities which, except for the company town development, were of an ongoing nature. U.S. Steel hired women in the 1900s as well as in 1950. But it was more important that people know how many women were hired during World War II. Similarly, society has recently placed more emphasis on pollution control. Also, internal pressures, quite likely from influential individuals, could reasonably be expected to have influenced the decisions to add certain data reporting and eliminate others at various points. From a long-run perspective, it appears that the company has become a much more "private" enterprise today than it was in 1900.

These findings suggest that corporate social accounting should not be seen simply as a new planning and control technique for helping contemporary managers "assume accountability for social and as well as economic objectives," as Carroll and Beiler (1975:597) conclude. It is also a practice, dating from the turn-of-the-century, which defines and illuminates the boundaries between the interpenetrating systems of business and the larger society. Analysis of the U.S. Steel experience reveals a long record of growth, decline, and evolution rather than a short period of recent one-way development.

ACKNOWLEDGMENT

The author wishes to thank the staff of the Office of the Secretary, United States Steel Corporation, for their assistance in furnishing documents for this research.

REFERENCES

Bauer, Raymond A., and Dan H. Fenn, *The Corporate Social Audit*. New York: The Russell Sage Foundation, 1972.

Blake, David H., William C. Frederick, and M. S. Meyers, *Social Auditing: Evaluating the Impact of Corporate Programs*. New York: Praeger, 1976.

Bowen, Howard R., *Social Responsibilities of Businessmen*. New York: Harper, 1953. As cited in Carroll, and Beiler, below.

Carroll, Archie B., and George W. Beiler, "Landmarks in the Evolution of the Social Audit." *Academy of Management Journal* (September, 1975):589–599.

Dierkes, Meinhoff, and Raymond Bauer (eds.), *Corporate Social Accounting*. New York: Praeger, 1973.

Jensen, Robert E., "Phantasmagoric Accounting: Research, and Analysis of Economic, Social, and Evironmental Impact of Corporate Business." *Studies in Accounting Research*, No. 14. Sarasota, Fl.: American Accounting Association, 1976.

Kreps, Theodore J., Measurement of the Social Performance of Business. Monograph No. 7, Investigation of Concentration of Economic Power for the Temporary National Economic Committee. Washington, D.C.: United States Government Printing Office, 1940.

Preston, Lee E., and James Post, *Private Management, and Public Policy*. Englewood Cliffs, NJ: Prentice-Hall, 1975.

Ramanathan, Kavasseri V., "Toward a Theory of Corporate Social Accounting." *The Accounting Review* (July, 1976):516–528.

Seidler, Lee J., and Lynn L. Seidler, *Social Accounting: Theory, Issues, and Cases*. Los Angeles: Melville, 1975.

Steiner, George A., "Should Business Adopt a Social Audit?" *The Conference Board Record* (May, 1972):7–10.

United States Steel Corporation, *Annual Reports 1902–1980*. Pittsburgh: 1903–1981.

Research in Corporate Social Performance and Policy

Edited by **Lee E. Preston**
Center for Business and Public Policy, University of Maryland, College Park

Volume 1, 1978, 291 pp.
ISBN 0-89232-069-9

CONTENTS: Introduction, *Lee E. Preston.* **Corporate Social Performance and Policy: A Synthetic Framework for Research and Analysis,** *Lee E. Preston, State University of New York — Buffalo.* **An Analytical Framework for Making Cross-Cultural Comparisons of Business Responses to Social Pressures: The Case of the United States and Japan,** *S. Prakash Sethi, University of Texas — Dallas.* **Research on Patterns of Corporate Response to Social Change,** *James E. Post, Boston University.* **Organizational Goals and Control Systems: Internal and External Considerations,** *Kenneth J. Arrow, Harvard University.* **The Corporate Response Process,** *Raymond A. Bauer, Harvard University.* **Auditing Corporate Social Performance: The Anatomy of a Social Research Project,** *William C. Frederick, University of Pittsburgh.* **Managerial Motivation and Ideology,** *Joseph W. McGuire, University of California — Irvine.* **Empirical Studies of Corporate Social Performance and Policy: A Survey of Problems and Results,** *Ramon J. Aldag, University of Wisconsin and Kathryn M. Bartol, University of Maryland.* **Social Policy as Business Policy,** *George A. Steiner, University of California — Los Angeles and John F. Steiner, California State University — Los Angeles.* **Government Regulation: Process and Substantive Impacts,** *Robert Chatov, State University of New York — Buffalo.* **Managerial Theory vs. Class Theory of Corporate Capitalism,** *Maurice Zeitlin, University of California — Los Angeles.* **Appendix A – The Management Process Audit Manual,** *Raymond Bauer, L. Terry Cauthorn and Ranne P. Warner, Harvard University.* **Appendix B – Canadian Corporate Social Responsibility Survey,** *Donald W. Kelly, Public Affairs International, Inc.* **Appendix C – Guidelines for Social Performance Case Studies,** *Donald W. Kelly, Public Affairs International, Inc. and R. Terrence McTaggant, The Niagare Institute.*

Volume 2, 1980, 352 pp.
ISBN 0-89232-133-4

CONTENTS: Introduction, *Lee E. Preston, University of New York — Buffalo.* **Business Political Activity: Research Approaches and Analytical Issues,** *Edwin M. Epstein, University of California — Berkeley.* **The Political Character of Business in an Organizational Regime,** *Malcolm D. Schlusberg, Syracuse University.* **The Persistence of the American Business Creed,** *David Vogel, University of California — Berkeley.* **The Management of Social Policy by Multinational Corporations: A Research Agenda,** *David H. Blake, University of Pittsburgh.* **State Owned Firms: A Review of the Data and Issues,** *R. Joseph Monsen and Kenneth D. Walters, University of Washington.* **Analyzing Complex Policy Problems: The Social Performance of the International Infant Formula Industry,** *James E. Post, Boston University and Edward Baer, New York, New York.* **Corporate Political Activity: An Exploratory Study in a Developing Industry,** *Steven N. Brenner, Portland State University.* **Social Responsibility in Large Electric Utility Firms: The Case for Philanthropy,** *Ferdinand K. Levy, Georgia Institute of Technology and Gloria M. Shatto, President Berry College.* **Corporate Social Performance and Reporting in France,** *Francoise Rey, Director ISSEC, Paris, France.* **Corporate Social Responsiveness to the Unemployment Issue: A British Perspective,** *Keith MacMillan, Administrative Staff College — Greenlands.*

Volume 3, 1981, 250 pp.
ISBN 0-89232-184-9

CONTENTS: Editor's Introduction, *Lee E. Preston, University of Maryland.* **Corporate Power and Social Performance: Approaches to Positive Analysis,** *Lee E. Preston, University of Maryland.* **The Process of Corporate Social Involvement: Five Case Studies,** *Michael J. Merenda, University of New Hampshire.* **Implementing Affirmative Action: Impetus and Enabling Factors in Five Organizations,** *Marilyn L. Taylor, University of Kansas.* **Corporate Law Violations and Executive Liability,** *S. Prakash Sethi, University of Texas—Dallas.* **Economy-Ecology Conflict: Analysis, Examples, and Policy Approaches,** *California State University and Stahrl W. Edmunds, University of California—Riverside.* **The Context of Social Performance: An Empirical Study of Texas Banks,** *Banwari L. Kedia, Louisiana State University, and Edwin C. Kuntz, S.E. Missouri State University.* **Public Issues Scanning,** *John E. Fleming, University of Southern California.* **Employer Policies and the Older Worker,** *Lois Farrer Copperman, Portland State University.* **MNC Responses to Equity-Sharing Policies: The Indonesian Experience,** *Robert B. Dickie, Boston University.* **Corporate Political Participation: From Tillman to the Eighties,** *Carl L. Swanson, University of Texas—Dallas.*

Research Annuals in
ECONOMICS

Consulting Editor for Economics
Paul Uselding
Chairman, Department of Economics
University of Illinois

Advances in Applied Micro-Economics
Series Editor: V. Kerry Smith,
University of North Carolina

Advances in Econometrics
Series Editors: R. L. Basmann,
Texas A & M University
and George F. Rhodes, Jr.,
Colorado State University

Advances in the Economics of Energy and Resources
Series Editor: John R. Moroney,
Tulane University

Advances in Health Economics and Health Services Research
(Volume 1 published as Research in Health Economics)
Series Editor: Richard M. Scheffler, *George Washington University.* Associate Series Editor:
Louis F. Rossiter, *National Center for Health Services Research*

Applications of Management Science
Series Editor: Randall L. Schultz, *University of Texas at Dallas*

Research in Corporate Social Performance and Policy
Series Editor: Lee E. Preston,
University of Maryland

Research in Domestic and International Agribusiness Management
Series Editor: Ray A. Goldberg,
Harvard University

Research in Economic Anthropology
Series Editor: George Dalton, *Northwestern University*

Research in Economic History
Series Editor: Paul Uselding,
University of Illinois

Research in Experimental Economics
Series Editor: Vernon L. Smith,
University of Arizona

Research in Finance
Series Editor: Haim Levy,
The Hebrew University

Research in Human Capital and Development
Series Editor: Ismail Sirageldin,
The Johns Hopkins University

Research in International Business and Finance
Series Editor: Robert G. Hawkins,
New York University

Research in Labor Economics
Series Editor: Ronald G. Ehrenberg, *Cornell University*

Research in Law and Economics
Series Editor: Richard O. Zerbe, Jr.,
University of Washington

Research in Marketing
Series Editor: Jagdish N. Sheth, *University of Illinois*

Research in Organizational Behavior
Series Editors: Barry M. Staw, *University of California at Berkeley*
and L. L. Cummings, *University of Wisconsin—Madison*

Research in Philosophy and Technology
Series Editor: Paul T. Durbin,
University of Delaware

Research in Political Economy
Series Editor: Paul Zarembka, *State University of New York—Buffalo*

Research in Population Economics
Series Editor: Julian L. Simon,
University of Illinois

Research in Public Policy Analysis and Management
Series Editor: John P. Crecine,
Carnegie-Mellon University

Research in Real Estate
Series Editor: C. F. Sirmans,
University of Georgia

Research in Urban Economics
Series Editor: J. Vernon Henderson, *Brown University*

Please inquire for detailed brochure on each series.

JAI PRESS INC.